Jim Keogh
Cracking the Project Management Interview

Jim Keogh

Cracking the Project Management Interview

——

DE GRUYTER

ISBN 978-1-5015-1514-9
e-ISBN (PDF) 978-1-5015-0622-2
e-ISBN (EPUB) 978-1-5015-0592-8

Library of Congress Control Number: 2019950122

Bibliographic information published by the Deutsche Nationalbibliothek
The Deutsche Nationalbibliothek lists this publication in the Deutsche Nationalbibliografie;
detailed bibliographic data are available on the internet at http://dnb.dnb.de.

This book is dedicated to Anne, Sandy, Joanne, Amber-Leigh Christine, Shawn, Eric and Amy. Without their help and support, this book couldn't have been written.

About the Author

Jim Keogh is an assistant professor at New York University where he teaches project management and other related courses. He was a principle developer of the Advanced Diploma in Project Management program at New York University and was on the team that introduced formal project management methodology to a leading Wall Street firm. Keogh is the author of nearly 100 books and introduced PC programming across America in his *Popular Electronics* magazine column in 1982, four years after Apple Computer started in a garage. He developed the Electronic Commerce Track at Columbia University and was a team member who built one of the first Windows applications by a Wall Street firm that was featured by Bill Gates in 1986 on Windows on Wall Street. Keogh wrote one of the first books that showed how to solve the Year 2000 problem. He appeared on CNN, FOX, *Good Day New York*, NBC's *Weekend Today*, and ABC's *World Wide Business Report*. His books are sold around the world and have been translated into Arabic, Thai, Romanian, French, Hungarian, Turkish, Portuguese, Russian, Italian, Spanish, Czechoslovakian, Chinese and Japanese. They can be found in leading university libraries including: Harvard Business School, MIT Barton Library, Yale University Library, Columbia University Library, Wharton Business School Lippincott Library, Beijing University, University of Cambridge, and University of Oxford.

https://doi.org/10.1515/9781501506222-202

Contents

Introduction: Cracking the PM Interview

You're hired!

The words every project manager wants to hear whether it is your first job as a new project manager or a seasoned professional looking to grow as a project manager within or outside your organization. There's a long pathway—some feel it is a mine field—to navigate from applying for a position to when you start work. Challenges begin by applying for the job and trying to be picked by the application tracking system—the computer program that "tells" the recruiter which candidates to look at first. Then there are interviews where your background and project management knowledge come under close scrutiny looking for reasons to disqualify you as a candidate—at least that is the feeling of some project managers who move through the onboarding gauntlet. It's a game of strategies where you anticipate the interviewer's moves and motivations, then try to respond appropriately knowing that the wrong word or gesture might injure your chances of being hired. And we shouldn't minimize pre-employment online tests—if there is one—that sends a chill through even the most experienced project managers who probably haven't been formally tested in years. Worse, some organizations report that more project managers fail than pass pre-employment online project management tests. The problem is that project managers don't prepare for the test.

Welcome to the new world of project management! *Cracking the Project Management Interview* is here to help by providing you with information you need to know about the interview process, sample questions and tips that likely will come up in the interview. Included are detailed review "cheat sheets" so that you will be prepared and confident, and more.

This book won't get you a project management job ... but the book provides insights and strategies that help you:
- Leverage your experience whether a novice or seasoned professional
- Beat the application tracking system at its own game with strategies that work
- Successfully surmount what might seem insurmountable interview hurdles
- Review material to help you pass pre-employment tests

This book was written to help you get the job you want. Much of what is written here may seem simple or even self-evident, but it is better to be prepared, confident and succeed than to lose a job because of something that could have easily been avoided. This applies to any existing project manager, project managers who may be looking for a job broader in scope than their current one, candidates looking for their first job, those still in school, looking forward to becoming a project manager or even those considering project management as a profession.

https://doi.org/10.1515/9781501506222-001

Proving Your Project Management Skills

It is common to think you can whiz through technical interviews with the hiring manager or answer questions on the pre-employment project management tests —if you have to take one. You are probably an excellent project manager, but it might have been a while since you've been quizzed on details (by the book) of project management. You may take shortcuts that pose no harm to the project, but you wouldn't pass muster if your project sponsor, or project management professor, was watching you. Furthermore, you don't know what you might be asked. We don't know what you'll be asked either. You probably need something to jog your memory. You'll find those memory-joggers in this book. You'll also brush up on some project management skills reflecting the PMP certification exams that may have slipped your mind. You will also see in Chapter 12 that we have incorporated help on the new PMP Certification that begins in December 2019, so you not only will get a quite detailed overview of the older PMP standards but also the new guidelines that will be part of the PMI test content for project management classrooms around the world and tests conducted by employers.

One thing is for certain: there are no standards when it comes to quizzing you about project management. In fact, you may be lucky and have no one challenge your knowledge—but somewhere along the onboarding process you'll probably be challenged about your project management knowledge and skills. This book helps prepares you. Don't panic—prepare!

Part One provides the knowledge of what the hiring manager is looking for, expectations, suggestions for interviews, getting selected by the application tracking system, and more. It will make you more confident and successful in selecting and deciding on the right job for you. You will gain an understanding of the motivations, or how to determine the motivations, of the hiring manager.

Part Two is an overview—a big cheat sheet or memory jogger—of what you may be expected to know in the interviews. It is a simple review of topics that will likely come up and, for ease of use, is broken down by project management methodology. Together, this book gives you what you need to know to successfully navigate through the interview process.

Chapter 1 The Project Manager Interview Process

There are hurdles you must jump through to let the organization know that you are the candidate for the job. There is no magic wand that can be waved that will lead you over the hurdles. There is no crystal ball that will tell you the words and the right moves to get you the job. However, understanding the project manager interview process gives you insights into developing your own strategies for getting noticed and jumping over the interviewing hurdles.

Topics covered are:
- How Project Manager Jobs Are Created
- Project Management Institute, PMBOK and the PMP Certification
- The Project Manager's Job Description
- Full-Time, Part-Time, Agency
- Independent Contractor
- Benefits and No-Benefits
- Union versus Non-Union
- Job Postings
- Applying In-house for a Position
- Applying from the Outside
- Networking Helps
- Who Will Interview You?
- Human Resources Interview
- Executive Interview
- Pre-employment Technical Tests
- Job Offer
- Pre-employment Health Exam
- Background Check
- Orientation and Probation

Chapter 2 Behind the Scenes of the Project Management Interview Process

Finding the right job is challenging for you, but also challenging for the recruiter. Finding the right project manager for the job can make a lot of difference. Project management is not a job that will be replaced by computers. It is the knowledge and the assets that an individual brings to the table that can be the difference between a success and a failure (or somewhere in between). It is your job to communicate those assets and the job of the recruiter to find them. So, your project is to get yourself hired for the job you want.

Topics covered are:
- The Challenges of Recruiting Project Managers
- The Ideal Project Manager
- How Decisions Are Made
- The Flow of Interviews
- Getting Lost in the Shuffle
- The Dreaded Application Tracking System

- Job Fairs
- The Background Check Anxiety
- Why You Didn't Get Hired

Chapter 3 The New Project Manager Interview

It's the old chicken or the egg debate: You can't qualify for a project manager position without experience as a project manager, and you can't get the experience without being hired as a project manager. So how do you get your first project management job? There should be an easy answer but the reality is that there isn't. It is about timing—being in the right place at the right time—but it is also about preparing to be the right person at that right time and place.

Formal project management training goes a long way for preparing to be a viable candidate by taking courses in project management and sitting for the PMP certification exam. Seeking positions working on projects in your current firm is a critical element in your preparation. Find something valuable that you can bring to the table, then let the project team launch you into a project management career that will qualify you for an entry-level project manager's position. You'll learn a few strategies in this chapter that can help you find and be offered your first project manager job.

Topics covered are:
- Before Applying
- What Type of Project Management Do You Want?
- You Don't Have Project Management Experience but You Have Experience
- The Search Begins
- Use Your Network
- What Recruiters Look For
- Selling Yourself in Your Resume and Job Application
- Cover Letter
- What to Expect During the Interview
- After the Interview
- A Second . . . or Third . . . or Fourth Career

Chapter 4 The Experienced Project Manager

As strange as it may sound, there isn't a clear definition of who is an experienced project manager. Some say that after six months you are no longer a new project manager, but six months is really not a lot of experience. And experience doing what? Is five years of experience as a project manager in running a relatively small project equivalent to five years of experience managing mission critical projects? Is five years of experience managing systems projects equivalent to five years of managing extreme projects? Probably not.

Defining an experienced project manager is baffling and frustrating when you are looking for a project management position. It is also baffling for the recruiter and hiring executive who look at experience from a practical—not academic—viewpoint. Both you and the recruiter want to know if you have the experience to do the job. The hiring executive knows the experience needed to do the job and has, with the help of the recruiter, defined the required experience in the job description.

You should decide if you can do most if not all tasks listed in the job description. The perfect candidate can do all tasks but the perfect candidate may not apply for the position, leaving the recruiter to select the candidate who can do most of the required tasks. Your next task is to show—in your resume and job application—the recruiter where your experience complements the required experience for the job.

Topics covered are:
- Are You an Experienced Project Manager?
- Risks of Changing Jobs
- Transfer or Seek a New Employer
- Resign or Be Terminated
- Mergers and Jobs
- Returning to Project Management
- Networking Helps
- Applying for a Transfer
- Applying for an Outside Position
- Cover Letter or No Cover Letter
- Reapplying to a Former Employer
- What to Expect During the Interview
- After the Interview
- Meeting the Hiring Manager

Chapter 5 Project Managers with Reputations or Recommendations

If you have been a project manager and have acquired a reputation or have been recommended for a given job, you may be treated slightly differently from a typical candidate. In the end, however, you must prove yourself as the right candidate. These advantages may help you, in the sense that you may not be asked to take the test that other candidates are required to take, but you must be prepared. The level of scrutiny likely depends on the duration of your employment or, if just a project, its importance. The organization may be more likely to accept your recommendations or reputation for a single project than for a long-term commitment. If you are looking at a single project, the position may be worthwhile if the project is to your advantage and offers you something (money, challenge, new connections). If so, then direct the conversation to your other commitments and foregoing them for the project at hand. You may be in a position to influence the nature of interviews by changing the dialog to what it will take for them to win you over. In this chapter, you'll learn what it takes to select your next firm and your next project by carefully examining details of the deal with your new firm. Details in your agreement may build a foundation for success or can scuttle your prospects from the outset.

Topics covered are:
- Myths vs. Facts About You
- Myths vs. Facts About the Firm
- Employee vs. Contractor
- Scope of Authority
- Management Support for the Project
- Management Support for You
- Financial Support for the Project
- Realistic Expectations: Challenge vs. Manageable
- Termination Terms
- Compensation
- Probe During the Interviewing Process
- Fact Finding Is Critical
- The Foundation for Negotiations
- Negotiations
- Your Pitch
- Keep Communication Focused on Need
- Dealing with Difficult People During the Interview and the Fact-Finding Process
- What Is Your Risk Tolerance?
- Joining as a Contractor

Chapter 6 Choosing a Project Management Specialty

Few project managers actually plan their project management career aside from training, earning the PMP certificate, and finding a first project management job. A project management career seems to evolve from circumstances and opportunities that happen, not planning. Downsizing may force you to explore a different type of project management. Openings within your firm may give you a chance to branch into a new specialty. However, you probably don't have a master plan or a career path.

A career path is a plan that states a goal and the tasks necessary to reach that goal. You had such a plan when you first thought about becoming a project manager. The goal was to become PMP-certified. You selected a training program, identified and completed pre-requests, and then passed each course required to complete the program. You prepped for the PMP certificate and you passed. You became a PMP-certified project manager.

Recruiters are noted for asking, "Where you do see yourself five years from now?" They want to determine if you have a career plan and whether or not the open position acts as a stepping stone for reaching your career goal. Some candidates simply fake a response to make themselves sound as though they have a well thought-out master plan for their career, ensuring that the open position is the next step in their career plan.

Topics covered are:
- Developing a Career Path
- Assess Your Current Project Management Career
- Changing Project Management Specialty
- Is Management for You?
- Working for a Project Management Consulting Firm
- Working for an Agency
- Agile Project Management
- Enterprise Project Management
- Extreme Project Management
- Construction Project Management
- Information Technology Project Management
- Engineering Project Management
- Project Management Educator
- Project Management Auditing

Chapter 7 Preparing for the Interview

Face it. You'll need to prepare for the pre-employment interviews. This can be challenging since you have no idea what you'll be asked during the interviews. Become a good sales representative for yourself by anticipating probable and possible questions that might be asked during your interviews. No one knows the questions that will be asked—sometimes the interviewer comes up with the question on the spot. However, in this chapter you'll learn how to anticipate typical questions asked in interviews and how to write "scripts" that can be used to tactfully express your strengths and weakness during the interviews.

Topics covered are:
- Preparing Your "Script"
- The Game Plan
- It's a Wrap
- Some Thorny Questions
- Bring a List of Questions to Ask
- And If the Interview Doesn't Go Well
- Be Prepared to Walk Away
- Prep for the Technical Interview

Chapter 8 Prepping for Project Manager Questions

This chapter looks at the possible types of questions you may be asked by the manager or members of the staff who have an understanding of the job. They will likely be more interested in knowing how you might handle situations, your approach to solving a problem, or your knowledge of specific areas required in the job. This chapter provides an overview of the essentials that you will need to know for your interview. The material covered in this chapter is fairly certain to be part of questions asked in your interview.

Topics covered are:
- A Project Management Review
- Work Breakdown Structure
- Task Relationships
- Reporting Progress
- The Acceptance Process
- Managing People
- Face-to-Face Meetings and Presentations
- Communications Plan
- Strategic Planning
- Leadership
- Project Management Models
- Extreme Project Management
- Inspiring the Project Team
- Risk Management
- Vendor Management

Chapter 9 Preparing for Test Questions

You won't know if a firm will ask you to take a pre-employment test on your project management knowledge until you're a promising candidate for the recruiter. Don't panic if you hear the surprising words, "Do you mind taking our project management test?" The recruiter and the hiring manager may be in a position to waive the test if your years of similar project management experience clearly demonstrate your in-depth understanding on how to effectively manage a project. Having a PMP certification *usually* trumps the need to take a test. However, taking the test may be a requirement for the position. Answer no and you'll probably kiss that project management opportunity goodbye.

You probably won't, but if asked, respond by inquiring more about the test. Be upfront and ask if all candidates are required to take the test or whether there is something in your background that raises doubt about your project management ability. The answer implies whether the test is required or not. If your background is an issue, you'll have an opportunity to verbally bolster your resume. If everyone takes the test, be positive and agree.

Follow up by gathering as much information as possible about the test. You'll probably learn that the test focuses on topics from the PMP exam and that questions resemble the PMP exam format, in which you are expected to use critical thinking skills and apply the Project Management Book of Knowledge (PMBOK) to respond to a test scenario. Expect to have multiple choice answers where at least two are correct. Your job is to select the one that is more correct than the other.

You might get lucky and the recruiter may provide you with a study guide, but don't count on it. If not, don't worry—this chapter reviews PMBOK concepts to give you a leg-up on any pre-employment project management test. No one knows what will be asked on a test if there is a test. However, focusing on terms and concepts will provide the foundation for responding to questions.

Topics covered are:
- Down to Basics
- Initiating the Project
- Planning the Project
- Managing the Project
- Monitoring the Project
- Closing the Project

Chapter 10 Project Management Calculations

You never know what you'll be asked during the interview or on a project management test, if you are given one. The previous chapters reviewed the basics that might be asked during a technical interview and more technical PMP exam topics. Think of these as items in your project manager's toolbox—items the interviewer may want you to know how to apply to a project.

Another thing that might come up is calculations. Yes, dreaded by many and embraced by few, there are budget and planning calculations that help to assess a project and make ongoing project management decisions—calculations that the interviewer may question you about. Calculations that are also in the project manager's toolbox.

In this chapter we'll review project management calculations and how and why to use them. Calculations focus on measuring the project—enabling the project manager to determine if the project is moving along as planned or how far ahead or behind the project is compared to the baseline schedule.

Calculations also estimate the future—not using a crystal ball but using statistics to project the project's trajectory. Many calculations focus on money—the budgets, investments, and contracts. Some firms expect the project manager to have a working knowledge of basic finance. Calculations shown in this chapter will give you a leg up on the basics.

You'll notice that calculations used for project management have their own terminology that you need to understand to properly use the calculations. A misunderstanding might lead to plugging in the wrong numbers in the formula resulting in the wrong value—not a good thing during the hiring process. You'll find the explanation of each calculation a great way to help you avoid traps that might trip you during the process.

Calculation names are followed by the abbreviation that is commonly used in formulas. Abbreviations have been excluded from the formulas to avoid confusion. However, you may find that firms will use only abbreviations on tests, if you are administered a pre-employment test. Next, you'll find an explanation of how the calculation is used to assess a project, and the formula. The formula illustrates values and calculations necessary to arrive at the result. Examples below each formula include a word problem and a solution using the calculation.

At the end of the chapter you'll see questions similar to questions found on project management tests, and answers with rationales on why the answer is correct.

Topics covered are:
- Planned Value (PV)
- Budget at Completion (BAC)
- Estimate at Completion (EAC)
- Earned Value (EV)
- Estimate to Complete (ETC)
- Actual Cost (AC)
- Variance at Completion (VAC)
- Cost Variance
- Cost Performance Index
- Schedule Variance
- Schedule Performance Index
- To Complete Performance Index

- Expected Monetary Value (EMV)
- Return on Investment
- Payback Period
- Risk Priority Number (RPN)
- Cost Plus Percentage of Cost (CPPC)
- Cost Plus Fixed Fee (CPFF)
- Cost Plus Award Fee (CPAF)
- Cost Plus Incentive Fee (CPIF)
- The Critical Path
- PERT Triangular Distribution
- PERT Beta Distribution
- Total Float (Slack)
- Number of Communication Channels
- Take the Challenge
- Answers and Rationales

Chapter 11 Enterprise, Extreme, Agile Project Management

If someone tells you she's a physician, after sharing your aches and pains with her, you'll probably ask what her specialty is. There are hundreds of medical specialties and specialties within specialties—probably some you've never heard of and haven't a clue what it is without an explanation.

Project managers are somewhat like physicians—not necessarily in pay and prestige, but in specialties. A specialty might be in an industry, managing projects for a Wall Street firm, or a discipline, managing computer systems projects that cross industries. Another type of specialty is in the project management framework used to manage a project. The most commonly used are the waterfall, enterprise, extreme, and agile project management frameworks. There are others, but these are the likely ones that come up during a project management interview.

The waterfall project management framework is discussed in detail in Chapter 7. Enterprise, extreme, and agile project management frameworks are also touched upon in Chapter 7 but you'll probably need more than a touch for the project manager interview. This chapter goes into more details about enterprise, extreme, and agile project management frameworks.

Topics covered are:
- Enterprise Project Management
- The Project Management Office (PMO)
- Types of Project Management Offices
- Select Projects for the Project Portfolio
- Breakeven Analysis
- Return on Investment (ROI)

Chapter 12 Staying on Top of Your Game with PMP Changes

A key to successfully landing your next project manager position is to demonstrate that your knowledge and skills have kept pace with changing project management techniques. Yesterday's approaches to project management may not meet today's out-of-the box critical thinking skills needed to deliver complex mission critical projects. You need a diverse approach as reflected in changes in the PMP exam.

The Project Management Institute recognized the next stage of the project management evolution is at hand. There is a new value spectrum for project management—

predictive project management approaches along with agile and a blend of predictive and agile approaches called the hybrid approach. Collectively these approaches align knowledge and skillsets with real-life practices of managing projects.

This chapter helps you sharpen your knowledge to speak intelligently about changes to the project management body of knowledge giving you an edge over project managers who are behind the times during job interviews.

Topics covered are:

- How Projects Are Really Managed
- New Domains
- Tasks and Enablers
- Need to Know for the Job Interview

Chapter 1
The Project Manager Interview Process

Looking for a job as a project manager is challenging, whether you are looking for your first entry into project management or an experienced project manager seeking to move on to hopefully a better opportunity. The organization is looking for a competent project manager to join their team and manage their projects. You might be competent and want to manage their projects. However, there are hurdles you must jump through to let the organization know that you are the candidate for the job. There is no magic wand that can be waved that will lead you over the hurdles. There is no crystal ball that will tell you the words and the right moves to get you the job. However, understanding the project manager interview process gives you insights into developing your own strategies for getting noticed and jumping over the interviewing hurdles.

How Project Manager Jobs Are Created

Traditionally, there are three reasons an organization creates a project manager position. The most common reason is the need to manage projects as a result of a project manager leaving the organization or transferring to another position within the organization. Another reason is growth of the organization into areas that are not currently provided by the organization. The organization increases the number of project managers to manage projects that help the organization grow. A third reason to hire new project managers is to ensure there is a pool of project managers in the future. Although executives typically focus on current staffing needs and needs for staffing in the near future, they realize that there is a sizable group of senior project managers who are nearing or beyond retirement age that may leave a relatively large gap in the workforce if they retire. Executives know they must invest in new project managers to fill that gap.

You may not care how the project manager's job opportunity came about—you simply need a job. However, you should care because the reason the position was created may provide a clue as to whether or not you should accept the position if it is offered to you. If the position was opened because the project manager transferred or was promoted, then there are opportunities for advancement within the organization. That's a good thing. If the current project manager left the organization, then you probably want to explore the reason for the departure. The work environment may have been unbearable or there were few or no opportunities to move around the organization.

https://doi.org/10.1515/9781501506222-002

Project Management Institute, PMBOK and the PMP Certification

The Project Management Institute creates standards that can be used across industries that can be used to teach people basic project management skills useful in a wide array of businesses. They essentially create the curriculum, train for it and have created a 700+ page book, the *PMBOK Guide,* that serves as a reference for the "standard." Most importantly, they provide the project management professional certification, the PMP, that 900,000 people in 210 countries and territories around the world have passed. Having this standard ensures a level of professionalism that is well known around the world. There are hundreds of books, videos and training courses around the world to teach the methods decided upon by a group of experts on project. management. Gaining the PMP requires study so that you know the range of possible questions that may be asked and so it requires a time and cost commitment that make the certification worth having. Many job descriptions list a PMP certification as a requirement. Certainly, if you are in a crowded job market and are new to project management, then a PMP can boost your chances of landing a job as a "project management practitioner."

The PMP certification, at this writing, is being revised for release by the time this book is released in very late 2019. The PMI has done extensive research into the issues surrounding project management and decided that a significant overhaul of their exam content was in order. As a result, they warn that the current sixth edition of PMBOK has significant variation from the new outline. The Exam Content Outline is presented upon accessing the PMI website. Its focus will be on People (42% of questions), 50% on Process, and 8% on Business Environment. A look at the Exam Content Outline would be wise for any applicant for a job in project management. They further say that they will split attention to agile project management 50–50 with predictive project management. If you are an existing PMP or in training to become one or simply looking for a project management job, looking into the changes is worth your time if you are looking for work.

The Project Manager's Job Description

The breadth of categories of project manager jobs is too broad to list in any book. It is safe to say that not all project manager jobs are the same, which makes it challenging for executives and project managers to find the right match for a project manager's position. The initial challenge is to describe the position in writing. The job description typically has at least two divisions: boilerplate and specific requirements for the actual position. Boilerplate is part of the job description that appears in all job descriptions for the organization and covers general requirements expected of candidates who apply for the position. Specific job requirements describe what the executive needs of the candidate. You need to focus on both the boiler-plate and the specific job requirements since these are required for the position.

Executives describe the ideal candidate for the position knowing that this candidate may not exist, but if one does exist they may be hired on the spot. The job description may list some requirements as "required" and other requirements as "preferred." Some organizations "require a PMP" while others "prefer a PMP." Organizations that require a PMP usually do so because of its status or because they are obligated by the organization's customers. Working toward a PMP usually works only if you are currently employed by the organization, although they may consider a project manager who is a candidate for a PMP (all requirements are met and you are waiting to take the PMP exam). Typically, the only way a candidate without a PMP is considered for an organization that requires a PMP is if the candidate has a unique skillset that is needed by the organization.

If you have a PMP, then you may be asked when you got it. You may not want to volunteer that information if it is more than four years ago and if you have not been consistently working project management since then. But you should know at least the month and year that you got the PMP. You will likely be asked, and it shows that you are sharp, or at least well prepared.

There are times when "required" requirements may be waived by the executive. This may happen when no candidate meets all the requirements for the position as described in the job description and the executive is pressured to fill the position. Unfortunately, applicants and potential applicants rarely know about the waivers. Some applicants apply even if they don't meet all the "required" requirements hoping that "required" requirements may be waived.

Preferred requirements are sometimes referred to as "tie-breakers." If two candidates are equally qualified and one has the preferred requirement, then the candidate with the preferred requirement is offered the position. Don't assume that a preferred requirement is "required." Some executives make a requirement preferred because few candidates who apply for the position meet the requirement. The executive doesn't want to discourage other candidates from applying, so they specify "preferred" requirements and "required" requirements.

Full-Time, Part-Time, Agency

Project manager jobs are also described by the number of hours that the executive allocated to the position. Most project manager positions are full-time. A full-time position is a position that is guaranteed 40 hours per week. (The actual number of hours may vary depending on what the organization considers full-time.) There are busy periods when the executives need extra help for a few hours per day. For example, an operations unit may have a relatively small, simple project. The executives may create a part-time project management position of 20 hours per week

(4 hours per day) to manage the project. The part-time project manager is guaranteed 20 hours of work per week.

An *agency project manager* is not an employee of the firm, but is an employee of an organization that is contracted by the firm to provide temporary or length of project help. The contracted organization may be a consulting organization that is brought in by the firm to help solve the firm's problem, such as developing and executing a project plan. The contracted organization may be more a personnel agency than a consulting organization and may focus on providing project managers and project teams to the firm rather than taking on the firm's entire problem. Project management is a lucrative business and credentialled employees are often in demand. The following is a list of some of the world's largest project management firms. Their area of specialization is varied and a PMP offers such an organization flexibility. Supplying resources to a firm can run the gamut from temps to multimillion dollar project managers. If you are specialized in an in-demand area, you may be used to gain a contract, so interpersonal skills are highly valued as an agency project manager.

Internally, project manager positions may be identified as a full-time equivalent. The project manager is a full-time employee of the firm but is assigned to projects sponsored by different executives. For example, the project manager's week may be allocated to five projects, each receiving the project manager's attention for a day. The organization may find it difficult finding five project managers who want to work one day a week. However, one position can be combined and split among the five projects.

Independent Contractor

Hiring a project manager as an independent contractor is a complex process and can be an issue in the US because the Internal Revenue Service (IRS) has strict rules on whether a person is an employee or an independent contractor. The firm hiring an independent contractor does not pay employer's taxes normally paid if the person was an employee. It is common for the firm to hire a person who works as an independent contractor through an agency where the person has a relationship (employee or independent contractor) with the agency and the agency has an independent contractor relationship with the firm.

Here are guidelines provided by the IRS:

With an employee, the firm:

- Controls every aspects of the person's performance.
- Decides when and where the employee will work.
- Provides tools to use.
- Includes detailed instructions on how to perform the work.

- Measures outcome of the person's work.
- Trains the person on how to perform the work.
- Reimburses for expenses.
- Provides employee-type benefits.
- Provides a guarantee payment (paycheck).

With an independent contractor, the firm:

- Provides broad instructions on how to perform the work.
- Focuses on outcome of the work, not the person doing the work.
- No reimbursement for expenses. The independent contractor has profit/loss opportunity.
- Provides payment based on terms of the contract. Paid for performance.
- The independent contractor can provide services to other clients.
- The independent contractor determines how and when work is performed and the independent contractor supplies tools needed to complete the work.

Benefits and No-Benefits

Benefits vary greatly. Don't assume all benefit packages are the same throughout the different industries. It is wise to carefully assess the benefit package when you are offered the position and compare the benefits package to the benefits offered by your current employer. A substantial decrease in benefits may be costly and negate any increase in pay that you received when changing jobs.

Not all project manager positions come with full benefits. A firm may offer benefits to full-time project managers. Part-time project managers may be offered pro-rated benefits that are offered to full-time project managers—or no benefits at all. Benefits are not offered to agency project managers primarily because agency project managers usually work full-time for the agency. Agencies may or may not offer benefits.

Make sure you find out when benefits begin and when they are terminated. Benefits may not kick in until you are off your probationary period, which can last three months, depending on the company policy. During that period you are expected to find your own coverage, or hope you don't become ill. The Consolidated Omnibus Budget Reconciliation Act of 1985 (COBRA) may enable you to temporarily continue your current employer's health insurance when you terminate employment. You'll be expected to pay the health insurance premium. Also, make sure you find out when benefits end. Some healthcare facilities stop benefits the day the employee is terminated. If you leave today, your benefits stop at midnight.

Union versus Non-Union

You may find that project team members in a firm are represented by a union. A union is an organization of employees (called a bargaining unit) that negotiate terms of employment (called a collective bargaining agreement) for its members. The bargaining unit is usually affiliated with a state or national organization that has similar affiliations with bargaining units in other healthcare facilities. The state or national organization provides professional labor and legal services that guide local affiliates through the bargaining process and management of the collective bargain agreement.

The collective bargaining agreement typically specifies positions that are covered by the collective bargaining agreement. Terms of employment for covered positions are specified in the collective bargaining agreement. Project managers are usually considered management and are not covered by a bargaining unit. However, if you apply for a project team position covered by the collective bargaining agreement, you must abide by terms of employment specified in the collective bargaining agreement. You will not be able to negotiate other terms of employment nor will the organization be able to do so.

During the first few days of orientation, you will meet with a union representative who will explain the benefits of joining the union. If you agree to join, you'll complete paperwork that permits the organization to deduct union dues from your pay and give the dues to the union. You'll have rights to participate in union activities without retribution from management. Under the National Labor Relations Act (NLRA), you have the right to refuse to join the union without any repercussions from the organization or the union. However, the NLRA permits the organization and the bargaining unit to enter into a union security agreement. The union security agreement requires employees who hold positions covered by the bargaining agreement and who are not union members to pay an agency fee to the union as a condition of employment. The agency fee is usually a substantial percentage of the union dues paid per pay period to the union for services in negotiating terms of your employment. You are bound by the collective bargaining agreement but you don't have any rights to participate in union activities since you are not member of the union.

Some states have passed right-to-work laws that prohibit a bargaining unit from collecting an agency fee from non-union members who hold positions covered by the bargaining agreement. This means that the organization is an open shop where project managers are free to choose when or not to join the bargaining unit. You'll probably be told by the organization if the organization is an open shop. You can also use online resources to find out if the state where you intend to work is a right-to-work state.

Job Postings

Once the executives receive approval for the project management position, Human Resources follows the firm's policies and procedures—to search for candidates. The initial search begins internally, by posting the position on the firm's internal website and posting the position on designated sites throughout the firm. Current employees can contact Human Resources directly or apply online through the firm's internal website. Internal applicants must meet the same criteria as external applicants. After a period of time specified in the firm's policy, the internal posting is removed and the position is made available to both internal candidates and to candidates who are not associated with the firm.

Firms tend to be more favorable to current employees who want to transfer into a position than to outside candidates for a number of reasons. Current employees develop a reputation—hopefully a positive one—which executives can use as an indicator of future performance in the new position. The current employee is already vetted—no background check is required—and is available to begin work once the transfer process is completed. Firms tend to encourage current employees to grow within the organization. Current employees do have the inside track. This is especially true for new project managers who are employed in other positions in the firm. A project team member may find it easier to transfer into a project manager's position within the firm than finding the first-time project manager position outside the facility especially if they are familiar with the firm's processes.

However, being a current employee may work against the employee from being offered the position. The employee's perceived skillset and worth ethics may not be looked upon as favorable. Unfortunately, unofficial decisions are made based on perception of executives rather than objectively made on facts. Furthermore, management may feel that replacing the employee is difficult and deny the transfer. In some situations, the executive has an outside candidate who is ideal for the position. The executive will then find reasons to disqualify current employees.

Applying In-house for a Position

Be prepared to go through the interviewing process if you apply for a position within your current firm. You'll probably be asked to complete an abbreviated application form and submit your resume again. The application is likely called a transfer request and probably requires notification of your present manager. Printed transfer forms typically require your manager's signature. Online transfer forms are probably sent to your manager at some point during the process. Human Resources tends to want the transfer process transparent so there are no surprises.

There will be requirements that you must meet before your transfer application is processed. Typically your job evaluations must be acceptable and any disciplinary action will likely kill your transfer opportunities for the near future. You will also be expected to complete annual requirements for your current position.

There is always the dilemma about sharing your desire to transfer with your current manager before you are offered the new position. If you do so, your manager may feel that you are disloyal and treat you differently if you don't get you get the position. If you don't, your manager may feel slighted, especially when the manager hears of your transfer application from Human Resources. Transparency is usually the better choice because in many cases, your manager can provide you with insights into the other position that may affect your decision. Your manager may very well informally give you a great recommendation to the hiring manager.

Applying from the Outside

Applying for a position is challenging and requires patience because the human factor is removed from the beginning of the process. Whether or not you visit the Human Resources department personally, you will probably be told that applications are accepted only online. If you tried dropping off a resume, you might be politely pointed to a computer where you can access the facility's website and begin the application process.

Human Resources can receive thousands of resumes, and the only practical way of processing them is through the use of an application tracking system (ATS). The ATS is the computer program that displays job postings on the facility's website and collects applications from candidates. There is actually much more to an ATS, which will be explored in Chapter 2, Behind the Scenes of the Project Manager Interview Process.

Applying online for a position is less personal than submitting your resume to a person, but it does have advantages—at least for Human Resources. The recruiter may quickly review at least a few hundred resumes of candidates who apply for a position. Paper resumes are not uniform, requiring the recruiter to hunt through the resume for information about the candidate that indicates if the candidate meets the minimum qualifications for the position. The ATS sifts through resumes and applications, and then displays qualified candidates to the recruiter. Furthermore, the online application process flags missing critical information from the application before the application is accepted by the ATS. The candidate must supply the missing information in order to submit the application.

The ATS also enables Human Resources to track the application throughout the hiring process. Paper resumes always have the chance of getting lost in the process, especially if the resume is passed along to several hiring managers. Some ATS alert Human Resources when a resume hasn't been reviewed by the hiring manager. Furthermore, the hiring executive can view resumes online and electronically respond to Human Resources.

Networking Helps

Does knowing someone who works at the firm help you get the job? This is arguably one of the most commonly asked questions by candidates. The answer is maybe—however, the candidate must still be qualified for the position. If you know the hiring executive and the executive wants to offer you the position, then knowing the executive helped get you the job.

More often than not, you don't know the hiring executive—at least not enough for the executive to give you the job. There is a better chance that you know someone else who works at the firm who can recommend you to either Human Resources or the hiring executive. You'll probably be told to apply online like everyone else. Let your contact know when the application is filled out so your contact can alert Human Resources or the hiring executive. It is at this point when the recruiter or the hiring executive will use the ATS to display your resume and bypass the normal search, basically placing your resume on top of the pile.

And this is about all the help you'll get. Your resume will be compared with the job requirements and possibly with other candidates. If you qualify for the job even marginally, then you'll probably be called in for the first round of interviews. If your qualifications don't match the requirements of the job, you may receive a courtesy phone call from the recruiter who will explain your situation.

Who Will Interview You?

First, it depends on the size of the company and the importance or duration. Are you to be full time, part time, or a contract worker? What is the job about? Who will you be interviewing with? Do they need samples of your work? These are all questions that will help you prepare for the interview. If you go into an interview and know little about the company, then the interviewer is likely to think you are not interested or were not willing for whatever reason to prepare.

The more important you are to them, the more they will want to be careful to pick the right person. You may be interviewing with a start-up. In that case you are likely interviewing with the founder. That person wants to make sure you are the best that can be found and so confidence is key. There may not yet be an HR department and so you may be interviewed with everyone. Having some good cases related to the company's business in mind can be very effective in this situation. The more you can command the interview, the less likely they are to be asking the hard questions.

If you are going to be a freelance worker or work for hire, there is a chance that you may not be interviewed by HR at all. If not, you will almost assuredly be interviewed by the person who will be your boss, a person in a similar position that you are hiring for and a head of department to make sure that they will be getting their money's worth.

You likely will be interviewed by a recruiter. Often if the open job is typical, the HR person is likely to have expertise in the area and may have hard questions to ask you. Again, if you have some experiences to call on with stories similar to what they are looking for, all the better. As a project manager, they are looking for someone who is impressive, and can work with people. So, listening well, and asking good questions should gain a good impression. But, rambling on may work against a project manager who must ultimately be responsible for schedules and getting the best work out of people.

If you are introduced to a group of people concentrate on names and repeat them when you leave them. Group interviews are generally easier, though it does give each participant time to think while you talk.

In all of these cases, it is highly likely that you will have some kind of test, so that the company is not making a mistake in hiring a project manager. You may avoid that if you are certified, but otherwise, be ready for a test. Later in this book in Chapter 8 we offer review material that is likely to be the subject of such tests.

A test that you can't study for is informal and is probably given each time you are interviewed. Each person interviewing you decides if you fit the organization's and department's culture. Do you fit the group? There is no technical definition of fit but it usually focuses on personality, the way you interact with others (the team, stakeholders), the way you carry yourself, and other elements that are not easily defined—but the interviewer knows it when she sees it. If you don't pass the fit test, then for many organizations you don't get the job regardless of your background and skills—with some exceptions. If you have extraordinary talent that the organization needs, then they may work around the fit. You won't know you're taking the fit test therefore it is critical that you be yourself throughout the interviewing process. Let the interviewers see you for you and make the decision on whether you are a fit—or not.

Human Resources Interview

Once your application has caught the eye of the recruiter and you seem qualified for the position, the interview process begins. The first stop is usually Human Resources to meet the recruiter. Some recruiters may hold a telephone interview before inviting you to a face-to-face interview. The telephone interview may be informal where the recruiter asks "showstopper" questions. These are areas where there is no room for negotiations. For example, traveling may be mandatory, so the recruiter makes sure that you can fulfill your obligations during the phone interview. If you can't, then going further with the interviewing process is a waste of time.

The in-person interview with the recruiter is a get-together where the recruiter gets a feeling of how you are as a person. Are you pleasant? Can you communicate well? Can you think on your feet? Responses to these and many more questions help the recruiter know if you may be a fit to work within the culture of the firm. The recruiter also reviews with you the requirements of the position, giving you the opportunity to explain how you meet those requirements. This is where both you and the recruiter determine if you should continue with the interview process. You'll find a lot more about the interviewing in Chapter 3, The New Project Manager Interview and Chapter 4, The Experienced Project Manager Interview.

The interview with the recruiter may last 30 minutes or less. Don't read too much into the length of the interview. Some candidates believe a longer interview means that they are being seen as a good candidate and short interviews means they are not. Each recruiter has her own style of interviewing. A short interview might mean that you are a good candidate and there is no need to extend the interview. A long interview might indicate that the recruit is giving you more time to sell yourself and to show that you meet the job requirements. And in some firms, the recruiter is more a facilitator than a decision maker so the initial interview is relatively short. The candidate is then brought to the executive for the longer, more formal interview. The executive decides whether or not to hire the candidate. The recruiter can veto the decision if the candidate fails to meet pre-employment requirements of the company.

Executive Interview

The interview with the executive is where you get to shine. The executive is usually the person who decides who is offered the position, with some exceptions. The executive probably can't overrule Human Resources' objections to failure to meet requirements established by the firm. Furthermore, the executive may have little choice if the position is covered by a bargaining agreement. The bargaining agreement may contain rules for selecting a candidate, especially if an in-house staff member wants to transfer into the position. If the staff member meets the qualifications for the position; has no disciplinary actions; and has seniority among other in-house candidates, then the position must be offered to the candidate.

Expect anything to happen during the interview with the executive. That's the only thing that can be said with confidence about the interview. Although Human Resources may give guidance, the executive determines how the interview will be conducted. An experienced executive may have their own formal process. An inexperienced executive may be learning how to interview prospective employees. In the end, the executive must decide if you are a fit for the position. "Fit" doesn't necessarily mean that you are a super project manager, but usually answers the question: will you fit into the culture?

If the answer is yes, then the executive typically focuses on your judgment. If the answer is no, then the executive may forgo exploring your project management skills because the executive's foremost responsibility is to build a cohesive team that works together. Unfortunately, you need to show that you fit without knowing much about the team. You'll find out how to deal with that situation in Chapter 4.

Getting a call back from Human Resources following the executive interview is obviously a good sign that you still are in the running for the position. However, there are more hurdles ahead of you, some of which may quickly knock you out of contention with little or no recourse.

Pre-employment Technical Tests

One of those hurdles is pre-employment tests that some (not all) firms require of candidates who have performed well during the interview process. These are usually formal tests conducted online in Human Resources. Tests are created and maintained by an outside organization that specializes on testing employment candidates.

Pre-employment tests focus on the basics and may explore your knowledge of project management. Typically, if you have passed the PMP exam, you will not need to take the test. However, they may be testing for your reactions to situations and so those simply require you to think on your feet. It is always a good practice to prep on the project management body of knowledge before interviewing and before taking any test on project management. Human Resources may offer a reference on the areas that you'll be tested. Chapter 6, Prepping for the Interview and Chapter 7, Technical Questions, along with other chapters in this book will help you prepare for technical questions that may appear on a formal test and may be asked during interviews.

Why should you be tested on skills that you've been successfully using for years? This question is asked often. Although the recruiter and the executive recognize your achievements, both need a clear way to document your knowledge and prove that you are a competent project manager. The relatively standardized test is an objective way to measure your knowledge compared to other candidates. The firm establishes the passing grade based on whatever criteria they deem appropriate. Passing the test determines whether you continue to be considered a viable candidate for the position. Human Resources may give you several opportunities to retake the test. If you fail to pass, then you are no longer a candidate.

Job Offer

With interviews and pre-employment technical testing out of the way, Human Resources and the executive make the decision about who to hire. All hope that there is one obvious choice among the remaining candidates. Sometimes there is a tossup—and in a few cases there is a literal toss up of a coin. The goal is to offer the position to the candidate who has good judgment and who is likely to work well within the culture. Achieving a perfect score on pre-employment technical tests is less important than fitting into the culture. You still have to pass those pre-employment technical tests.

The job offer is typically informally made over the phone by the recruiter. The recruiter will clearly emphasize requirements that might become problematic, such as traveling—including no health insurance—until the probationary period is completed. Job offers are conditional, which will be explained by the recruiter. You may have to pass a pre-employment health exam and pass a background check. The pre-employment health exam will usually be scheduled while you are on the phone with the recruiter. You should know the results of the pre-employment health exam before you resign from your current position. However, the background check may take a while before the recruiter receives the result. You may have started orientation by that time.

Your official offer is sent in the form of a letter that contains your date of employment, position title, compensation, and any conditions of employment such as passing the pre-employment health exam, passing the drug test and the background check. Furthermore, the offer letter will tell you how to arrange for the pre-employment health exam and drug testing, if it wasn't scheduled by the recruiter. The letter also states the date, time, and where to report to work. You are expected to accept the offer in writing within a reasonable time period.

Pre-employment Health Exam

In some firms you'll need clearance from Employee Health. The goal of a pre-employment physical is to determine if you are healthy enough to do the job except to be given a drug toxicology test, which is commonly in the form of a urine toxicology screening. This is a carefully orchestrated test that may be performed shortly after the job offer and before the pre-employment health examination. You are usually asked for a list of medications that you are taking. Be sure to include all natural supplements since natural supplements may have trace substances that may lead to a positive test result. No doubt, you'll have to empty your pockets before being led into a designated bathroom for the test. Usually, there is no running water. You'll be expected to fill a specimen container with fresh urine, and you're not permitted to flush the toilet. The sample will be taken by the nurse or medical assistant for testing. You'll be given hand sanitizer to wash your hands after you submit the sample. You'll be notified if the result is positive. If so, you'll be given an opportunity to explain what may have caused a positive result, assuming that you are not taking non-prescribed medications that would set off a positive result. Healthcare facilities are usually reasonable and may give you the benefit of the doubt—however, you still must either pass the toxicology screening or provide convincing evidence from a practitioner explaining why the result is positive.

Background Check

A firm usually runs a background check on all employees, regardless of their position within the organization. The actual background check is typically conducted by a vendor that searches public records, online sources, and previous employers to verify information that you provided on the application and on your resume. No background check is conducted without your written permission, which is normally obtained either at the time you apply for the position or when you accept the offer. Some firms request that you give them access to your Facebook page and other online accounts. You don't have to give permission for a background check, but the employer may reject your application as a result.

The background check usually involves review of your credit rating, your history of debt and repayment of debt, and other financial information that might give the firm an indication of how well you honor your obligations. There is also a criminal background check to see if you have ever been convicted of a crime. Any legal action against you, such as being sued, will usually be reported in the background check.

It is usually legal for an employer to ask you background information during the hiring process. An employer is not permitted to ask medical information until you receive a job offer. Even after the job offer they can't ask you information about family medical history or genetic information, except in very limited circumstances. The background check must be conducted on everyone who is hired for the same position. The employer is not permitted to select you for a background check based on race, national origin, color, sex, religion, disability, genetic information, or age.

Human Resources receives a background report, usually made available online by the vendor. You will receive a copy of the background report if something in the background report causes the company to withdraw your offer. You will also receive a notice of rights at that time that contains information on how you can contact the vendor who made the report to challenge the findings. Sometimes there are errors. Point out the error to the vendor and ask the vendor to fix the background report and send a corrected copy of the background report to the company. Notify the recruiter about the error and steps you are taking to have the error corrected. If there is something in the background report that concerns the nurse recruiter, you will likely be given an opportunity to explain the situation and why it will not affect your ability to perform the job.

There can be concern about what a previous employer may say about you. There are few laws that prohibit a former employer to voice an honest opinion about you or state documented facts such as your time and attendance record. However, firms and other organizations typically have policies that limit the information that they share about you. Typically, a former employer will share your dates of employment. Other information such as reason for termination and performance evaluations may not be shared. More on background checks is described in Chapter 2.

Orientation and Probation

Your next hurdle is orientation. Orientation is the process where you become familiar with the operations of the firm and your position. There might be a few days of classes and presentations where you'll be introduced to policies and procedures of the firm, Human Resources rules and benefits, and the firm's computer system. There is a growing tendency to use more online courses than classroom courses. Less staff is required, and at times you'll be asked to take online courses on your own time, shortening the orientation period and saving money for the hiring organization. You probably won't get paid for taking online courses on your own time.

Each area of the firm has its own orientation process. Sometimes you are teamed with a colleague who will show you the ropes—other times you're simply thrown into the job, expected to hit the road running directly into your first meeting. You are expected to ask many questions until you can perform tasks independently. Don't hesitate to do so, because you probably won't have this opportunity once orientation is completed.

There will be a list of tasks that you must successfully perform in order to complete orientation. There are also lists for Human Resources to complete and lists for your boss to complete. Most of these are checkboxes indicating that you were told the firm's policies and procedures.

And your last hurdle is getting through the probation period. The probation period is when you can be terminated with or without cause with little or no recourse. Many positions in a firm are technically a day-to-day position even if no one really considers the position as such. Some project managers receive an employment contract when hired that contains expectations of both the firm and the employee. The contract has a date when the contract begins and when the contract terminates. The project manager is guaranteed the job as long as the project manager doesn't violate terms of the contract. Most project managers don't have an *employment contract*. Instead, the project manager—as all employees—has an employment letter. An employment letter spells out the terms for employment but isn't a formal contract where there is a termination date—afterward, the firm and the employee terminate the relationship, unless both parties agree to another contract.

If there is a union involved, the project team members—usually not the project manager—have a bargaining unit position and also have a contract with the firm, which is better known as the *bargaining agreement*. The bargaining agreement is between the bargaining unit (the union) and the firm and contains terms of employment for the length of the contract. The bargaining agreement typically specifies procedures for disciplining team members who underperform and procedures for terminating employment. However, the bargaining agreement usually states that those procedures do not come into play until after the probationary period is completed. In essence, the union can do little for you until the probationary period is over.

You work at the discretion of the facility if you are not covered under a contract or bargaining agreement. You are most vulnerable during the probationary period when you can be terminated at will with little or no notice. Once the probationary period concludes, there are policies and procedures in place that specify how management must deal with underperforming staff. Sometimes executives are required to give a verbal warning, then a written warning, and possibly develop a performance improvement plan to rectify the issue. Termination usually follows failure of the performance improvement plan to improve the situation.

The recruiter and executive want you to be successful. They need you and spend an appreciable amount of time and money to recruit you and get you through orientation. The last thing they want is to terminate you and start the recruitment process over. However, they will terminate and cut their losses if there isn't promise that you will succeed. Some executives are quick to terminate and not throwing good money after bad by continuing your employment. Other executives will give you time to assimilate to your position and the culture of the firm. They may ask the recruiter to help find you another position in the organization if you are not a good fit for the current position.

Be proactive if you feel the position is overly challenging. You'll quickly know that the fit isn't a good one. The executive and your colleagues will know so too. Open a dialog with your executive and your colleagues soon after you complete orientation. Share your challenges and encourage them to help you meet them. This shows that you are well aware of the situation and you are willing to ask for help. The goal is to incorporate advice into your practice so that you can work relatively independently.

Chapter 2
Behind the Scenes of the Project Manager
Interview Process

Finding the right job is challenging for you, but also challenging for the recruiter. Finding the right project manager for the job can make a lot of difference. Project management is not a job that will be replaced by computers. It is the knowledge and the assets that an individual brings to the table that can be the difference between a success and a failure (or somewhere in between). It is your job to communicate those assets and the job of the recruiter to find them. So, your project is to get yourself hired for the job you want.[1]

You might apply to a few firms within commuting distance from your home for a project manager position. However, on the other end, a recruiter for each firm receives hundreds of applications for multiple project manager positions and must identify the best fits and contact each potential candidate, arrange for interviews, coordinate interviews with executives, and work through each step of the recruiting process. In this chapter, you'll take a brief look at what goes on behind the scenes after you submit your application to a firm. This behind-the-scenes look will give you insight into presenting your skills in a letter and resume and developing strategies for interacting with the recruiter and hiring executive.

The Challenges of Recruiting Project Managers

Applying for a project manager position can become frustrating. You submit your application and then wait—sometimes with no response at all, and other times, receiving an automatic response generated by the application tracking system. You call Human Resources only to be told that your application was received and is being processed. And you continue to wait. Weeks and in some cases months go by before you hear back. The response might be a general thank you for applying but that the position has been filled. If you get lucky, you might get a call from the recruiter, which is the beginning of a long onboarding process that can stop at any point along the way.

Let's take a moment to see what might be happening with Human Resources. Typically there is one recruiter who might also be recruiting for project managers. The recruiter's job is to find, vet, and hire qualified candidates after the executive receives approval to fill a position. There are likely many positions that the recruiter

---

1 In this chapter, we will refer to the recruiter as your contact, but it could be anyone seeking a candidate for employment.

https://doi.org/10.1515/9781501506222-003

must fill—not just your position. At times, the recruiter may feel between a rock and a hard place. Qualified and unqualified candidates are knocking at the door, trying to get a few minutes to pitch their resume. Executives are knocking at the door, wanting to know why the recruiter hasn't filled positions for the executive. In addition to locating the right candidate, the recruiter must coordinate the onboarding process—collecting paperwork, coordinating background checks, scheduling pre-employment physicals, and scheduling orientations for applicants who received job offers. If they have a high volume of projects to source, you can see why they may wish to work with firms specializing in project management to meet their requirements. It is also easy to see why having a candidate with certification has an appeal as they have shown that they should be able to take on a wide array of project management jobs.

The application tracking system is a computer program that handles the chore of sifting through the hundreds of resumes and applications (more on the application tracking system later in this chapter), assisting the recruiter to identify seemingly qualified applicants who will be invited in for interviews. The decision of who to invite is coordinated with the hiring executive, who also reviews resumes and applications. The recruiter does this for all open positions. Coordinating applications can be a nightmare. Even with today's sophisticated HR applications the recruiter often plays email and phone tag, getting the hiring executive to agree on which candidates will be called for an interview. And then it is finding time to schedule those interviews. Juggling these tasks is likely the reason for many of the delays you encounter after you submit the application online.

Once the first round of interviews—by phone or in person—are completed, the recruiter and the hiring executive decide who to eliminate and who should be brought back for another round of interviews (sometimes there is one round) and for pre-employment testing. A few days or weeks may go by before they make a decision. It is then when the recruiter schedules follow-up activities. All this goes on while applicants and executives are knocking on the recruiter's door, asking for a status update on their application and when the executive will fill the opening. This is why you receive an abrupt and cold response from the recruiter when you finally get through to her.

Finding a qualitied project manager isn't easy. The recruiter works with the hiring executive to define the qualifications for the position, salary, full- or part-time, and other information the recruiter needs to advertise the position. The position may have to be posted internally for ten days before the position is available to project managers outside the firm. The recruiter must field inquiries from current employees who tend to stop by unannounced or call. Others in the organization suggest candidates as informal recommendations—not just for one position, but for all open positions. Current employees expect to be treated as a colleague and as a friend—a level above someone from outside the organization. The recruiter tries her best to meet expectations while trying to respond efficiently, which can be a nightmare.

The Ideal Project Manager

Executives and recruiters all look for the perfect project manager. Who is the perfect project manager? Probably the project manager who the executive felt was doing a great job, and who transferred or resigned from the position. The executive and the recruiter must define in words the characteristics of the perfect project manager and use them in the job description and as a guide for when interviewing potential candidates.

Although each project manager job is unique to the project, there is a tendency for the executives and the recruiter to develop a general description of the ideal project manager description to describe every project manager position. You'll find this at the beginning of the job description. Unique requirements for the position are found toward the end of the job description.

So what are the executive and recruiter looking for? Project management skills is a given but. being a team player and having a stable work history lead the list. If you are not a team player then you probably won't fit with the culture in the firm. Unless you have a unique skill not widely found in the marketplace, you'll probably be knocked out of the running by a project manager who fits in.

Having a stable work history is critical, even if you are a team player. A stable work history implies that other organizations found your work acceptable—you showed up for work and performed a decent job. If you have worked as an independent contractor between full time jobs, then that should be expressed in your resume. This is a good reason for you to have created your own business so that those time slots in your resume are accounted for in a professional manner. Each of us has our own definition of a stable work history and you'll see indications of the executives' and recruiter's definition in the job description. Project managers are given leeway in that they move from project to project and so that can mean moving from job to job. Your recruiter will likely investigate gaps to fully understand your work history. Your goal is to show that you don't jump around from job to job—including within the organization. For example, spending a year managing projects in the finance department, then moving to the marketing department for another year, and then working in the distribution department for the past year may seem like you widened your experience, but may also imply that some jobs didn't work out. Instead of terminating you, they sent you to Marketing, and when that didn't work out you ended up in the distribution department, which does not seem to be working out either because you are looking for a job outside the firm. On the other hand, you might be a great talent who was urgently needed to fill jobs that were difficult to fill. Maybe you got tired of jumping around and you now want to settle down in one position, but that opportunity doesn't present itself within your current organization. Each of these scenarios is supported by your work history; however, the recruiter is likely to assume the worst without a clear, rational explanation in your application. They will also be contacting references and if you are in a "tight" industry, they might contact people they know. So it is important to honestly portray your work history.

Next is: Do you have the skills to do the job? This does not necessarily mean that you can run meetings, identify specifications, and complete the project. The executive and recruiter are looking for a candidate who has critical thinking skills, can solve problems, can deal with conflicts, and work independently. They want you to be customer-centered and an advocate for the customer. You see project management as a profession and not simply a job.

Strong communication skills are high on the list of requirements. The executive and recruiter both want a project manager who can express themselves logically, actively listen to customers and colleagues, and respond appropriately using both written and oral communication. Your resume, application, and cover letter are the first clues of your communication skills. Each conversation with the recruiter and the executive demonstrates your oral communication skills as you follow directions they give you throughout the recruiting process. Each encounter with the executive, recruiter, and other staff helps them learn who you are.

As you move down the requirements list you'll find basic requirements, such as current project manager experience and working in the firm's industry. Education requirements may appear as basic requirements or preferred, depending on the firm and position. Firms that have or strive for a high professional status have specific educational requirements, including Project Management Professional (PMP) certification. Some firms require PMP certification for project managers because their clients require it. A firm that does not require a PMP certification may say the certification is preferred or must be obtained within a set time period following employment.

The executives and the recruiter are looking for competent project managers who show up to work, work independently, think on their feet and are willing to help the firm address the needs of clients. The project managers should have realistic expectations of compensation, work schedule, travel requirements, and their role on the team. Your job is to convey these requirements in your resume, job application, and during each encounter with the executive and recruiter.

How Decisions Are Made

After breaking through the application tracking system; passing interviews with the executives and the recruiter; and passing pre-employment tests, a decision is made to offer you (or someone else) the position. It seems to be a simple decision—pick the candidate who is most qualified. Sometimes it isn't that simple.

Human Resources makes sure that the candidate is qualified based on policies and regulatory requirements imposed on the firm. Employee Health decides if the candidate is physically capable of doing the job. The executive decides if the candidate is a good fit for the team. Although the executive makes the hiring decision, Human Resources and Employee Health can veto the decision.

The process of determining who is hired is similar across firms; however, each firm has its own quirks in the process. For example, an executive noticed that a new project manager hired for her area had started orientation. She didn't remember hiring the project manager, although Human Resources said she did. The executive had interviewed many candidates for the position and told Human Resources the candidates she wanted to hire. Yes, *candidates* (plural). The executives went through this exercise a few times because each candidate she selected couldn't pass the pre-employment tests. Months went by until a selected candidate passed the test. By that time, the manager lost track and forgot which candidate she selected.

The Flow of Interviews

Generally, there is a lot of planning that goes into interviewing candidates. But that may not always be the case. Interviews performed by the recruiter are generally professional and well-organized. Time is slotted for the interview and the recruiter has a proven strategy for conducting the interview. The same may not be said about the hiring executive. The hiring executive may not be available for the interview at the scheduled time because of operational issues, or simply due to conflicts related to poor planning. You might be asked to reschedule the interview or, more likely, you might be interviewed by another executive who is "stepping in" for the hiring executive. Whether this is a good or bad thing is debatable. Will a hiring executive agree to hire a project manager who she did not interview? It depends on the hiring executive but you may get an offer to come back or arrange for a phone interview with the hiring executive.

At times, you may be interviewed by two or more executives in the same interview. This happens when the hiring executive is a relatively new executive and may not be comfortable with interviewing project managers. Other times, it just so happens that the other executive is in the room. For example, the interview may take place in the conference room rather than the hiring executive's office and other executives may happen to be there. This tends to be a good thing because you have a chance to impress multiple executives. Hopefully one of them will advocate for you in a discussion with the hiring executive and the recruiter after the interview concludes.

A few firms encourage the hiring executives to arrange a group interview with staff. You get to meet your potential colleagues and subordinates and they get to meet you. On a positive note, you get to ask questions about how the team works and they have an opportunity to set realistic expectations. Focus is about the types of projects. Your colleagues can't hire you, but they can let the hiring executive know if they think you are a good fit. The downside of a group interview with (hopefully) your future colleagues and subordinates is that information contained on your re-sume may have been shared with them before the interview. You may not want some information shared.

Getting Lost in the Shuffle

One of the horrors of applying for a position is that your application may get lost—and it does happen. An executive shares the frustrations of the hiring process. The executive has a million things to do—hiring is just one of them. They must deal with client conflicts, physical issues, leaking pipes, complaints from staff, going to meetings, budgeting, staff evaluations, and so on.

Yes, the executive must find time to hire a project manager. Resumes and appli-cations arrive electronically once the executive arranges for Human Resources to post the position. In some firms, Human Resources takes the lead by looking through applications and then suggesting a few candidates to the executives. In other organ-izations, the executive sifts through online applications to find likely candidates. In this case, the executive stated the executive usually forgets to check the application tracking system for applications. Weeks might go by without him checking. He re-members to check once there are complaints that the project hasn't started yet.

He states that he doesn't arrange the interview. Instead, he sends an email to the recruiter, who contacts the candidate. The executive's request gets placed some-where on the recruiter's to-do list, and the executive focuses on other things until the recruiter gets back to him. All this time, the candidate's frustration level in-creases to the point when the candidate stops sending emails and stops calling Human Resources—the candidate simply gives up, assuming that the position was filled and that they hadn't yet taken down the job posting.

Things get worse when the executive interviews several candidates over a few days. The executive admits that sometimes he gets resumes and the candidates mixed up in the days following the interviews. He is left with resumes and must try and remember his impression of each candidate. Under these circumstances he may tell Human Resources to hire the wrong person, not realizing until the person begins orientation.

Can you get lost in the hiring process shuffle? Yes, and unfortunately, there is little you can do about it.

The Dreaded Application Tracking System

With hundreds of resumes and multiple project manager positions (among other positions) open, there is no practical way to manage applications without using the application tracking system. Recruiters will admit that the application tracking system removes the human factor from the initial recruiting process; however, there is a benefit. The application tracking system helps to sift through hundreds of resumes and applications to find candidates that seem qualified for a specific position. "Seem qualified" is the key phrase. The application tracking system is likely to overlook qualified applicants primarily because their resumes and applications don't match the search criteria used by the application tracking system. Think of it this way: A recruiter quickly scans resumes to filter unqualified applicants, and so does the application tracking system. However, the application tracking system literally matches applications and resumes with the words in the job description. It usually doesn't recognize synonyms for those words, so qualified candidates can be overlooked.

The application tracking system also helps the recruiter manage applications. The recruiter can quickly display your resume on the computer when you call instead of having to sift through a large pile of resumes. The hiring executive can also review resumes on the computer without having to obtain copies from Human Resources. Chances are slim that your resume will be lost. In addition, the application tracking system helps the firm comply with anti-discrimination laws in hiring and assist in compliance reporting.

The application tracking system works by searching resumes and applications for contextual keywords and phrases. Simply inserting keywords probably won't help get your resume selected. Keywords must be used in context. Each keyword and phrase is assigned a value, sometimes referred to as a *weight*. Words and phrases considered more significant to the job qualification receive a higher weight. Sometimes the weight is based on the number of times the keyword or phrase is used in the resume.

The search result appears as a score based on the relevancy to a specific open position. Applicants with the highest scores are sent to the recruiter. Human Resources determines qualifying scores. It does not necessarily mean that applicants with lower scores are not qualified. It simply means that the application tracking system was unable to find a match for contextual keywords and phrases in the resume or application. The resume or application may have been poorly written or poorly formatted.

The recruiter, with input from the hiring executive, determines the contextual keywords and phrases used to identify resumes and applications of potentially qualified candidates. This information will not be shared with you. You must anticipate the search criteria and make sure those keywords and phrases appear clearly in your resume and application. Furthermore, you must avoid things that might confuse the application tracking system, such as fancy formatting of your resume. This may work well with humans, but it can confuse the application tracking system. Here are some tips that may help you to catch the "eye" of the application tracking system.

Keep your resume simple—no graphs, tables, illustrations, headers and footers, columns, special characters, or multiple fonts. Use standard resume formatting and include sections such as "Work Experience" and "Education." Use commonly used fonts such as Arial, Courier, or Times New Roman, and no smaller than 11-point size. Start your work experience with your employer's name, then your title, and then dates of employment—each can be on its own line, making it easy for the application tracking system to read.

Use bullet points to highlight key information. This helps when the recruiter needs to call you in for an interview. Uploading your resume in a Word document or rich text document may work better than using a PDF file. Some application tracking systems may have difficulty parsing a PDF file. Typically the application tracking system will display your parsed resume in the system's format. Carefully review the parsed document and make any corrections. This is the document that will be searched and scored by the application tracking system, and this will probably be your last chance to tweak your information.

You'll need to guess at the contextual keywords and phrases that will be used in the search. Chances are pretty good that the verbiage found in the job description on the organization's website will be incorporated into the search criteria. Therefore, you should use some of the verbiage in your resume and application. Use both acronyms and the full spelling of words that make up the acronym—the application tracking system may search for one and not the other. Make sure that your resume doesn't have typos and misspellings and that you use proper capitalization. The application tracking system doesn't use a spell checker and will give you a low score if it is unable to understand what you are trying to say. Furthermore, the recruiter is likely to reject your misspelled resume should it get through the application tracking system.

Keep in mind that the resume parsed by the application tracking system will be read by the recruiter, should it be selected. Therefore, don't simply stuff contextual keywords and phrases from the job description into your resume—this will become too obvious. Sophisticated application tracking systems may pick up on this and give your resume a low score. Instead, use contextual keywords and phrases no more than three times. The length of your resume doesn't matter because the application tracking system will parse resumes of any length.

When the application tracking system identifies your resume as a good match, it brings your resume to the attention of the recruiter. Depending on the application tracking system, the recruiter may be presented with information that the applicant tracking system retrieved from the resume, and not the entire resume. Key information may be inadvertently excluded by the application tracking system, especially if you don't use a standard resume format. Some application tracking systems also automatically email the applicant if the application was rejected; however, this may be sent in error and the applicant could later receive an invitation to meet the recruiter.

Application tracking systems typically are position-oriented, in that they search resumes of applicants for a specific open position. It doesn't search resumes of candidates who applied for a different position. Therefore, you need to indicate positions that you want to apply for.

Application tracking systems use optical character recognition (OCR) technology to scan your resume and statistical natural language processing (SNLP) to score your resume. Here's how some application tracking systems work:

1. Remove all formatting from the resume
2. Locate contextual keywords and key phrases
3. Organize the resume into specific categories based on contextual keywords and phrases:

   - Work Experience
   - Education
   - Contact Information
   - Skills

4. Match contextual keywords and phrases to the job requirements
5. Give the resume a score based on matches
6. The recruiter selects the highest scored resumes to review

Avoid gaming the system by using tactics such as white words—copying the job description to the bottom of your resume and changing the color of the type to white to blend in with the white background of the screen or paper. The application tracking system will be able to read them. Newer application tracking systems are aware of such tactics. Your resume may receive a lower than expected score for trying to manipulate the system.

Job Fairs

Job fairs are gatherings of recruiters who are looking for project managers and project managers who "might be" looking to change positions (some recruiters are there to support the sponsor of the job fair).

Here are some hints if you attend a job fair:

1. Attend at the beginning of the job fair when recruiters are still enthusiastic about attending the job fair. Halfway through the job fair, recruiters are likely to lose interest. Standing in the booth seeing an endless sea of potential candidates and answering the same questions hundreds of times an hour takes a toll.
2. You need to make an impression. This is going to be challenging, because you may be one of a few hundred applicants trying to do the same thing. Dress professionally. Keep your pitch short since the recruiter is probably going to forget you as soon as you walk away. Tell the recruiter something about you

that differentiates you from the other applicants who visit the booth, such as, "I use to be a client representative for Wall Street firms but then switched to project management." Later you can mention this in emails, phone calls, or even on your application to jog the recruiter's memory.

3. Set realistic goals for yourself at the job fair. You can submit your resume to the recruiter but there is a good chance it will get lost. Your resume is one of hundreds in a pile and chances are pretty good that the pile will be the last thing the recruiter wants to sift through when returning to the office. It is best to submit your resume and application using the application tracking system on the = website. Spend your brief moments with the recruiter to find out what jobs they are trying to fill. The recruiter will likely be anxious to talk about those jobs. You can also use this time to ask questions that you are probably hesitant to ask in an interview for fear of sending the wrong message. For example, how much traveling is required? Can your travel schedule be worked around your family schedule? Questions like these might be interview stoppers. Chances might be good that the recruiter wouldn't remember you asking those questions if they were asked at a job fair.

4. You won't be interviewed at the job fair, so keep your conversation brief and to the point.

5. You may want to contact the recruiter, but they may not want to be contacted. Don't take this personally. From reading this chapter you probably realize that the recruiter has a very busy job and the last thing they want is to spend time responding to phone calls and emails from everyone they met at the job fair. If they ask you to contact them, then do so—otherwise, apply online.

Maybe the recruiter is not looking to recruit project managers at the job fair. Instead, the firm may have sent the recruiter to the job fair to support the organization sponsoring the job fair. The goal was not to recruit project managers but to keep the name of the firm in front of project managers, other firms, and support organizers of the job fair.

The Background Check Anxiety

The hunt isn't over once you've beaten the application tracking system; impressed the recruiter and the executive during interviews; passed pre-employment tests; and received an offer and possibly a start date. You still must pass the background check. The background check isn't a "from birth" background check that potential federal agents must pass, but. our project supports business operations and affects clients and investors. The primary goal of the background check is to protect the firm. However, a background check may be extensive and require security clearance if the project is related to national security.

Human Resources may or may not conduct background checks depending on the depth of the check they require. A vendor is often hired to perform more detailed background checks. The vendor uses multiple sources to verify your background. For the most part, the background check verifies everything you have on your application, resume, and sometimes what you said during your interviews. The best advice is summed in a line from the award-winning movie *Moonstruck*: "Tell him the truth. They find out anyway."

The background check cannot be conducted without your written permission. One of the documents that you are asked to sign once you are offered the position is a consent form authorizing the firm to conduct the background check. You have the right to refuse to sign the consent form; however, the job offer will probably be rescinded. Your arm is not being twisted to sign. It is simply that the firm is protecting clients, investors, and employees.

A background check typically includes searches of:

- Court records (criminal and civil)
- Credit reports
- Motor vehicle reports
- Verification of your education and employment record
- Actions against your license
- Employment eligibility verification (I-9, E-Verify)
- Identity verification

Background checks cannot include:

- Any negative information that occurred from incidents after seven years except criminal convictions
- Bankruptcies that occurred after ten years
- Civil suits, civil judgments, and arrests that are after seven years
- Tax liens (paid) after seven years
- Incidents of credit collections after seven years

Nearly all background checks are conducted electronically, depending on whether data is electronically availability to the vendor. Results are usually presented electronically to Human Resources within a week. The report typically identifies discrepancies between your application and resume and what the vendor found. The report also identifies derogatory results that came up during the background check. A derogatory result is when someone—an acquaintance, ex-significant other—said something negative about you. Human Resources determines if any negative result from a background check warrants your disqualification from working at the firm.

The recruiter carefully follows the firm's policy before taking steps to rescind your job offer. The recruiter doesn't want to start the recruiting process over if you are an acceptable candidate. The recruiter verifies that the vendor's background check report was reported on the correct candidate. The recruiter typically uses a decision matrix to decide whether negative items on the background check report are within the hiring criteria for your position. The decision matrix ensures that the firm has consistent hiring practices.

If the job offer is rescinded because of a negative background check, Human Resources will send you a pre-adverse action letter, a copy of the background report, and a copy of the summary of your rights under the Fair Credit Reporting Act. You will be given a reasonable time to explain elements of the background report that would disqualify you from the position. The recruiter realizes that a background check is sometimes not 100 percent accurate. For example, you might be a victim of identity theft without knowing. You will be given a reasonable time to address discrepancies with the recruiter and/or the vendor who conducted the background check.

If you don't make any attempt to explain discrepancies or if your explanations do not satisfy Human Resources, you will receive an adverse action letter. The adverse action letter states that the job offer is rescinded based on either in whole or part of the information provided in the background report. The letter will contain the vendor's contact information so you can further explore the matter with the vendor.

A criminal conviction may or may not disqualify you, depending on the nature of the crime. Even if you have a criminal conviction that would impede hiring, you might be able to have that conviction expunged, depending on the nature of the crime and regulations within your state.

Lying on your resume is a common finding on a background check. What is a lie versus an exaggeration? The recruiter must determine it. Where you worked, your title, and dates of employment and compensation are hard to exaggerate. Likewise, schools you attended, dates you attended, and degrees earned are also factual. The actual work you did can be exaggerated to some extent. Lying can be attributed to your character. The recruiter and executive expect a little exaggeration about your experience, but outright lying implies that you are dishonest and that you can't be trusted. Remember that the recruiter and executive decide the extent to which an exaggeration is a lie. What might seem minor to you may be major to them.

Will your current and former employers say something that will prevent you from getting another job? Possibly, but not necessarily. Many firms have a policy of verifying employment by confirming your job title, dates of employment, and salary. Characterizing your work performance may expose the firm to libel claims and lawsuits by trying to prevent you from finding work. Some executives may still give an opinion about you when requested, regardless of policy.

References that you supply the recruiter will be contacted and presumably will give you a good reference. However, many industries are relatively small and are well-networked, where someone working in the firm probably knows someone you know. It is not too uncommon for the hiring executive to call a friend who might know a friend who works in your current firm and ask for an informal reference. The response—or lack of a response after acknowledging that they know you—may play heavily on the hiring executive's decision about you, long before a decision is made on a candidate for the position.

Be aware that your Facebook account, tweets, blogs, videos, and other things you post on the internet might end up in your background check. Some firms find that your Facebook account and other online postings provide more insight into your character than other items in the background check. Reference to heavy drinking, violence, or sexually offensive material in your postings might quickly eliminate you from consideration for the position. However, employers must be careful doing so, because your online content might reveal political, religious, ethnicity, existing medical conditions, and other information that legally cannot be revealed to your employer until after you are hired. Some employers pressure candidates to provide ID and passwords to their online accounts. There is legislation pending in several states to ban this practice.

You are entitled to receive a free copy of your background check report even if there is no adverse action expected. It might be wise to ask Human Resources for a copy of your present background check report to get an idea of what your employer sees. If you see any problems that weren't brought to your attention, you may still want to explore why they occurred, even if you don't share it with Human Resources. Once the background check is completed and you are offered the job, there is no need to address anything negative in your background check since it did not stop you from getting the job.

Be prepared to honestly explain items in your background that are hazy during your initial interviews with the recruiter, and be prepared to do so well before the background check. No one has perfect background, and the recruiter knows this. Being honest—not elusive—goes a long way to show your true character. If you worked for three months and left the position, point this out to the recruiter and explain what occurred and why it probably won't occur again. For example, things may not have worked out on your first project manager job and you left the job. You could say this was too much too soon and that you and the executive realized you were in over your head. You might explain that since then, you have been successful in more appropriate positions.

Why You Didn't Get Hired

You were perfect for the job. Interviews went well. Both the recruiter and executive gave you the feeling that you were a good fit for the job. So why didn't you get the job? Let's begin with the interviews. A good interviewer will leave you with a positive feeling after an interview unless you are obviously not qualified for the job.

If you are unqualified, the interviewer is likely to describe what the project manager will be doing, painting a picture that lets you discover for yourself that you probably can't do the job. If you might be qualified for the job, then the interviewer wants to keep you motivated to continue to explore the opportunity, even if the interviewer realizes you are the fourth most qualified candidate for the position. The first three may not accept the job offer so they don't want to be too quick to discourage you.

So what are some reasons for not getting the job? It might be something you said during the interview. You may have narrowed your requirements such as limited travel availability that gave the perception that you are not flexible. Furthermore, you might have trashed your former employer and manager during the interview. No matter how true it might be, the recruiter and executive may feel that you are too negative. Keep your discussion on a professional level when speaking about your current or former jobs.

Failure to communicate effectively during your interview is another reason some recruiters reject applications. Your background on the resume might be perfect, but you may be unable to effectively discuss your background with the recruiter or executive. The recruiter is hiring a person, not your resume. Your goal is to tell your story within the first ten minutes of the interview. Hit only the highlights. Save the details for when the recruiter or executive asks questions. Don't focus on one factor of the job such as compensation or schedule. Prepare for the interview. Research the company. Ask questions about issues that might be affecting the company, such as potential takeovers.

Dressing inappropriately can kill your hiring prospects as soon as the recruiter sees you. Explain in advance of the interview that you are coming from work and will be in your work attire, if that is the case. Ask if this will be a problem—if so, reschedule the interview. Your work attire is likely acceptable but it is always wise to make this known ahead of time—restate this at the beginning of the interview. You might say, "Excuse my attire, I'm coming directly from the airport after a long flight, as I mentioned during our phone call."

Finally, maybe the recruiter or the manager didn't feel you were the right fit for the job. What that means is that they may not have liked you well enough, not that you can't do the job. Something might have turned them off about you during the interviews. You might have said something inappropriate, lacked motivation, or failed to express yourself. Some executives place themselves in the position of a customer and ask themselves whether they would want you to manage their project. If the answer isn't a solid "yes," you probably won't get the job. And then maybe it just so happened that they liked another candidate more than you.

Chapter 3
The New Project Manager Interview

It's the old chicken or the egg debate: You can't qualify for a project manager position without experience as a project manager, and you can't get the experience without being hired as a project manager. So how do you get your first project management job? There should be an easy answer but the reality is that there isn't. It is about timing—being in the right time at the right place—but it is also preparing to be the right person at that right time and place.

Formal project management training goes a long way for preparing to be a viable candidate by taking courses in project management and sitting for the PMP certification exam. Seeking positions working on projects in your current firm is a critical element in your preparation. Find something valuable that you can bring to the table, then let the project team launch you into a project management career that will qualify you for an entry-level project manager's position. You'll learn a few strategies in this chapter that can help you find and be offered your first project manager job.

Before Applying

Be proactive. Start building a network of contacts while you are in other roles within the organization. Each position presents hands-on learning experiences and the opportunity of introducing yourself to staff throughout the firm. You can be just another colleague to the staff, or you can be a colleague that they'll remember—especially should you want to join or lead their project team.

Each opportunity gives you a chance to meet the executive of the area. Don't be afraid to briefly stop the executive in the hallway or politely knock on the executive's office door and introduce yourself. But make sure you are not going around the executive's assistant. Executives tend to look forward to meeting staff that have talent and the desire to grow within the firm. Many want to be a good host and share experiences, and executives are always on the prowl for potential candidates even if there are no current openings. Be quite sensitive to how busy that executive is.

Once you have met, don't stalk the executive and don't ask for a job. Build a casual relationship since you are likely to see the executive throughout the firm. Make small talk. Find out something unique about the executive—whether they have pets or hobbies—just like you would when you meet a new colleague. Give an impression that you are already part of the staff. Ask the executive a few meaningful questions about the area or the clientele. This demonstrates your sincere interest in clients. Keep questions short. Listen carefully to the reply and give the executive feedback that you understood the answer. Keep the conversation short. Politely

https://doi.org/10.1515/9781501506222-004

interrupt if the conversation goes long. Say, "This is very interesting. I have to get back to my work, but I would love to continue this later." The interruption demonstrates that you can prioritize your job first. You are simply planting a seed that may or may not grow into an opportunity in the future. Get a sense of how interested the executive might be in you. Consider how you might use that to your benefit. If you "bump into" the executive, make small talk and asking something unique that you remember about the executive. Keep the conversation short. Don't sit down in the office. Don't bring up anything about a job. The goal is simply to show your face and return to your job. Stay in touch but don't be too forward. The executive doesn't want to be your best friend or a pen-pal via email.

Consider joining employee activities, especially during off hours. Some firms have sporting activities or fantasy sports (unofficially) where you can get to know colleagues throughout the firm. Although this is mostly social, these activities help you create a network within the firm that can be used to assist you get your first project management job. Show your personality and a readiness to learn. You'll have many chances to connect with folks who know someone who knows someone who might have a project manager's job opening.

You can also go to conferences and educational programs to expand your network outside your firm. Your goal is to develop relationships and keep in touch with those you meet—keep building your network.

What Type of Project Management Do You Want?

Prepare yourself for questions that recruiters, executives, and members of your contact network will likely ask you. The first is: What type of project management do you want? You may be thinking, "Any project management job," but don't say this. They realize that finding your first project management job is challenging and that you will probably accept the first job that is offered. However, the real question is: Have you given any thought to the kind of project management that you might do in the future?

Working at various positions in different firms expose you to the most common project management areas, giving you some foundation to choose a path. Decide on an industry and then an area within the industry such as finance, marketing, sales, engineering, operations, distribution, information systems, and human resources. There are also opportunities in consulting firms that serve the industry. Consulting firms are prime training grounds for project managers—they ensure that their project managers and project teams employ best practices.

And what type of project manager do you see in your future? Agile projects, enterprise projects, extreme projects, global projects, and traditional projects—there is an endless list of specialties from which to choose. The recruiters, executives, and members of your contact network don't expect you to have your whole project management career mapped out. Instead, they simply want to see what area piques your interest so far and that you are thinking ahead about planning to build your project manager career.

Answer questions honestly. Don't try to tailor your answers based on what you think the recruiters, executives, and members of your contact network want to hear. You don't have to pick any area of project management at this point. A good response is to say you want to be a good project manager and that you are looking for a position that will help you develop good project management skills. Mention specialty areas that interest you. Try not to commit to one specialty unless you've worked in it as a project manager.

You Don't Have Project Management Experience but You Have Experience

The recruiter knows you are a new project manager without any project management experience—although you are basically competent as a project manager once you've gained project management knowledge and have limited experience, executives see you as a liability and a relatively expensive project manager to hire. New project managers make a lot of mistakes—it is all part of learning. Clients and business operations may be adversely affected by mistakes made by a new project manager. Therefore, a new project manager typically is given less intensive projects to manage than an experienced project manager, which is expensive. The new project manager is likely assigned to work closely with one of the firm's experienced project managers. The experienced project manager is responsible for overseeing the new project manager's project—assessing the new project manager's skills at every turn and always ready to jump in to keep the project on course. Both project managers receive full salary. In essence, the firm is paying for two project managers for a project that is normally managed by one project manager. Months can go by before the new project manager proves her project management skills and is permitted to work independently.

The executive knows that the facility must invest in onboarding new project managers; otherwise the pool of available experienced project managers will shrink in the future as current project managers move on and retire. However, the executive and the recruiter are very selective as to which new project managers will be offered the opportunity to join their firm. The selection process is challenging because the new project manager lacks proven work experience in this role.

Your job is to show the recruiter that you are a good investment by demonstrating how your successful non-project manager experience can be an asset in your project manager role. What you did is less important than how you did it. The recruiter is looking for a new project manager that has a good work ethic. You show up for work and call in well in advance if you can't, to give the staff time to fill your void. You complete each assigned task. You demonstrate critical thinking. You follow procedures. There are times when procedures are not appropriate, and you must identify them and ask for direction. You'll encounter similar situations as a new project manager. Questioning something that isn't right based on your limited project manager knowledge is important to the recruiter because you asked for help rather than risking a mistake that may have a profound effect on the firm. As you gain experience, your critical thinking becomes the basis for solving those problems independently. Tell the recruiter how you incorporated good customer service in your previous experiences. Show how you went that extra mile for customers in your previous jobs.

Your work in a project team is important to share with the recruiter. Direct project experience such as a system analyst, technician, or a project team role is a good foundation for a project manager. Other jobs—such as being a coordinator who assisted the project team but not a member of the team—also help to convince the recruiter that you are a good investment. The recruiter is not looking for you to have top notch project manager skills but is looking for you to have a good work ethic, critical thinking skills, good customer service skills, and be willing to continue learning. There is a lot to learn as a new project manager.

The Search Begins

Your search begins within your firm. Make it known that you want to be a project manager. Don't keep it a secret. Also be realistic that just because you want the position doesn't mean you'll get it—at least not right away. Keep your eyes and ears open for hints of the formation of a new project team, and then volunteer to join the team not as the project manager but as a team member. Find something that you can bring to the table. You probably have unique knowledge of operations, procedures, or stakeholders that can be used by the team. You can maneuver into a leadership position—not the project manager—during the life of the project. This provides a solid foundation for getting your own project as a project manager.

Also keep alert for new smaller projects that are sometimes not even considered official projects. These are projects that you can lead while in your current position by mostly coordinating activities resources from other departments or vendors. You are responsible for the project but other departments or vendors are managing the project. You can practice your project management skills and become the go-to person for delivering projects—granted, relatively small projects, but this too lays the foundation for taking on more complex projects.

It goes without saying that you should look at online job postings within your industry. Your knowledge of the industry helps to offset your project management skills.

Don't apply for advanced project manager positions. This is a waste of time. Rarely will a posting will say "new project managers invited to apply." More often, the recruiter may consider a new project manager who has experience in the industry—not as a project manager—but this is not mentioned in the job posting. How do you find out? There is no magic answer. Email the recruiter and ask.

An online search or a call to Human Resources is the best way to identify the recruiter. You may find the recruiter's email that way too. Alternatively, you can probably guess the recruiter's email address by finding the email address of someone else who works at the firm. For example, looking at the press contact section of the firm's website, you'll find names of the Public Relations staff and their email addresses (mjones@myfirm.com). Chances are good that recruiter Mary Smith's email address is msmith@myfirm.com.

Keep your email short and to the point. You are one of hundreds received by the recruiter. The subject line is very important. Don't hide the fact you are a new project manager in the body of the email. State something like "brief question from a project manager" in the subject line. This helps the recruiter prioritize your email—you'll have a relatively low priority but that doesn't mean that you won't receive a response. If you recently completed a project management program, then naming your school in the subject line may help. Firms sometimes have a formal or informal connection with schools. Responding to your email might be viewed by the recruiter as maintaining that connection.

Be patient for a response! It may take a few weeks or you may never receive a response—then again, the response may be immediate. The recruiter can easily get your email out of the inbox by hitting reply and writing a few words. With luck, the response will include instructions on how to apply.

Should you visit human resources personally? Yes, but not to apply for a job. Many firms use an online application tracking system to handle applications (see Chapter 2). Instead visit Human Resources to inquire if the firm has a job fair and if so, whether you could get information about it. You'll probably be speaking with a receptionist, but there is always a chance you'll get to chat with the recruiter.

Be realistic on where you want to work. It would be great to find a job in a local firm, but you and other new project managers from your area all have the same thought. There aren't enough positions to hire all of you immediately. Consider broadening your search area. You may have to explore opportunities at firms in a different part of your state, in other states or outside the country.

Be honest with yourself. Working for a firm outside where you live may require you to move. Traveling three or four hours to work every day may not make sense. Your commuting expenses will be high, traffic may delay your trip, and it might be a nightmare commuting during inclement weather. Relocating may be the only feasible option if you find a job outside your current area.

Use Your Network

Completing formal project manager training does not guarantee you a project manager's job. It is time to let the world know that you are a new project manager looking for your first project manager's job. Don't keep it a secret. Friends, friends of friends, neighbors, family acquaintances, someone may know someone associated with a firm who can help you contact the recruiter. They may even know the recruiter. Chances may be slim, but you never know who may help you open the door to your first project manager's job.

Your best opportunity is working the network you built during formal training. Email managers and other staff who you met at your firm or at other firms. Don't think that you can simply knock on their door and ask when you start. It doesn't work that way. Even if the executive wants to hire you, there first must be an open position—that opening may not exist. Give members of your network time to help you.

Email your network (especially managers) asking for advice, not a job. Ask if they have any suggestions on how to find your first project manager's job. They'll know you are looking for a job. You don't have to mention it. Make reference to your previous contacts with them. For example, "You might recall that we met at a client conference." Be sure to include anything that may uniquely identify you from others who they might have met. Hopefully, you planted that seed then and now it is time for the seed to start to germinate.

Don't become a nuisance. Send the email and be patient. You can follow up in a couple of weeks with another short email updating them on your search. Keep it light and a little humorous. The goal is to remind them that you are still looking.

What Recruiters Look For

So what might a recruiter look for in a new project manager? Each recruiter has their own requirements—some set by policy, some set by requirements of the hiring executive, and some that are subjective. No one can tell you exactly what criteria the recruiter is looking for but there is a good chance they include these characteristics.

- Brief and to the point when communicating (i.e., emails, phone conversations) with the recruiter.
- Show respect for the recruiter by not stalking. Don't send follow-up emails daily. Give them time to process your request. You are probably not their top priority.
- Read the job description. Clearly relate something in your background that matches the job description even if that experience isn't exactly a perfect match. Drawing the link between your non-project management background

and the job description helps the recruiter justify to the hiring executive to bring you in for an interview.

- Positive attitude. You know enough about project management to be minimally competent. You know you have a lot to learn and you are willing to learn.
- Good work ethic. You are punctual and arrive early, anticipating that you may get lost or that traffic may delay your arrival.
- Team player. You are willing to do things outside your job description.
- Honesty. You know your strengths and weaknesses. You want to be a great project manager, but you have a long way to go and need everyone's help to get there. You will make mistakes. However, you acknowledge them and ask others to help you rectify the mistakes. Learning from your mistakes shows that you are accountable for your actions.
- Understand job requirements. You know that you'll be working weekends and long days, including times when you are on the road. You don't get to pick those weekends and days. You won't have personal days and vacation until you are off of probation. Let the recruiter know upfront if you have plans already made such as a wedding or vacation. The recruiter may or may not be able to accommodate you.

Selling Yourself in Your Resume and Job Application

Your email opens the door and your resume is an advertisement that tells the recruiter, "Stop looking—I'm your new project manager." This might be a little wishful thinking; however, your resume should give a sales pitch that encourages the recruiter to take a closer look at you and invite you in for an interview. Likewise, the same is true about your job application that you submit on the firm's website.

Take a tip from advertisers. Advertisers tailor each advertisement for a specific group of customers. The group has needs that the advertiser can fulfill. The advertisement shows how the advertiser can fulfill those needs. The description of the open position identifies the needs of the recruiter. You can fulfill those needs. Your resume and job application show how you can meet those needs.

Each resume and job application must be tailored to a specific job posting. Yes, this is time-consuming, but you'll have a better chance of success than sending a general resume. The recruiter has a list of job requirements for a position, and minimal time to review the qualifications of each applicant. The application tracking system (see Chapter 2) will do the first review of candidates.

Format your resume in common sections:

- Contact Information
- Work Experience
  - Employer's name, your title, dates

    – Education
    – Skills

Make a list of job requirements. Next to each job requirement, enter something in your background that meets the requirement. Keep entries brief and to the point. Be honest. Leave it blank if you don't meet a specific job requirement. Rarely is there a candidate who meets all job requirements.

Next, write those entries incorporating the exact words and phrases that are used in the job description. The goal is to use keywords found in the job description at least three times in your resume or job application. This makes it easier for application tracking system to give your resume/application a high score.

The recruiter matches the job description to information in the candidate's resume and application. You make the recruiter's job easier if you do the matching for them in your resume/application. The recruiter can scan your resume/application quickly without having to read long descriptions of your work history. Remember that non-project management experience is important for the recruiter. A new project manager will be unlikely to have project management experience.

This is same strategy advertisers use to encourage potential customers to take a closer look at their product. Advertisers identify the customer's need (job description) and pointedly demonstrate how their product (you) meets each need (your resume/job application). Advertisers leave little room for the customer (recruiter) to misinterpret the message.

Practice! Go online and find job postings at your local firm's website even if you are not going to apply for the position. List job requirements and match your background to them using words and phrases contained in the job posting. Next, look at their job application. Jot down the information on the job application. Prepare your responses offline. Remember, this is an exercise and you're not applying for the position. Few new project managers do this and end up filling out the application online without much forethought.

Here is a sample job requirement for a new grad position.

Job Summary

Project manager is responsible for managing small- to medium-size information systems projects. The project manager will be responsible for providing and supervising direct and indirect interactions with project sponsors, stakeholders, and members of a small project team. The ideal candidate will have two years' experience as a member of a project team and one year of experience in a leadership role on a project team. New project managers are welcome to apply.

Education/Certification

    – Bachelor's degree in business, information technology, or engineering
    – PMP Certification or working towards the PMP Certification (preferred)

Job Responsibilities

Completes timely assessments of project requirements. Sets measureable and achievable short- and long-range goals for the project team based on the assessment. Selects the proper project management methodology for the project. Develops and implements a project plan. Manages the project team toward meeting project objectives. Manages expectations of stakeholders. Develops and manages a project budget. Negotiates with vendors and manages vendor contracts as related to the project. Effectively communicates with stakeholders and the project team. Comfortable using project management applications.

Here is an illustration of a simple resume that is designed to be "read" by an application tracking system. Notice that words and phrases from the job posting are used in the description of work experience. Remember that the initial goal is to have your resume selected by the application tracking system and then read by a human. You can modify the format of the resume and elaborate on your experience as needed, but make sure you include words and phrases that appear in the job posting.

Mary Jones
555 Any Street, Any City, Any State 55555
Phone: (555)-555-5555 Email: MaryJones@domain.com

Work Experience

My Firm, Some City, Some State 55555

   Project Leader, January Year to Present

Manage the day-to-day operations of a group of professionals within a large project team that is working on mission critical information systems for the firm. Assist in the development and planning of the project plan and project budget. Coordinate project activities with the project sponsor, vendors, and stakeholders. Adjust the project plan to ensure that the project remains on-target, meeting milestones, deliverables, and stakeholders' expectations.

Some Firm, Some City, Some State 55555

   Systems Analyst, Year to Year

   Worked with the project sponsor and stakeholders to identify current workflows and devised improvements in workflows that were incorporated into small- and medium-size projects. Translated workflows into project specifications used by other members of the project team to develop and implement projects. Assisted with end-user training.

Education/Certification

Bachelor of Science in Business Administration

   My School, Some City, Some State 55555

Expect to receive the PMP Certification within two years

Cover Letter

Some candidates might feel that a cover letter is relevant if you are sending a paper resume to the recruiter. Rarely is this done today with the introduction of the online application tracking system. The application tracking system has streamlined the process, doing away with unnecessary paperwork such as the cover letter.

An application tracking system may give you an opportunity to upload a cover letter. If it does, then create and upload a cover letter. The cover letter is an introduction to your resume—not a replacement for your resume—that encourages the recruiter to read your resume. Tailor the cover letter to the job posting. Avoid generic cover letters. Keep the cover letter brief and to the point. The cover letter should be one page.

Use the recruiter's name in the salutation, such as "Dear Ms. Smith." Identify who you are and the position for which you are applying. Tell your story in one paragraph. Conclude with a paragraph stating that you applied online and you would like to meet in person to discuss opportunities at the firm.

Here is a sample email cover letter that you can upload with your application and/or email directly to the recruiter.

Dear Ms. Smith,

As a project management professional, I am confident that my talents make me an excellent candidate for your project manager position based on requirements stated in the job posting.

My online application is completed and I have uploaded my resume. You will notice that I have a solid foundation working in different roles that progressively trained me for a position in project management. For several years I was a systems analyst on several project teams where I worked with project sponsors and stakeholders to identify and improve workflows that later became key operational procedures. Management recognized my talents and promoted me to a leadership position within a large project team where I manage a group that is responsible for the development and implementation of key components of mission critical information technology projects.

My application provides a glimpse into my enthusiasm for project management. I look forward to a time when we can further discuss how my background and qualifications compliment the requirements of your project manager position. I can be reached at (555) 555-5555 or email me at MaryJones@domain.com.

I look forward to hearing from you.

Sincerely,

Mary Jones

What to Expect During the Interview

Get to the firm half an hour before the interview. This gives you time to get lost and find your way. Arrive at Human Resources fifteen minutes before your scheduled appointment. There is a chance you can get in to see the recruiter earlier than scheduled. This benefits the recruiter because it keeps them ahead of what is usually a very busy schedule.

You get one chance at making a first impression, so dress the part of a new project manager. Dress in business attire. Every detail of your appearance counts. Keep nails short and nothing fancy. Good grooming is your calling card. It is a bonus if the recruiter sees that you dressed for work as a project manager.

Stand, extend your hand, make eye contact, put on a smile, and introduce yourself to the recruiter. Consider the recruiter a friend that you are meeting for the first time rather than the person who will decide to give you your first project manager job. A new project manager once commented that she didn't expect to be offered the job so she relaxed and was herself during the interview. The worst that could happen was that her expectations were met. Any other outcome surpassed her expectations. Most important in how you are perceived is your appearance and how you handle yourself. Business attire and a relaxed respective demeanor can project the type of person you really are to the recruiter.

Open the conversation with small talk—short and to the point—such as how you found traveling to the firm. Speaking up first shows that you are comfortable communicating with strangers. Let the recruiter take the lead from there. There is a tendency for the recruiter to find out about you before describing the position and the firm. Some recruiters tell you about the position only if what you say makes you a good candidate for the position. Otherwise, you might be told that this position probably isn't a good fit.

After a minute or so of small talk, the recruiter asks the first of many open questions. The objective is to find out who you are but also to decide if you meet the job requirements and will fit in with the firm's culture. The former is a checklist, the latter is a gut feeling. The recruiter looks for gaps in your background too. Be honest. A gap isn't a deal breaker as long as you are upfront and can explain the gap.

The first question might be, "Why did you become a project manager?" Answer honestly and logically. You may have coordinated with a project team and then became interested and joined as a team member. Project management seemed to be the next logical step. You may have relatives who are project managers who shared the rewards and trials of being a project manager. Whatever the reason, the recruiter will be very interested in how you communicate. Did you listen to the question and did your response make sense? Be sure to speak in complete sentences and use conversational words. Project management terms are fine but the recruiter is more interested in you telling a complete story using words that others will understand.

The next question might be, "What are your career goals?" Even some experienced project managers find this question difficult to answer, and as a new project manager, you probably don't know. You haven't as yet worked as a project manager. Again, be honest. You've been exposed to different types of projects but not all kinds of projects. You might respond by saying, "I found working as a project team member on upgrading the accounting system rewarding; however, once I get experience as a project manager I'll be in a better position to know which types of projects are for me." Even if you are set on a specific area of project management, tell the recruiter that you want to develop a good foundation in project management before moving into your dream project management job.

Another commonly asked question is, "What are your strengths and weaknesses?" This is a tricky question to answer because you are being asked to identify weaknesses that you probably want to keep to yourself for fear of losing the opportunity for the job. Don't put a spin on your weaknesses—recruiters may feel you are being dishonest. You may answer by saying, "I worked well in pressure situations, paying great attention to details. When things are slow I get bored. However, I have learned to spend those moments talking with my stakeholders." You provided both a strength and weakness. You also explained how you work toward strengthening your weakness.

Be prepared to answer the frequently asked question, "What makes you a good person for the job?" Tell the recruiter why you think you'll be a good fit for the job. Base your response on experience working on a project as a coordinator for a client or on the project team. You experienced the type of clients and you've seen the quality level of projects expected of the staff. You got to meet the staff and saw how they worked as a team, and you feel you fit nicely. Restate that you have a strong work ethic and are eager to learn and build your project manager knowledge and skills.

"What do you expect to learn from your colleagues once you join our staff?" You might be asked this question. An objective of asking you this question is to determine if you understand that you have a lot to learn about project management. The recruiter is not looking for specifics. Instead, the recruiter is looking for you to briefly describe what you don't know but want to learn. Speak about quality project management and types of project manager skills that you haven't mastered. You might want to conclude by saying, "I expect to learn how to be a good project manager. I know there are things I don't know—I want my colleagues to help me learn those things."

Another commonly asked question is, "How did your education prepare you for your first project manager job?" This is your opportunity to credit your instructors for doing a great job. You were a beginner the first day of school and knew nothing about project management. The faculty and your hard work helped to develop the skills needed to begin your career as a project manager.

Speak with confidence about your abilities and experiences. Be social and humorous at times, but serious when answering the core of questions. Avoid negative comments even when you are being humorous. Negative remarks may be misinterpreted, and you have no way of correcting the misinterpretation.

The direction of the interview may switch from you selling yourself to the recruiter selling the firm and position to you. This may be a signal that you convinced the recruiter that you are a viable candidate, but you still have a long road ahead before you receive a job offer. However, the recruiter explaining the firm and the job might simply be their signaling that the interview is over.

Stand. Maintain eye contact. Extend your hand and thank the recruiter for spending this time with you. State that you realize that other candidates are being interviewed. Ask the recruiter what the next step in the process will be. The response will give you a hint about what you should do next. The recruiter should tell you approximately when you should be hearing from them so you won't harass the recruiter with emails and phone calls. On occasion, the recruiter may be honest about the process. You might be told that there is a stronger candidate but that they haven't reached a decision yet. This helps you set realistic expectations about your prospects of getting the job.

After the Interview

Be patient! It is unrealistic to expect a call from the recruiter when you get home from the interview. Don't harass the recruiter. Send a brief email the day following the interview thanking the recruiter for the opportunity to meet and discuss the position. Include three brief examples of how your background compliments the requirements of the position. Conclude by saying that you are looking forward to continuing the interviewing process in the near future.

You will be contacted if the recruiter feels that you are a viable candidate for the position. However, there is no set time period for the recruiter to get back to you. You are one of many candidates for the position, and there are many positions that the recruiter needs to fill. There are a lot of things going on behind the scenes (see Chapter 2) that may delay the recruiter from responding to you.

Plan to send a follow-up email about a week to ten days after the interview. Ask a question relevant to the position in the email such as, "Is traveling usually within the United States or abroad?" or "Is tuition reimbursement available?" These are reasonable questions that require the recruiter to respond. The response may include the status of your application.

A long delay in a response doesn't mean that another candidate was selected for the position—although that might be the case. Rejection emails are typically sent automatically by the application tracking system once a decision is made on your application. A delay for a couple of months might be normal for the firm. It takes time for the recruiter to complete the first round of interviews and to arrange for interviews with the hiring executive. You may be a viable candidate but not in the top three candidates who probably will get the first crack at interviewing with the hiring executive. You'll likely be called if the hiring executive rejects one of the three.

The best course of action is to keep looking for your first project manager job. Continue to look at job postings at firms where you were interviewed. Send an email to the recruiter—who likely remembers you from the interview—that you are also qualified for the other position. Name the position in the email.

Continue to send a follow-up email every week to ten days inquiring about the status of your application. This is a reasonable request and won't be considered harassment by the recruiter. At some point you'll either be invited back for an interview with the hiring executive or will receive a rejection. Don't be discouraged by rejections. You are a new project manager looking for a firm that is willing to invest in you. Keep widening your search to include firms outside of your desired industry. Don't overlook smaller firms—they present golden opportunities for a new project manager. You are looking for your first project manager's job, not your perfect project manager's job. And there is a project manager job for you—you just have to find it.

A Second . . . or Third . . . or Fourth Career

Let's say you are a new project manager and are much older than others in your class because you already had a career or more in fields other than project management. Your kids are grown and out of college—now it's your turn. The economic downturn wiped out any opportunity to continue in your previous career. You retired relatively young and you don't want to sit home. Or maybe it is just time for a change. Whatever the reason, you tried project management.

The school was tougher than you imagined. Training in project management is an equalizer. Young or old, everyone had to take the same courses and pass the same tests. Age probably seemed to disappear as collectively everyone in the class looked for ways to increase their chances of passing.

Some project management schools tend to have an up-or-out policy. You pass the course and move on to the next course, or you fail and you're out of the program—although some schools give you one chance to recover by retaking the course. This applies to everyone regardless of age. At the beginning of each term, you and your younger colleagues probably counted heads to see who made the cut.

Passing each course may not have been as easy as passing courses for your previous career(s). Many college courses use the horseshoe method of passing. Getting close to the peg (passing) usually means that you pass. Instructors have a tendency to curve actual grades that give borderline students a boost to a passing grade. Not so in a project management program. That was probably an eye opener—no curves. The Project Management Professional exam tests your critical thinking—how you apply the knowledge, not the knowledge itself. Each question has two answers that are correct, and you have to select the answer that is more correct than the other.

Likewise, there are no curves when it comes to getting your first project manager job. You'll go through the same application and interview process as everyone else. The recruiter is prohibited by law to consider age as a qualification for the position. However, maturity is on your side in another way. You are probably very comfortable speaking with strangers (e.g., the recruiter, hiring executive) because you've done so in your previous career(s). Furthermore, you can tap into experiences dealing with people in your other career(s) that can carry over to the job at hand.

Although you connect with the recruiter on a mature level, you'll still need to answer questions that are asked of all candidates (see "What to Expect During the Interview"). Why did you leave your previous career? Why do you think project management is better than continuing your previous career? Do you plan to go back to your previous career? These are all questions that you must be prepared to answer.

Develop a one-minute response that explains your transition to project management. For example, you might say that your previous career was developing computer applications. The economic downturn hit and companies cut those jobs. Project management seemed to be a great opportunity to continue caring for people so you decided to change careers. You really enjoyed project management courses and feel that this path is a perfect career choice.

Be sure to link experiences in your career to requirements of the project manager job. Experiences and skills that were honed in other industries can be applicable to project management. You need to make the connection in your cover letter, resume, and during the interview.

You are still a new project manager and are prone to all weaknesses of being new. Don't be afraid to admit that you have a lot to learn about project management. Briefly tell the recruiter about how you had to adjust to returning to school and meeting the challenges of project management training. This demonstrates that you recognize that you have to change, and that you successfully met those challenges by graduating and passing the PMP exams (or how you are planning to take them).[1]

---

[1] It is difficult to know how many project managers are in the world, but PMI estimates that there are 16.5 million of which roughly 900,000 are certified.

Chapter 4
The Experienced Project Manager

Are You an Experienced Project Manager?

As strange as it may sound, there isn't a clear definition of who is an experienced project manager. Some say that after six months you are no longer a new project manager, but six months is really not a lot of experience. And experience doing what? Is five years of experience as a project manager in running a relatively small project equivalent to five years of experience managing mission critical projects? Is five years of experience managing systems projects equivalent to five years of managing extreme projects? Probably not.

Some firms have adopted an experience ladder that describes levels of project management experience that associate each level with progressively higher compensation. Levels are identified by the level number. Each level is usually described in a paragraph that describes the characteristics of the project manager. Here's a brief sample of a ladder.

I.   A new project manager who is being oriented and has not completed the probation period.

II. A project manager who has developed sound practice skills and assumes primary responsibility for small routine projects. The project manager must have successfully completed the probation period and is prepared to learn greater responsibilities of being a project manager.

III. A project manager who has demonstrated in-depth knowledge of project management and is considered a proficient project manager. The project manager has demonstrated good critical thinking skills and developed good judgment. The project manager can effectively handle unanticipated problems and emergencies.

IV. A project manager who is considered an expert in project management. The project manager has a comprehensive knowledge base. The project manager is innovative, self-directed, and can respond to complex and rapidly changing situations. The project manager makes things happen.

This seems a logically structured approach to define project management experience, but there are challenges with the ladder. Many characteristics are difficult to objectively define and measure. For example, whether or not a project manager is considered a proficient project manager is a judgment call–not something that is usually measurable. The ladder also has an undesirable consequence of limiting project managers from exploring other areas beyond the project manager's current projects. For example, level IV project managers who manage agile projects but who wants to manage an extreme projects may find themselves moving to a lower

https://doi.org/10.1515/9781501506222-005

level in the ladder. These project managers must develop new skills and are technically at level I for an extreme project—compensation should be adjusted for their new level.

Some say an experienced project manager should have worked their way up from various roles on the project team and on various complex projects for a period of time. This exposes the project manager to a breadth of experiences and enables the project manager to develop a skillset that is transferrable to all aspects of project management. While true, the question remains: How many months of project management experience is necessary to be considered an experience project manager?

And can project management experience be summarized as months or years of experience? There are project managers who work successfully on small routine projects for years and have little experience managing more complex projects. Based on the needs of the current employer, a project manager may rarely have the opportunity to lead more challenging projects.

There are new project managers who have better project manager skills—including critical thinking—than project managers with years of experience. New project managers are taught the latest project management skills and their knowledge is thoroughly tested. Experienced project managers may not have kept up with changes in project management and rarely is their knowledge thoroughly tested.

Defining an experienced project manager is baffling and frustrating when you are looking for a project management position. It is also baffling for the recruiter and hiring executive who look at experience from a practical—not academic—viewpoint. Both you and the recruiter want to know if you have the experience to do the job. The hiring executive knows the experience needed to do the job and has, with the help of the recruiter, defined the required experience in the job description.

You should decide if you can do most if not all tasks listed in the job description. The perfect candidate can do all tasks but the perfect candidate may not apply for the position, leaving the recruiter to select the candidate who can do most of the required tasks. Your next task is to show—in your resume and job application—the recruiter where your experience complements the required experience for the job.

Risks of Changing Jobs

If only you had a crystal ball to tell you whether that new job is really a good fit for you. There is no crystal ball, and you'll never know if the job is a good fit unless you try it out. What happens if it isn't a good fit? Can you return to your old job? This is a dilemma facing everyone who considers changing a project management job. When you are unemployed or a new project manager you have nothing to lose by taking a new job, but you have everything to lose if you are giving up your current job for the prospects of a new position.

Decide why you want to change jobs before applying for a new job. There are lifestyle reasons for moving on, such as a change in shift for child care, working closer to home, or poor compensation. There are also work environment reasons for a change. You may dislike your boss or your colleagues, the work rules imposed by the firm could be burdensome, or maybe you are simply overwhelmed. And maybe it is time for a change.

The primary risk of changing a job inside a firm is that the job isn't a good fit and you are terminated not only from the job, but also from the firm. You and your new manager want you to succeed, but you have to prove to yourself and to the hiring executive that you can do the job any time you change positions. There will be an orientation and a period of probation during which you can be terminated with or without cause. Under these circumstances, you would be unemployed—no income nor benefits—and prospects of finding a new job may be months away. And you'll have to prove yourself all over again once you find a new job.

If you left for a new firm and have a problem, then you'll probably be offered several opportunities to improve your performance as part of a performance improvement plan. The performance improvement plan will contain specific measurable objectives that are to be completed at specific milestones and a date when you and the executive will review your performance. If milestones are met, then you're probably out of the woods—otherwise, you may well probably be terminated. There is no guarantee that the new job is a fit. There is no gray area. Either the job is a fit or it isn't a fit. The manager—not you—makes this decision.

Identify the reason you want to change jobs. Is that reason worth the risks associated with a change? Try addressing the reason that you want to leave your current position before you begin looking for a new job. Assuming your manager isn't the issue, voicing your concerns to your manager may lead to solutions that can be implemented while you remain in your job. The manager may welcome the conversation because finding your replacement is the last thing the manager wants to do if you are doing a good job. You may avoid the risks associated with changing jobs by working out your issues with your manager.

Transfer or Seek a New Employer

Transferring to a project manager position within the organization is a way to accommodate your personal needs, such as taking an evening position so you're available to take your children to school. Likewise, you'll probably have opportunities to learn new specialties while minimizing the risk of changing positions if you transfer within the firm.

The rumor mill usually announces availability of a potential position well before the position is posted by Human Resources because the project manager leaving the position is given a going away or retirement party. Open positions are usually posted internally ten days before the position is announced to the public.

If you transferred to the new position, you may be able to return to your old position—assuming the position is available. Alternatively, you may be offered to apply to other open positions—some of which may not be desirable because of the nature of the project or your role in the project. And you may be terminated, although a good firm will try not to penalize a good project manager who fails at a new position, but don't count on that.

Next, looking for positions within your firm is usually a "safer" choice compared to seeking a project manager job elsewhere. You have a track record within your firm, plus friends and colleagues—including your manager—who may informally help introduce you to the hiring manager. And the recruiter and managers may help you find another spot within the firm if the job isn't a fit for you. Be prepared to take what may be considered a less desirable position in this situation.

Lastly, look for a position in another firm. This is the riskiest option because your termination is a likely result if you are not a fit for the position, unless Human Resources encourages you to apply to a more appropriate open position if one is available.

Resign or Be Terminated

Your job is not forever. All of us end up leaving a job for some reason. The US Bureau of Labor Statistics reported that Americans quit over 40 million jobs (up from 22 million in 2010)[1] while 20 million were fired or laid off in 2018. Leaving a job can be voluntary or forced. This section discusses the latter.

Losing your job can be hard to accept especially if you have years of success in the same position. However, there may come a time when you are no longer a fit for the job—at least according to your manager. It may be simply that the manager feels it is a time for a change—a change that doesn't include you continuing in your current role. A new manager may have taken over and set performance expectations that you are unable or unwilling to meet. You may receive hints that your performance is lacking and receive suggestions on how to improve from the new manager before the manager starts to officially document your performance deficits.

Next comes the official verbal warning followed by the written warning and then the dreaded performance improvement plan. Each business has its own process, giving time for the project manager to improve, but there is a clear decision point defined. If you meet performance goals as specified in the performance improvement

---

1 https://www.shrm.org/resourcesandtools/hr-topics/talent-acquisition/pages/workers-are-quitting-jobs-record-numbers.aspx (captured 8/24/2019)

plan, then you'll be back on course. If not, you'll likely be terminated. There are lots of different criteria around the world for dealing with this situation having to do with labor regulations, unions and other legislation that may affect the process described here, typically on a country basis.

Even if you meet performance improvement goals, you may want to consider looking for another job outside of the firm because your reputation may be tarnished within the organization unless other managers perceive that you were treated wrongfully. Time might diminish any prolonged effect of a disciplinary action if no additional disciplinary action occurs.

Should you resign before getting fired? This isn't an easy question to answer. Resigning may be easier to explain to a prospective employer than a termination. However, a resignation may prevent you from collecting unemployment insurance. You still have to pay your bills. Termination usually enables you to collect unemployment insurance.

If you wait for termination, then you need to explain the termination to a prospective employer. Don't badmouth your former firm or your manager. Instead, simply state that the job was no longer a fit and explain the reason. Mention that there were no other suitable positions within the organization, if that was the case. The recruiter may still be suspicious, so expect to focus on your successful work history, especially if you had a long run at the firm.

The best approach is to acknowledge to your manager and Human Resources that the job requirements of your present position seem to have changed and that it would be mutually beneficial if you looked for another position within and outside the organization. Negotiate a time period for your job search. Be reasonable, but the longer time you have, the better off you'll be. The manager and Human Resources will probably be open to negotiation. They don't have to pressure you to leave, which is just as uncomfortable for them as it is for you. There is an end date when their problem employee (you) will no longer be a problem. More importantly, it is a win-win for everyone. You have time to find another job and Human Resources and your manager will support you in your endeavors.

Speak with Human Resources and ask a few important questions. First, will you be on the "do not rehire" list? Yes, there is such as list. Unless you have a bad track record with the organization, you probably won't be on the list. The job was simply no longer a fit but something more suitable might open in the future. Ask what Human Resources will release to a prospective employer. This is always good to know when writing your resume and applying for another job to ensure that what you say about your former position coincides with what your former employer says about you. Human Resources usually releases date of service, last job title, and confirmation of salary. Sometimes Human Resources may state if termination was voluntary or involuntary.

Mergers and Jobs

Mergers occur primarily for sustainability. Consolidation enables the firm to offer expanded services under one roof, giving an advantage when attracting and negotiating with new clients. Furthermore, consolidation usually places the firm in a stronger financial position when negotiating terms for loans within the financial community.

Consolidation, however, may place the staff at a disadvantage. The realignment of services may result in layoffs. Staffing requirements are based on clients' needs, regulatory requirements, and contractual obligations. If consolidation re sults in a discontinuance of a service, then positions that support the service are no longer required, and staff members who hold those positions may be laid off. Consolidation may also result in duplicate services. This may not result in layoffs if the new organization serves different clientele or if there is no change in demand for current services. Layoffs may occur if both organizations provide duplicate services.

Layoffs may be based on seniority, depending on the firm's policy. However, there are limits to seniority. Project managers with seniority must also be qualified for the remaining project management positions. Some firms will train the project manager for the position rather than laying off the project manager, but don't count on it.

Alternatively, the firm's leaders may offer project managers to transfer to positions in other project manager positions that fall under the new consolidated organization rather than be laid off. There are challenges with this option. Positions may be at a different location where commuting may be a concern. Also, there may be a culture difference, and you'll find yourself having to prove yourself all over again.

One of the least mentioned but arguably the most important factor about consolidation is the impact it has on project management opportunities. Consolidation tends to result in one cohesive organization with one culture and one set of policies. There are limited opportunities for a project manager who doesn't fit into the new organization. Furthermore, choices of employers are especially reduced if there are ongoing consolidations of the industry.

Furthermore, a project manager on the consolidated firm's "do not hire" list may have to move out of the area to find a project management position since the list applies to the consolidated firm. There may be no alternatives to working for the consolidated firm. Consolidation may have created a de facto monopoly within your commuting area.

Returning to Project Management

It's time to get back into project management. Maybe you've cared for your kids or your parents and now you want to restart your project management career. This can be a challenge if you haven't held a project management job for years. You're not a new project manager, yet your project management skills are not current. You are competing for project manager positions with project managers who have current project manager skills. Your primary job is convincing the recruiter that you still have good project manager skills and can do the job.

Be realistic. You may not be the ideal candidate, especially if you've been away from project management for years; this shoe doesn't fit according to the recruiter whose job it is to match the shoe with the right employee. Place yourself in the position of the recruiter who is required to find a project manager. You have a resume from a project manager who is currently working and has five years of experience managing projects similar to the firm's projects. You also have a resume from a project manager who has ten years of successful project manager experience but who hasn't worked as a project manager for the past five years. Who would you invite for an interview? What would it take for you to hire the one who had been off for five years?

Finding your first project manager job after a hiatus is daunting. Older project managers working through retirement age and more new project managers than there are positions only further complicate your situation. This is to be expected. You have value to offer the recruiter, especially if you specialized in a certain type of project that is in short supply. Your job is to convince the recruiter and the hiring manager to select you.

Study! Your personal goal is to regain the confidence as a project manager and hone your critical thinking abilities. You will likely be asked to demonstrate your project management knowledge. It is critical that you keep your project management knowledge current. A refresher course—even if not required—may be something you want to attend.

Research the requirements for returning to project management. There may be penalties if you were absent from project management for more than five years, especially if you have a PMP certificate that needs renewing. Make sure that you have the required continuing education—60 professional development units over a three-year period. This is a worldwide requirement. You may require refresher courses before you can return to project management.

Contact your network of colleagues, especially the recruiter from your last project management job. With luck, the recruiter may try to find a position for you. Even if you are not remembered, there is a connection between you and the firm that may place your application at the top of the pile. Attend job fairs where you'll have the opportunity to ask recruiters for advice, not a job. This is a great place to get advice from the person who hires project managers. You never know—the recruiter might have a position that's right for you.

Keep in mind that you don't have to return to the same project management specialty that you left. Look for a position that will give you time to dust off your project management skills. Some firms hire part-time project managers during peak periods and for one-off special projects. This is a perfect position for a returning project manager.

Networking Helps

Network, network, network. You have probably heard this said countless times when you have spoken to colleagues about finding another project manager job. Although many experienced project managers find project manager jobs by searching websites of firms, many are referred to a recruiter by a colleague or by a friend of a friend.

You probably have a network that can help you get your foot in the door of a new firm. Former classmates are part of your network. Even if you haven't contacted them in years, they still might remember you if you rekindle the relationship. Your former instructors are a good networking source. Current and former colleagues are part of your network. Don't overlook friends, family, and your former bosses. They too might directly or indirectly have contacts at firms.

Realistically, your network will not get you a project manager job unless a member of the network is in the position to arrange for you to be directly hired. This rarely occurs. However, your network may get your application (yes, you still need to apply) in front of the recruiter or hiring manager without overcoming the challenges posed by the application tracking system.

The conversation will probably go something like:

"Mary is an excellent project manager and is perfect for your spot."
"Tell her to apply online and email me when she completes the online application."

The hiring manager will then pull up the application from the application tracking system, circumventing the application tracking system selection process. Your application will be placed at the top of the pile and will be seen by the hiring manager or recruiter. You don't have to manipulate the application tracking system.

But that's all you can expect to occur. Your resume and application will be seen, but you still must sell yourself to the hiring manager and recruiter. Your background will be compared with other applicants, then a decision is made as to who to invite for an interview. You may be called for an interview if your background is marginally acceptable because you've been recommended for the position. The hiring manager or recruiter may feel obligated to see you. Although the interview might be a courtesy, you still have the opportunity to give the hiring manager or recruiter your sales pitch. You may change the courtesy interview into a project management job by selling yourself.

The courtesy interview is also a time to explore other potential opportunities within the firm and to develop a rapport with the hiring manager or recruiter. Acknowledge that the current position may not be a fit. This shows that you have realistic expectations. Ask the recruiter which types of positions within the firm would be a better fit for you, and how frequently those positions become available. The answers will help to manage your expectations. Remember, the hiring manager and the recruiter just became new members of your network.

Applying for a Transfer

Transferring to a different position within your organization has many of the same requirements as applying from the outside. You'll need to check the internal posting board for open positions, then typically complete a transfer application and send it and your resume to the recruiter. This is all done electronically in many companies; however, you probably won't have the hassles associated with an application tracking system, since less than a handful of staff apply internally for the position. All internal applications are likely reviewed by the recruiter.

However, transferring has its own challenges. Don't be surprised if there is a waiting period (about 6 to 12 months) before you can apply for a transfer. The period begins when you are originally hired or when you last transferred. You are likely expected to achieve a specific performance level in your last performance review. Usually an acceptable performance level is the minimum criteria. This may pose what might seem to be an insurmountable obstacle if your present job isn't a fit. You want to transfer to a better fitting job, yet you can't if you're having trouble with your present job and receive less than an acceptable performance level on your review. Speak with your manager and Human Resources if you find yourself in this predicament. Many times, the manager and Human Resources want to find a mutually beneficial way of resolving the situation so they may agree to help you transfer to a more appropriate position and waive the waiting period.

Another challenge is that your manager may need to agree to the transfer. If you're doing a good job, chances are that the manager may never want to lose you. Senior management of the facility is usually aware that this conflict may arise and have established policies and procedures to handle it. Some firms require the manager to make a compelling case to block the transfer, otherwise the transfer process continues. The manager may have only one block—after that, the manager needs to develop a contingency plan that allows you to transfer in the future.

Seniority is another challenge when transferring within an organization. If two internal candidates meet the job requirements, then policy may dictate that the candidate with the higher seniority is offered the position. Seniority is usually defined in the policy. It might be length of employment in the firm. Alternatively, it might be the length of time as a project manager within the facility. For example, a project manager may have started as an executive assistant, and then worked as a team leader on a project before becoming a project manager. Seniority may begin from the time the person was hired as an executive assistant. Alternatively, seniority might begin when that person received their PMP certificate and worked as a project manager in the firm. Time worked as an executive assistant and team leader does not count toward seniority. Clarify the seniority policy with Human Resources when you apply for a transfer.

Another possible tie-breaker with two equally qualified applicants applying to transfer to the same position is the date and time of the transfer application. The applicant who applied first gets the position. It is not unusual that each transfer application is time-stamped when the computer saves the application. The Human Resources staff usually handwrites the date and time on paper transfer applications. Ask Human Resources if such a policy exists within your firm well before you consider applying for a transfer. This becomes important when the rumor mill speaks about a position opening—it is not as yet posted. You can easily forget to keep checking the internal posting board and someone else might apply for the position before you do.

Does someone have the inside track for the position? They could. There are times when the manager or higher-level managers have a candidate in mind for a project management position, and in some cases the position is created for that candidate. The challenge is to offer the position and stay within the firm's policies. This is even more difficult if the position comes under the bargaining unit where the bargaining agreement specifies the process for transferring employees. Not all positions must be posted, but bargaining unit positions are likely required to be posted.

The manager and Human Resources may keep the opening quiet if they have a candidate in mind for the position. The hope is that the position will get lost in all the open positions and no one on staff will notice the posting. Requirements for the position may be based on the candidate's qualifications. Only that candidate meets the requirements for the position. Another strategy for limiting the applicant pool is for the manager to talk other candidates out of applying for the position by over-emphasizing all the negative aspects of the position in interviews with candidates. There is only one candidate remaining at the end—the candidate that the manager wanted before the position was posted.

Applying for an Outside Position

Applying for a position outside of your firm has its own challenges. In essence, you are starting over and have to convince the recruiter, the manager and possibly the application tracking system, that you are a good candidate for the job—all in writing. You'll need to apply for the job in the form required: by letter, email, or online using the application tracking system regardless of your experience or who referred you for the position. The application tracking system matches your application to job requirements set by the recruiter (see Chapter 2).

Your initial objective is to match elements in your background to each requirement specified in the job posting. Do this in both the application and in your resume.

Take time and tailor your resume to complement the job posting. If you submit a generic resume, you leave matching your background to the job requirements to the application tracking system and the recruiter. You'll have better results if you do the matching to ensure that nothing was overlooked in the application process.

Create three columns. List each requirement for the job in the first column and how you meet the requirement in the second column. Realistically, you may not meet each job requirement—nor will other candidates—so be honest with yourself. If you don't meet the requirement then leave it blank. Write the exact wording that you'll use to describe your background in the third column. Incorporate words and phrases that you find in the job description at least three times. This helps the application tracking system give your application a high matching score when searching for qualified applications.

Rewrite your resume using text that you've written in the third column. Format your resume in commonly used sections to make it easy for the application tracking system to parse your resume into sections of the application. Don't begin an entry with dates. Place dates at the end of the entry. Here is an example of sections of a resume.

- Contact Information
- Work Experience

    - Employer's name, your title, dates

- Education
- Skills

Here is a sample job requirement for an experienced PM.

Job Summary

The project manager functions as the manager who can translate a business idea into a project plan then develop and implement the project to achieve desired outcomes. This position directs and oversees the project management team. This position effectively coordinates project activities among executives, business managers, and support services.

Required Experience

- Consistently and independently prioritizes and delivers dependable and effective project management
- Performs ongoing project assessment
- Plans and implements individualized project requirements to meet immediate needs in collaboration with the interdisciplinary team
- Evaluates the project team's response to project tasks and adjust the project plan as necessary
- Documents the project activities
- Communicates effectively
- Identifies and brings ethical issues to the attention team members

- Utilizes project management policies/procedures
- Incorporates evidence-based practice in project management
- Responds to opportunities to enhance stakeholder satisfaction

Education

- BS in business or engineering
- MS or MBA preferred
- Minimum of 5 years of prior project management experience

Licenses and Certifications

- PMP Certification

Here is a sample resume designed to be parsed by an application tracking system. You'll notice that words and phrases are included from the description of the job in the job posting. Keep in mind that the initial goal is to have the application tracking system give your resume—once imported into the system—a high score. Elaborate on your experience but make sure your resume contains the key words and phrases that appear in the job posting.

Mary Jones

555 Some Street, Some City, Some State 55555

Phone: (555) 555-5555 Email: MaryJones@domain.com

Work Experience

My Firm, My City, My State 55555

    Project Manager January Year to Present

    Provided independent, dependable, and effective project management as a project manager to projects of the financial division. Performed project assessment as part of ongoing evidence-based practice. Worked with and communicated effectively with an interdisciplinary team to plan, develop, and implement projects that met the immediate needs of stakeholders. Evaluated the project teams and stakeholder response to the project and made adjustments to the project plan. Documented components of the project based on the firm's policy and procedures.

Some Firm, Some City, Some State 55555

    Project Leader Year to Year

As a project leader of a mission critical project, I provided independent, dependable, and effective management and performed ongoing project assessment for a major subset of the project. Evaluation of the project team's and stakeholder responses to the ongoing development of the project based on the firm's policies and procedures were documented and effectively communicated to the interdisciplinary team that managed the mission critical project. Recommendations were made to the interdisciplinary team to adjust the overall project plan.

Any Firm, Some City, Some State 55555

    Project Team Member Year to Year

    In the information technology department, I provided independent, dependable, and effective systems analysis based on ongoing evidence-based practices as a member of the project team. I effectively communicated and interacted with all levels of stakeholders to develop detailed workflows of all business processes that were automated by the project. Recommendations were made to the interdisciplinary team to modify the project plan to meet new workflows and related policies and procedures.

Education/Certifications

Bachelor of Science in Business Administration (BS)

    My School, Some City, Some State 55555

Master of Business Administration (MBA) in progress

PMP Certification

Cover Letter or No Cover Letter

In the days before submitting resumes electronically, resumes were sent on paper through the postal service—sometimes referred to as "snail mail." In those days, you greeted the recruiter for the first time in a cover letter that briefly introduced yourself to the recruiter, told the recruiter why you were contacting them, and asked the recruiter to read your enclosed resume.

Today, fewer candidates send resumes by mail because recruiters often prefer—or may demand—that all inquiries about jobs to be made electronically using the application tracking system that is available on the firm's website. An email is accepted, but the usual reply politely redirects you to the application tracking system. Keep in mind that you may be one of hundreds applying for the many positions posted on the firm's website.

The application tracking system usually offers the option to upload a cover letter. It may seem a waste of time to do so since the application tracking system parsed your resume into the application form that was then searched for key words and phrases to match your application against requirements for the job. For the most part, the application tracking system decides which applicants are presented to the recruiter. The cover letter seems irrelevant.

But is the cover letter *really* irrelevant? Maybe not, considering a good number of applications don't upload one in the application tracking system. You might stand out if you include a cover letter. The cover letter must be brief and customized to the position. The salutation should use the recruiter's name, if available, such as "Dear Ms. Smith." State that you are an experienced project manager and list the position for which you are applying. The next paragraph should tell your story using some of the terms found in the job description. You want to make it easy for the recruiter to match your background to the job requirements. The last paragraph encourages the recruiter to invite you for an interview. Here is a sample email cover letter.

Dear Ms. Smith,

For the previous seven years, I have been a PMP certified project manager working in the financial industry and would like to be considered for your project manager position.

As you will note in my resume, I provide independent, dependable, and effective project management based on ongoing evidence-based practices as a project manager. I am an effective member of an interdisciplinary team that performs ongoing assessment, planning, and implementation of projects.

I look forward to meeting you in person to further explore your needs for a project manager. I can be reached at (555) 555-5555 or by email at MaryJones@domain.com.

Yours truly,

Mary Jones, BS PMP

Reapplying to a Former Employer

Every sales person knows that it is easier to sell to a previous customer than to a new customer as long as the previous customer had a good experience with you. You are your own salesperson, and convincing the recruiter to rehire you is less challenging than convincing a recruiter from a different firm that you are the perfect candidate for a project manager position.

In some firms, a terminated employee—and resigning is a form of termination—may be placed on the do-not-rehire list, depending on the employee's evaluation and reason for termination. Anyone not on this list might be considered for future positions within the firm. This typically means that the recruiter considers your application along with other applicants.

Recruiters and managers realize that good project managers leave for new opportunities. As long as the parting was amicable, there is an excellent chance that the project manager can return to their previous employer. Did you leave on good terms? Many times the answer depends on the recruiter and the manager(s). This may go beyond your last evaluations and not being on the do-not-rehire list. It may be based on perceptions (or misperceptions) of your performance.

If you didn't have any time management or attendance problems, you performed what was seen as quality work, and you didn't complain, then you are likely to be viewed as a good project manager—rehiring is a viable option. Likewise, if you were a team player, pitched in without being asked to do so, and were a problem-solver, then you probably were seen as a super project manager. There is no question about rehiring you—in fact, you might be actively recruited.

However, the slightest negative perception by a manager may present a barrier to being rehired. The hiring manager may ask her colleague, "Did you know Mary Jones? She worked in Information Technology three years ago and applied for my project manager's position." Any negative response may cast doubt on the viability of her candidacy for the position—even if her colleague confused Mary Jones with Mary Adams, who was a terrible project manager.

Apply to your former employer using the application tracking system if you feel you fit the open position. Contact former colleagues who still work there and ask if they can recommend you to the recruiter or the hiring manager. The goal is to have the recruiter or the hiring manager retrieve your application from the application tracking system so you don't have to gamble that the application tracking system will select your application.

You have a track record with the organization that the recruiter can easily review. Even a moderately successful experience may get you an interview with the recruiter. However, you have to sell yourself during the interviewing process. Just because you worked there before and know the staff and managers doesn't mean that you'll be hired. Sell yourself as if this was your first interview by following the steps mentioned in this chapter. Don't assume they know you—they may have misperceptions about you that you can correct during the interview.

What to Expect During the Interview

You get one chance to make a first impression, so treat your first interview with the recruiter as something special. Let the recruiter know if you are coming or going to work after or before the interview. This is understandable, and giving the recruiter a heads-up before the interview sets expectations and your time limits. Dress professionally.

Arrive early for the interview, giving you time to find your way, should you get lost or have difficulty finding a parking space. Arriving early may get your interview started early if the recruiter is running ahead of schedule. This is usually a plus for the recruiter. Be patient if the recruiter is running late — and late might be over an hour. Sit calmly and avoid complaining. Ask the receptionist if you can reschedule your interview if you have a pressing appointment.

Smile and introduce yourself to the recruiter, being sure to make eye contact at all times. Be friendly and consider the recruiter as a new colleague—you hope. Your body language and the tone in your voice projects your character more than what you say during the initial encounter with the recruiter.

Start with small talk—your experiences finding the facility, parking, and locating Human Resources. Don't be afraid to open the conversation. Speak in complete sentences. This shows that you are comfortable taking the lead when engaging with a stranger. Project managers do this all the time. Small talk will gradually move into the substance of the interview when the recruiter takes the lead in the conversation.

The recruiter wants to know you, the person behind the application—they might begin with an open-ended question, "So what makes you think our project manager's job is right for you?" Keep in mind that the recruiter already knows that your background is a fit based on your application. The recruiter is really asking you to demonstrate your communication skills and how you think on your feet.

An open-ended question gives you the opportunity to sell yourself. The best way to do this is to connect your experience to each job requirement. Be honest and let the recruiter know which are a perfect fit, close fit, or no fit at all. Don't hide the fact that you don't meet every requirement of the job, but do show how the requirements you do meet overshadow those requirements that you do not meet.

This approach helps the recruiter in a number of ways. First, you've read the job requirements. Next, you know you're qualified because you matched your background to each job requirement. And you helped the recruiter match your background to the job requirements. In essence, you've done part of the recruiter's job for them. Expect to be challenged on your comparisons to the job requirements, especially those requirements that don't appear to match with your background. You'll know where these are and should have a prepared response if you've done your homework prior to the interview. Speak with confidence about your abilities and experiences. Be social and humorous at times, but serious when answering the core of questions.

Next, the recruiter is likely to look for holes in your application by chronologically looking at your background. Gaps in employment or short periods of employment are fine as long as you have a rational explanation. However, a series of short periods of employment is a red flag and is probably difficult to explain. Recruiters are less concerned about the length of employment because it has become more acceptable for a person to remain in a position of a year or two and then move on to a better position.

The recruiter would like to know why you want to leave your current position. Keep in mind that if you work in an industry that has a few firms, the recruiter probably knows a lot about your current firm. Industries are small communities where employees move from firm to firm several times during their career.

Respond professionally. Avoid bad-mouthing your former boss and firm because the recruiter will probably ask, "What makes you think things will be different here?" That's tough to answer since you haven't worked there yet. Saying that you are looking for a change is an acceptable response. Moving to a different area of project management not presently available at your current employer is also a reasonable response. A change in schedule such as traveling is another reasonable response. You might be looking to travel more or less often.

The recruiter may ask you about your career goals. The recruiter is trying to find out if you think of project management as a job or a profession. Some experienced candidates simply want to do a great job managing a project and then go home. Other experienced candidates may do the same and look toward improving their professional skills through education and other professional activities away from the job. The recruiter may think both of these experienced candidates are qualified for the position. There is no right or wrong answer.

At some point, the interview could change direction from you selling yourself to the recruiter telling you about the job. The recruiter might tell you that this position probably isn't a good fit, might thank you for coming, or suggest that you keep looking at job postings for other positions. However, the recruiter may start selling you on the job if you convinced them that you are a viable candidate for the position. Don't read too much into the recruiter's sales pitch. You still have a lot of hurdles to jump over before you receive a job offer. And the recruiter might be keeping your hopes up while they search for the perfect candidate.

Always thank the recruiter for their time with you regardless of whether or not the interview ended on a positive note. Ask about the next step in the process and approximately how long it might be before you hear back from her. If you weren't a fit for this position, ask the recruiter if you should apply for more appropriate positions in the future. A positive response might indicate that you handled yourself professionally and that there were no gaping holes in your resume that will prevent you from applying for another position.

After the Interview

The hardest part of the interviewing process is waiting patiently for a response from the recruiter, especially if your interview ended on an upbeat note. Expecting a call from the recruiter when you get home is unrealistic. A week or more may go by without any indication on the status of your application. You may be one of possibly a hundred or so candidates applying for the many jobs that are posted on the firm's website. The recruiter usually waits until all interviews are completed before arranging for the next round of interviews with prospective candidates.

Send a brief thank you email to the recruiter, listing three examples of how you meet the job requirements. At the end of the email, indicate that you look forward to meeting with the recruiter again in the future to discuss the position. Don't expect a reply. The recruiter knows that you are anxious to pursue the position, but let the recruiter process all the applications—including yours.

You will be contacted if the recruiter feels you are a viable candidate, but there is no set time period for this to happen. Much is happening behind the scenes (see Chapter 2). Your application, along with other those of qualified candidates, is sent for review to the hiring manager. The manager may get back to the recruiter within a few hours, or a few weeks.

Don't harass the recruiter! Wait ten days after the interview and send the recruiter an email asking a relevant follow-up question about the position, not whether you are still being considered. Be sure to clearly identify the position by name, since the recruiter is likely interviewing many candidates for many different positions. The follow-up question might be about tuition reimbursement, the use of seniority for scheduling, or health insurance benefits. It is reasonable for you to clarify these issues. The recruiter might provide the status of your application when answering your email.

Don't stop looking for a position! Although you may think you're the perfect candidate, you have no facts to compare yourself to the other candidates. They too may be perfect candidates. The recruiter and the hiring manager typically select three or four candidates for the next round of interviews. You'll probably receive a rejection email quickly if you are not one of those selected. However, some recruiters don't send rejection emails to viable candidates until a candidate accepts the job offer. This is one reason there might be a delay in hearing from the recruiter after your last interview. At some point you'll be invited to meet with the hiring manager or be told that someone more qualified for the position accepted the job offer.

Meeting the Hiring Manager

Getting a call rather than an email from the recruiter is a sign that you still are in the running for the position. The next step is meeting the hiring manager. The manager is looking for an experienced project manager who will fit well with the current team. Unfortunately there is no checklist that helps decide if you are a fit. However, the manager wants you to communicate well, listen carefully, demonstrate that you understand what is being said, and respond professionally. A manager typically goes with their gut feeling when choosing a project manager to join the team.

Follow the same procedures you did for your interview with the recruiter. Give yourself time to get lost and find your way. Arrive for the interview about fifteen minutes early. Greet the manager with small talk, always making eye contact and speaking in complete sentences. The manager may or may not ask similar questions posed by the recruiter. Each manager has their own style of interviewing and has far less experience interviewing than the recruiter.

Some managers may describe their unit and the open position to you before asking you any questions. Don't take this as an indication that you are a good candidate for the position. Instead, the manager may simply be managing your expectations, describing the positives and the challenges about the job before asking you to present yourself.

Feel free to ask the manager specifics about the unit and the position before responding to questions. You can always tell the manager that you want to frame your answers based on the needs of the department. Prepare to give a two-minute synopsis of your story tailored to what you know of the department and position. Focus on your recent project management experience. Try to include something humorous but not negative. Describe how you are a team player in your current position. Give examples of how you use critical thinking when meeting the challenges of a project. Fill in information that the manager probably needs to know about you but may have forgotten to ask you. Your goal is to show the manager that you are a skilled project manager who will be a valued asset to the manager's team.

Summarize your understanding of the position and how your background complements the job requirements at the conclusion of the interview. Tell the manager whether or not you think this is a fit. Be honest. Raise any deal-breakers for you before the end of the interview. The manager may or may not be able to accommodate you. If no accommodations can be made, then you are not a fit for the job, but the manager or recruiter may have other job openings in the future that are a fit. So leave on an upbeat note.

Follow up with an email to the manager after the interview. Also email the recruiter describing how well your interview went with the manager. Give the manager and recruiter time to make a decision. This may take several weeks. You'll have to sit tight; however, emailing the manager after ten days. Asking a relevant question is permissible, such as, what project management software is used for the project? You might be given an inkling of the status of your application.

Chapter 5
Project Managers with Reputations
or Recommendations

If you have been a project manager and have acquired a reputation or have been recommended for a given job, you may be treated slightly differently from a typical candidate. In the end, however, you must prove yourself as the right candidate. These advantages may help you, in the sense that you may not be asked to take the test that other candidates are required to take, but you must be prepared. The level of scrutiny likely depends on the duration of your employment or, if just a project, its importance. The organization may be more likely to accept your recommendations or reputation for a single project than for a long-term commitment. If you are looking at a single project, the position may be worthwhile if the project is to your advantage and offers you something (money, challenge, new connections). If so, then direct the conversation to your other commitments and foregoing them for the project at hand. You may be in a position to influence the nature of interviews by changing the dialog to what it will take for them to win you over. In this chapter, you'll learn what it takes to select your next firm and your next project by carefully examining details of the deal with your new firm. Details in your agreement may build a foundation for success or can scuttle your prospects from the outset.

Myths vs. Facts About You

Reputations tend to be a mix of myths and facts, especially if executives of the new firm haven't worked directly with you. Myths are usually shrouded in hyperbole by your champions within the firm who advocate for you as the go-to person. Some pre-selling is needed. It is like the warm-up act for a concert—everyone may be convinced that the main act (you) will deliver the knockout punch. Executives are conditioned to believe in you well before your first face-to-face meeting.

Facts are based in reality. Can you live up to your reputation? Are you being oversold? These are not easy questions to answer, because you didn't write, approve, or deliver the sales pitch, and you were probably not in the room when the sales pitch was given. Your advocate is sold, but your advocate doesn't have to deliver results. You must decide if you can deliver.

Knowing myth from fact is challenging because you must take a sobering look at your previous projects. How much of your project's success was based on you, and how much of the success was greatly influenced by others? Were you really the super star that drove home those projects, or were you in the right place at the right time and/or had the right team to do the heavy lifting? It is important to know

https://doi.org/10.1515/9781501506222-006

yourself and what your strengths and weaknesses are. No one is perfect and your purpose is to convince the interviewer that you are the best person for the job. That said, no matter your background or reputation, it is important to decide on a job or a project with a realistic understanding of your capabilities.

The success of a project is influenced by many factors. Here are a few of them:

The staff: You hired the team and then created the environment within which they could deliver the project. They did most if not all of the work while you got out of their way. Your contribution to the success of the project was to hire the right staff and let them do the job. In a sense, the staff ensured success—not necessarily you. This, however, is one of the most important traits of a good project manager.

Definition of success: Success is defined by meeting expectations of the project sponsor and stakeholders. Were your previous projects successful because you met the original expectations, or were expectations lowered once the project got under-way to ensure that the project was successful? Project sponsors don't want it known that they sponsored projects that fail. It is not at all uncommon for project sponsors to change project requirements to meet what the project manager can deliver, leading everyone to believe the project was successful. This is known as *moving the goal post*.

Executive backing: It is often the case that projects are successful because the project manager was given all resources and financial backing needed to complete the project, even when the project looked like a failure. In a sense, a touted project manager is given the resources to correct mistakes that occurred during the project. Those mistakes might have happened because of unrealistic project requirements or poor planning. In such cases, the project manager might be given a blank check to ensure success when, without strong executive backing, the project would have failed. In such a case, the managers who helped the project get through likely did it with their own interests in mind and most likely have a good understanding of what it takes to make it work out.

Politics: Your success may be a result of friends in high places—friends that are not there to help you in your new firm. It may be important for you to establish those relationships with the new organization.

Luck: Everything seemed to work out on your projects. It was the right time, right project, right project sponsor, right stakeholders, and right staff. Success hap-pened because all the stars aligned. Will the stars align again? How responsible are you for your own successes? What can you do to repeat your successes? Do you have a specialty that you are especially good at? What are your weaknesses?

Take a sobering look at the basis for your reputation and decide for yourself to what extent your talent was the key ingredient to the success of your projects. Or was it your staff, moving the goal post, strong executive backing, friends in the right positions, or luck? Project management is a role where knowing your own ca-pabilities and the people you work with are critical to success.

If possible, find out what executives in the new firm know about you. What did your advocate say? What information caused executives to decide that you are a candidate for the position? Answering these questions combined with an honest look at yourself gives insight into whether you'll succeed.

Myths vs. Facts About the Firm

Is the firm's reputation based on myths or facts? In a sense, you are hiring the firm. Do research before meeting executives of the firm. There are countless well-known, highly reputable firms who find competing in today's market a challenge to the firm's sustainability. Simply speaking, the old way of doing business may no longer work and change may be too difficult or too late.

You may not want to join a firm whose real reputation will tarnish your reputation, even if your project is successful. Industry sources developed throughout your career can provide insight both into the industry and firms within the industry. Ask your contacts about the executive who is sponsoring the project and hiring you. Find out if the executive is up to the task. Hanging on to a rising star is more desirable than a falling star who has lost support of the firm's leadership.

For public companies, there is a wealth of Wall Street analysis available of both the industry and publicly held firms. Read back issues of business publications to gain a sense of what those in the know feel about the firm. Keep in mind that shareholders typically look for short-term gains and sour on firms that don't hit their expected numbers. This doesn't mean the firm is bad. The firm may have longer-term opportunities—one may be your project that turns around the firm.

You are a project manager, not a stock analyst—however, you need to be concerned about the well-being of the firm. It pays to know if there are issues that might impact your project, which might include possible takeovers or doubts about the current management, layoffs, or other events, as new projects are likely high on the list when cost-cutting is needed.

Employee vs. Contractor

Your reputation places you in a unique situation within the firm because executives see you as a person who can solve a critical problem facing the firm. Within reason, you can write your own ticket. Executives may be of the opinion that they'll pay any price to fix the problem, and you are the fixer.

You may have the option to join the firm as an employee or a contractor. There is a significant difference. Either can be the right fit for you. Here are a few points to consider.

Employee:
- You need to fit within the firm's structure.

- There is a hierarchy, compensation bands, and related perks that guide executives through negotiations of where to place you within the organization. Rarely is there really a blank check.
- You'll have benefits similar to other employees within your compensation band.
- Employees are the first paid.
- Some policies and procedures that govern employment may be waived because of your status while others won't be changed.
- The terms of employment letter is the official offer that explains expectations of the employer and the employee. Both parties must live within these terms. It is here where you see agreement to your terms; scope of control over the project; pay and bonus; and termination arrangements.
- Liability rests with the firm and not the employee.
- You are reimbursed for business related expenses.
- Bringing the project in under budget may not change your compensation based on your terms of employment.
- There may be an expectation of permanency once the project is completed. You stay on with the firm.

Contractor:
- You are independent.
- You are given an objective—the project deliverable—and you decide how to achieve the objective.
- Terms of your engagement are defined in a contract.
- You do not receive benefits.
- The only compensation you receive is defined in the contract.
- There is no expectation of permanency. Once terms of the contract are met, the relationship with the firm terminates.
- The contract may be terminated by the firm at any time with little or no notice. A termination clause in the contract determines terms and compensation at termination.
- You likely will pay all your business expenses unless otherwise provided for.
- You may employ employees and other subcontractors, depending on contract terms. They work for you, not the firm. In some projects, you may be using the firm's staff and resources to deliver the project.
- You are responsible for contingency plans and financing unless otherwise specified in the contract. You may incur the cost if your project plan falters and requires more resources than anticipated in your contract.
- Liability rests with you and not the firm.
- You may be required to reimburse the firm for using their resources (e.g., office space), depending on terms of the contract.

- Penalties may be imposed if you fail to deliver the project on time and on budget.
- Cash flow concerns. You are paid as a vendor within 30 days, 60 days, 90 days, or longer from the time the invoice is received. You must pay your expenses while waiting for payment from the firm.
- Revenue paid by the firm in excess of your expenses is profit and goes into your pocket.

Scope of Authority

Successfully managing a project requires that you have the authority to manage the project as you see fit. However, managing the project within the existing structure and politics of the firm can hamper your management ability. You want a widest possible scope of authority.

It's best to anticipate conflicts within the organization and negotiate a clear course to resolve potential conflicts as part of your onboarding agreement. There may be competing internal political interests within the firm that could impede your project, which is expected in many firms. Establishing the ground rules with executives prior to joining the firm goes a long way to circumventing disagreements.

Management Support for the Project

Explore the depth of management support for the project before you agree to join the firm. The number of executives who truly agree that the project is mission critical to the success of the firm defines the depth of support for the project. The key word is "truly" and not simply showing support to avoid signs of opposing influential executives. The best possible scenario is for everyone in the firm to agree that the project is the lifeblood of the firm and necessary to maintaining a competitive position in the market. The worse scenario is that only the executive hiring you has this belief and others passively differ, expecting to provide little support for the project once it gets underway.

It is difficult to estimate the depth of management support for the project, especially if executives are vocally championing the project. With the help of your contacts, industry sources, publications, and other information about the firm, competitors, and the marketplace, you should be able to identify problems facing the firm. You should be able to assess options the firm has to address those problems, one of which is the project. As a result, you'll be in a position to determine the strength of the project. There is a good chance that there is depth of management support for the project. However, expect support to wane if other options are equally viable, since there may be varied opinions on the benefit of the project or support for projects of more value to the organization.

Management Support for You

Executives may be in agreement that the project is important to the firm, but are they sold on you being the go-to project manager? Some executives might feel that there are likely others who are also viable candidates and who also have a solid reputation delivering mission-critical projects. Probe your advocate to identify your competition.

Don't assume that you are the only candidate for the position. This is rarely the case. You might be the strongest candidate, but protocol requires executives to consider other candidates to justify their selection. They can't say you are the best candidate if you are the only candidate for the position. If you are in a favorable position, do your research in the firm and make sure that any advantage you have is bolstered by your interest in the job, as evidenced by your knowledge of the organization. They may ask you harder questions specifically about the organization based on your presumed abilities.

Expect that internal and external candidates are each likely to have their own advocate who is selling their candidate behind the scenes. Unfortunately, you don't know whose advocate is the better salesperson. The best scenario is that your advocate is correct and you are the best choice because of your experience. The worst scenario is that your advocate bullied executives into choosing you. You might have gotten the position, but your advocate may have made enemies who could be lying in wait for opportunities to prove your advocate wrong.

It is not only executive support you'll need to successfully gain. You'll need other managers and staff who will directly or indirectly work on your project to support you too. Without the support of the other team members, your project might fail. Assessing your support before accepting the position goes a long way to determine the time and effort you'll need to be selling yourself during the first months of the project. Unfortunately, there is no easy way to learn how the staff and other managers will favor you until you get onboard.

Financial Support for the Project

Identify the financial commitment to the project during your interviewing process. Focus on magnitude, numbers, and contingencies rather than a budget. You are a star project manager who can estimate the size of the investment needed to produce the deliverable based on your previous projects or by estimating the cost of more recent projects in the industry. Your goal is to make executives aware of how much the project is realistically going to cost and the potential cost overruns.

It is important that they understand the full impact of their decision to move ahead with the project before you agree to manage the project. You are looking for a commitment upfront, not surprises after you sign on and once development is underway. Also estimate if the firm can afford the project. This isn't a consideration for larger firms who have the financial assets to undertake a mission-critical project. However, firms whose financial resources are already stretched, startups, and those who are looking for the project to get the firm back on strong footing may find financing the project a challenge.

Realistic Expectations: Challenge vs. Manageable

One of the most important decisions to make is determining if the project is viable. Is it a project that you can deliver? Your reputation, like most, is a blend of fact and myth. Your champions might paint you as a project manager able to deliver the most challenging project under any circumstance. Don't believe your press clippings. You're not a super hero. You are a smart project manager who selects projects that are meaningful to the organization and doable.

Is this project a challenge for you or a project that is manageable? A challenging project is one that pushes your skillset beyond your comfort zone. It is risky because of the many unknowns that you haven't encountered in your career. Delivering a challenging project enhances your reputation as a go-to project manager, but also increases the risk of failure that may tarnish your reputation.

The perfect project is one that others find challenging and you find manageable because your project manager's toolbox is loaded with proven tricks that can get you out of potential disasters. These are strategies known only to a few of your colleagues. Decide if you want a truly challenging project or one that seems challenging, but is doable.

Termination Terms

Nothing is forever. At some point, either your services will no longer be required or you'll find better opportunities outside the firm. Hopefully this occurs once the project is successfully completed. Realistically, termination can happen at any time, so it is best to mutually decide the parting terms during the negotiations to join the firm.

Termination is dissolving the relationship for whatever reason. It can occur at key points in the relationship, such as when the project deliverable is accepted by users. It can be a time period (such as a year) after which point you and executives of the firm revisit your arrangement. And it can happen when either you or executives decide that the relationship is no long advantageous for either or both of you.

Any termination is awkward unless you or executives planned for the termination as part of your terms of employment. Since you are coming onboard as a desired project manager, you can negotiate favorable termination terms. Here are a few factors to consider.

– Compensation: You can have a financial cushion when your employment terminates. Ask for compensation that will keep you financially stable until you settle down in a new position. The amount of compensation to ask for depends on the length of time it takes to find the next opportunity. Don't underestimate the gap. You have a solid reputation and draw high compensation; however, you need to find a firm that needs your talent at the same time when you're looking for a new job. The stars might take months or longer to align.

– Contingencies: Consider all the possible reasons for termination in your agreement. There might be a high-level management change, leading to a new direction for the firm. As a result, your mission-critical project is no longer critical and may be curtailed. The firm might be acquired by or merged with another organization. And your supporters may be terminated, leaving you exposed and without an advocate.

– Payment: You'll need to agree on when you'll receive termination compensation. It can be a lump sum or a continuation of your regular pay periods.

– Relationship: Termination means that your relationship with the firm ends. However, you can negotiate that you remain on as a consultant or work on "special projects," which really means that your employment continues for an agreed upon period as you hunt for new opportunities. These new opportunities might lie elsewhere in the firm.

– Benefits: Come to terms on when your health insurance and other benefits terminate. Try to have benefits extend for 12 months or more to cover you until you settle down.

– Confidentiality/Nondisclosure: You'll be expected to sign confidentiality and nondisclosure agreements when you join the firm. These are designed to protect the firm; however, consider including terms that limit what the firm and its employees can say about you too. You have a reputation to uphold and you need to restrain any potential negative comments that may tarnish your reputation. This is especially critical if the project should fail. Mission-critical projects for leading firms typically become well known in the industry. Failure of the project may lead to despairing remarks about you, the project leader. An agreement of what can be said should the project fail to meet expectations goes a long way to protecting your reputation, especially if factors outside your control caused the failure.

Compensation

What compensation do you want for managing the firm's mission-critical project? You'll need to decide the numbers, but you should consider various compensation structures that might be available. Much of what is listed here is not going to be available to a typical project manager, but they are included here for those who are in favorable negotiating situations. Here are types of elements that you should consider:

- Signing bonus: A signing bonus is a fixed amount that is given to you for agreeing to work for the firm. This is a sweetener that helps you make your decision and is usually a fixed amount that might be a percentage of your annual salary.
- Salary: Assuming you are employed by the firm and are not a consultant, expect to receive a salary. The salary is a fixed amount that is given to you at regular periods during the year that is usually determined by the firm's policy. Your salary usually needs to fit within the salary structure of the firm. The salary structure is defined as a compensation grade, with each compensation grade having a salary range and other perks. The hiring executives will assign you to the appropriate compensation grade based on your position within the firm and the agreed upon compensation package.
- Stock Options: You might be offered stock options. A stock option is the right to purchase a share of stock at a specified price, called the *strike price*. You can exercise the right based on terms set by the firm. In theory, your efforts will increase the value of the firm and as a result, the stock price will also increase. Once you are permitted to exercise your rights, you can purchase the stock at the strike price. The difference between the strike price and the current price is your profit. Of course, this assumes that the stock price increased beyond the strike price, which is referred to as "in the money." The stock price may fall below the strike price, making your stock options worthless.
- Stock: You might be offered stock known as *restricted stock*. Restricted stock is stock you own but must hold for a specific time period before you can sell the stock. The firm has stock that the firm owns, called *treasury stock*. You may be assigned a specific number of treasury stock shares. Once the restricted period expires, you are given the stock that you can place in your stock portfolio or sell. The firm might give you the cash value of the stock based on current market value, if you wish.
- Performance Bonus: A performance bonus is additional compensation—money, stock option, or stock—that you receive for reaching a goal (long-term incentive). The goal might be the delivery of the project deliverable or reaching a milestone on time and on budget (short-term incentive). A performance bonus might also be awarded for bringing the project in sooner and at a lower cost than expected. Depending on the industry, a performance bonus may be the

bulk of your compensation. For example, Wall Street firms pay bonuses that are multiple times the base salary for certain categories of employees. The theory is that you shared in the firm's profit as long as the firm made a profit.

- Retention Bonus: A retention bonus is an amount paid to retain your services once the project concludes. The firm may want to keep you on once your goal is achieved, rather than lose you to another firm. Think of a retention bonus as a sign-on bonus for the next project.

- Consultation Bonus: A consultation bonus might be offered once the project is delivered, but the firm does not want to retain you in your role as a project manager. Instead they want you to be available to consult on the deliverable after the project is implemented. You might be expected to be on-site for a time period or at least be available by phone to address any issues that might occur during the post-implementation period.

- Increases: Consider asking for compensation increases, especially if you are working on a multi-year project.

- Gross Up: In reality, you'll never see the dollar amount of your compensation unless you are a consultant because of various normal deductions and taxes. Gross up is an accounting technique that adjusts your compensation for deductions and taxes. Let's say you want $150,000 cash and normal deductions and taxes are 50 percent. Knowing this, you can use the gross up technique and ask for $300,000 so that after normal deductions and taxes, you'll receive $150,000 cash.

- Deferred Compensation: Deferred compensation is compensation that you earned but are paid after your employment is terminated. You might be able to defer receiving bonuses and stock after you leave the firm in order to possibly reduce the tax liability of receiving a lump sum. This provides ongoing cash flow for you, regardless of your current employment opportunities.

- Annuity: The firm might be open to purchasing you a fully paid annuity as part of your compensation. An annuity is an agreement with a financial firm such as an insurer for fixed, guaranteed future payments of cash based on current payments to the insurer. In this case, the firm makes one full payment guarantee to you for the flow of cash, beginning at a point of time in the future.

Probe during the Interviewing Process

A key objective is to learn as much about the firm and how the firm operates, especially the operations that will be affected by your project. Doing this helps you assess some of the important challenges you'll face once you sign on to the job. Executives can provide information about policies, procedures, and how decisions are made within the firm. Some may even give you information about the politics within the organization. Questions you may be asked are likely to be scenarios surrounding the company that also point to your preparedness for the interview.

You'll also want to speak with other project stakeholders, such as the process managers who can walk you through operational processes that will become directly part of the project. If possible, consider asking to meet process supervisors. These are staff who understand the day-to-day details of operations. They can tell you exactly how processes are performed.

As you meet with executives, key managers, and operational staff of the firm, look for barriers that may impede or prevent you and your project team from meeting expectations. Also assess if you have the skills necessary to meet these challenges.

Try to identify decision makers and probe their involvement in your project. How much do they influence the project? Are they in favor of, against, or have no opinion about the project? And who actually makes the final decisions? Answers to these questions help you determine whether the project is doable and if you are the right person to manage the project.

Try to find out what value the project is to each stakeholder and what it will take to make the project more valuable to stakeholders who appear against the project. Determine if you will be able to prove to them that the project is an improvement to their current situation.

If possible, brainstorm with your advocate. Identify influential stakeholders and their position on the project and about you. One of your goals is to identify each key stakeholder's expectations and create a list of potential problems and assess whether you can solve those problems.

Fact Finding Is Critical

Although the position might be tempting to accept, you must identify facts about the firm, executive leadership, stakeholders, and your chances of succeeding. Take control of the pre-employment interview process. You are just as much in charge of the interviewing process as executives are. Right or wrong, it is your decision to accept the position, and you need all the available information to make that decision.

Stay objective and don't become emotionally involved. Don't take anything to heart. Listen and fact-find. Stay flexible and change direction if needed during this process. Avoid talking unless you're looking for specific information because more information is gleaned from listening than talking. Be cordial but also firm when asking for specific information that you'll need to make a decision about joining the firm.

It is also critical that you make yourself appear different from others. You are a leader trying to help the firm solve a mission-critical problem. Your reputation also tells them that you are the go-to project manager. Now you must show them through your actions during fact-finding.

The Foundation for Negotiations

Probing and fact-finding during the interview process becomes the foundations for negotiating terms of employment. Always speak with authority and use a firm tone when speaking during the interview process, even when you are unsure of yourself. Here are a few facts that help you develop a negotiation strategy.

- Know the value of the firm to you: You've built a solid career in project management—one that has been recognized by leaders in your industry. Assess how much working for the new firm and managing the new project will advance your career and your financial future.
- Know the value of the project to the firm: Determine whether this is really a mission-critical project or a project that the project sponsor is hailing as mission-critical in order to better the project sponsor's career. Is the mission-critical aspect of the project more hype than fact?
- Know your value to the firm: Assess if you are really one of the few project managers who can deliver the project on time and on budget.
- Know your breakpoint: The breakpoint is the least terms you will accept. Failure of the firm to meet those terms will result in you walking away from the offer. Be ready to walk away if negotiations go beyond the breakpoint.
- Know your bargaining range: Bargaining range is the negotiable area between your opening position and your breakpoint.

Negotiations

Once you have the facts and know the value of each element and your breakpoint, decide if the position is right for you. Be objective. Walk away if you don't have all the facts or support from the firm's leadership. Also walk away if the project is too challenging. A key to success is to select projects that are within your capabilities to deliver.

Executives should be primed for negotiations. They already have a good impression about you, thanks to whoever advocated for you to join the firm. You are negotiating with the others who are sold on you. This is called sensation transference, which is used by consumer product companies. The packaging—the hype provided by your advocate—has left executives with a good impression about you. In a sense, this may be your job to lose.

Present yourself as a professional, showing you are confident, knowledgeable, and trusting. If you've done your homework, you should be able to explain your knowledge of how the firm works today and the challenges facing the firm in the future. Focus by explaining how you understand that the project will meet those challenges, ensuring that the firm will be sustainable and will grow in the future.

Should you and executives decide that the position is a fit, the negotiation process will begin. The party who speaks first and places an offer on the table is said to be at a disadvantage because by doing so, they set a value of the arrangement. For example, both sides have a salary in mind, but neither side knows if the salary is too little or too much until one side proposes the salary. You might want $175,000 and the firm might be offering $250,000. If you mention the salary first, chances are good that you might lose $75,000 annually.

Executives are likely to create an environment within which to discuss their needs, your role, and terms that will be negotiated. The stage is set for successful negotiations. However, look for signs that might scuttle negotiations before discussions begin. Don't be afraid to postpone negotiations to another time when executives are more receptive to receiving your message, or a time to negotiate without distractions. An angry executive is not going to listen attentively. An executive with a time constraint is unlikely to give you full attention.

Here are a few points to remember when negotiating.

- The winning strategy is to be well organized and prepared to respond to questions.
- Be professional, calm, efficient, persistent, and assertive.
- Don't feel intimidated, rushed, or emotionally involved.
- Strike a balance between assertiveness and respect and understanding.
- Never discuss anything until you are ready to discuss it.
- Be prepared before discussing anything. Do your homework.
- Open discussions on an upbeat.
- Avoid all discussions if the other person is unreasonable.
- Let the other side talk first and encourage them to make the opening offer. Remember that their opening offer is usually not their best and final offer. This is a position to begin discussions.
- Estimate their bargaining room. There might be elements that you require, but executives are unable to comply with such as managing the project out of your own office.
- Determine elements that are important to executives and the firm. These may not be important to you and can be used as bargaining chips to gain something that is important to you.
- If you find yourself having to present your position first, open with your maximum sustainable position. Ask for what you really want and then some. The firm can always counteroffer. Don't make your opening close to your breakpoint. If you do, then you will not have enough bargaining room.
- Think along lines of bartering when negotiating. There are things that are of low value to you and high value to the vendor, and things that are of high

value to you and low value to the vendor. Sometimes these are referred to as "sweeteners."
- Be alert for unclear terms, which are common pitfalls in negotiations. Every term should be clearly defined so there can be no chance of misunderstanding, which might lead to the failure of the project.

Your Pitch

Although executives may be pre-sold at some level, they haven't reached an agreement as yet. Exccutives go through the stages of adoption that lead them to hiring you. You need to lead them through the stages of adoption by explaining how you can manage the project to deliver the outcome that helps the firm meet its challenges.

Here's an outline that helps you walk executives through adopting the project and hiring you.

- Aware: Executives must be aware that a problem exists, the project is a solution, and you are the person to lead the project.
- Evaluation: Executives take a superficial look at the solution to see if it really solves the problem. This might have been done previously to you being considered as the project manager. They are looking at the puzzle pieces fitting.
- Examination: A closer look is taken, focusing on uncovering reasons why you and the project aren't the solution. They are looking at why the puzzle pieces won't fit.
- Testing: If executives determine that the project is likely a solution with few reasons for failure, attention turns to critical thinking and testing the solution based on facts known to executives.
- Adoption: Executives sign on to the project and to you as the project manager.

Keep Communication Focused on Need

You should have a strategy when communicating with executives during the preonboard process that anticipates their need for information. Your goal is to provide executives with just the information they need at the moment. Too much information is confusing. Too little information leads to questions. You want to stay in control of the information provided to executives.

One common strategy is SBAR. SBAR is a communication format that presents pieces of a problem in logical order to lead a person to support your conclusion. SBAR stands for situation, background, assessment, and recommendation. When a decision maker is presented with a problem (situation), attention is focused on the background and what led up to the situation. Once the background is known, the focus moves on to assessing the situation and looking for viable solutions before ending up with a recommendation to address the problem. Your goal is to compose all elements of SBAR before making the decision maker aware of the situation. You then reveal each element at the appropriate time, leading the decision maker to quickly focus on the recommended solution. The goal is to have the decision maker focus only on the decision and not spend time focused on identifying information required to make this decision. To make a decision, the decision maker needs to know the situation and background, then assess the facts and maybe ask experts for a recommendation. You are doing the legwork by providing the situation and background, summarizing your analysis, then giving your expert recommendation. The focus is on your recommendation.

Another effective approach is to use the inverted pyramid style of communication, which is common to news writing. Start with the headline, then the sub-headline, followed by a high-level explanation of the story. Expand the story with additional facts, background, and supportive information should the executive require additional information. Stop if no additional information is requested.

Here are some other tips on effectively communicating with executives during the pre-onboarding process and through negotiations.

- Define words that may be misunderstood.
- Select words that executives will understand.
- Use simple language—avoid jargon. Some executives pretend to understand but really haven't a clue as to what you are saying.
- Be clear and precise—stay on-point and avoid negative stories or anecdotes.
- Avoid words that are difficult to pronounce—this distracts from the message. The listener changes focus to pronouncing the word rather than understanding it.
- Ask for feedback either during or after the presentation.
- *Listen* carefully to feedback—make eye contact and concentrate on what the person is saying.
- Let the person finish their comment even if their remarks are off-base.
- Focus on the message and not the speaker—keep an open mind and suspend judgment until you gather all the facts.
- Put yourself in the other person's position so you can understand their viewpoint. They may identify a flaw in your message.
- Always let the speaker save face even if their remarks are outrageous.

Dealing with Difficult People during the Interview and Fact-Finding Process

Not everyone you meet during the pre-employment process will be on their best behavior. Here are a few points to consider.

- Stand up to a difficult stakeholder. Be understanding, but don't appease the inappropriate behavior. You can't change their behavior. There is no justification for the behavior, so don't seek to rationalize it.
- Cranky stakeholders usually have internal problems and they use their behavior to get their way. Agree only with true statements made by the stakeholder—don't agree just to appease the stakeholder.
- Aggressive stakeholders expect you to run away from them or react with rage. Stand up to the stakeholder without arguing. Wait for the stakeholder to run out of steam. Call the stakeholder by name and voice your opinion with confidence.
- The subtle sniper stakeholder gives disapproving looks and uses a sarcastic tone when voicing humorous put-downs. Provide feedback on how you are receiving the stakeholder's message. Ask if you understood correctly. Don't overlook this inappropriate behavior.
- Some stakeholders seem to always complain, primarily because they focus on the negative effects of the change. Speak with optimism. Acknowledge the stakeholder's concerns but balance those concerns with a sense of reality.
- Silent stakeholders avoid conflicts and responsibility. Ask questions that require a full response, then wait for the response. Don't permit the stakeholder to remain silent.

What Is Your Risk Tolerance?

Joining a new firm in a highly visible, demanding position brings risk. Nothing is certain, even if you have an ironclad work agreement that specifies the terms of employment. After signing the agreement, there is a honeymoon period during which everyone is supportive—afterward, you are expected to deliver regardless of circumstances.

There is a higher risk if you are coming from a stable organization where you have proven your worth. Alternatively, the organization may be unstable or you may be currently unemployed. In one case, you don't have to move to a riskier situation, and in the other, your options are limited. In both cases, you have your reputation to maintain.

You are more than another employee to the firm. You are the person who consistently solves problems that jeopardize the firm's sustainability. You have special talents that are respected within the industry, making you a cut above other project managers. Unfortunately, there is a tendency to judge you by results of your last project rather than a long stream of successful projects and one failure.

Be on the alert for these red flags that might indicate that the prospective project is more risky than you can tolerate.

- No one is clear on the project's scope.
- Estimates are unreliable and unrealistic.
- Business needs are consistently changing.
- Communication among executives is poor.
- The firm uses outdated technology and updating technology is not part of the project.
- Staff members that you are required to use are incompetent or unmotivated.
- Directions received from the project sponsor or stakeholders are in conflict with the organization's policies.

Identify fail points in the proposed project. A fail point is a period in the process of developing and implementing a project in which things can go wrong. For example, identifying specifications is a task that requires the cooperation of managers and employees. Any delay or outright failure to cooperate might result in the project's failure. After identifying fail points, clarify your management scope to mitigating the risk of failure. For example, can you hire, bring on consultants, or create virtual teams of experts within and outside the firm to address problems immediately when roadblocks are encountered? If you can manage without a lot of red tape, you'll have the authority to address fail points—otherwise, the project might be risker than you can tolerate.

Look for values in the firm that focus on success. A value is principle that defines what is important. Values guide decision making on all levels of the firm. Here are some positive values that reduce risks.

- Participatory: Everyone should have meaningful participation in the project.
- Proactive: Employees should be creative and proactive when solving problems.
- Open: All information is shared, regardless if the information negatively impacts the project or the firm.
- Outward-oriented: Focus is on the outcome and not the process. For example, sharing a problem is more effective and efficient than one person spending an endless amount of time attempting to solve a problem in isolation.
- Trusting: Everyone is here to do the best possible job and must be trusted.

Joining as a Contractor

Signing on as a contractor rather than an employee has the advantage that you are a vendor responsible for delivering the project limited by the terms of the contract. As a vendor you are relatively free of constraints of an employee; however, you also don't receive the benefits of an employee. There is no health insurance, vacation time, sick time, or a regular paycheck.

Instead, you are paid the same way utilities are paid. You send the firm an invoice and then wait for the invoice to be processed before receiving your check. Processing can take weeks or sometimes months, depending on the firm's cash flow. If the firm has slow receivables from customers, then expect the firm to be slow in paying their vendors, including you.

Firms use an accounting process called *aging payables*. The oldest bill is paid first, which impacts your cash flow. Your cash flow is critical to your success, especially if you are expected to pay your staff and subcontractors. They don't want to wait until you receive cash. You're expected to pay in a timely manner—otherwise, they may stop providing services.

Consider the following factors when negotiating a contract with the firm.

- Decide how you would like to be paid. At the end of the project, when milestones are achieved (progressive payment), or monthly payments are all common methods of payment.
- Do you want average regular payments, or progressive payments whose amounts reflect the amount of work completed?
- Determine the firm's payment policy and procedure, and the expected payment period—30 days, 60 days, or 90 days.
- Does the firm respond favorably to discounts? You may offer a 1 percent discount from the invoice amount if the firm pays within 10 days. Be careful that some firms will take the discount but not pay within 10 days, anticipating that you will not take action against the firm.
- Understand the terms of the contract. Know what work is covered under the payment schedule and the work that is outside the contract.
- Work that is required to complete the project may not be included in the original contract. Some firms prefer to negotiate into the original contract compensation for contingency work. It is difficult to set a price for work that is not yet defined; however, firms may want to build time and material terms in the original contract. Time is set at an agreeable daily compensation rate. Materials are the actual cost of materials for the new work when the work is required.
- Know the industry standards for your job. Industry standards are acceptable practices for an industry that may have priority over terms that are not explicit in the contract. For example, you order a 2" x 4" piece of lumber. However, the size you receive is 1.5 x 3.5 inches. This is acceptable according to industry

standards. The original board was 2" x 4" but normal drying and planning of the board reduced its size. You might say that the vendor did not live up to the terms of the contract, but that's not true. It meets industry standards.

– Develop a fallback plan if anticipated cash flow doesn't occur. If the firm doesn't pay your invoice in a timely way, then what is your Plan B?

Your reputation precedes you, which may enable you to circumvent the Human Resources recruiting process and go directly to executives who have the direct authority to bring you on board. This can be a mixed blessing. Typically, staff members in the Human Resources department know little (or at least less) about project management and the real needs of the hiring executive. This is why Human Resources departments administer pre-employment tests. You'll probably skip over pre-employment testing.

The hiring executive is likely project management savvy and knows the project and the type of project manager to manage it. Clearly, nothing is taken lightly when hiring a project manager. Expect to be drilled about how much you know about project management, the industry, and the firm. Simply reciting facts and figures won't cut it. You'll be expected to demonstrate critical thinking and how you will apply your knowledge and skills to meet challenges that may occur during the new project.

Chapter 6
Choosing a Project Management Specialty

Developing a Career Path

Few project managers actually plan their project management career aside from training, earning the PMP certificate, and finding a first project management job. A project management career seems to evolve from circumstances and opportunities that happen, not planning. Downsizing may force you to explore a different type of project management. Openings within your firm may give you a chance to branch into a new specialty. However, you probably don't have a master plan or a career path.

A career path is a plan that states a goal and the tasks necessary to reach that goal. You had such a plan when you first thought about becoming a project manager. The goal was to become PMP-certified. You selected a training program, identified and completed pre-requests, and then passed each course required to complete the program. You prepped for the PMP certificate and you passed. You became a PMP-certified project manager.

Recruiters are noted for asking, "Where you do see yourself five years from now?" They want to determine if you have a career plan and whether or not the open position acts as a stepping stone for reaching your career goal. Some candidates simply fake a response to make themselves sound as though they have a well-thought-out master plan for their career, ensuring that the open position is the next step in their career plan.

Consider asking yourself where you want to be in five years. Your answer may surprise you. You might want to pursue information technology application projects, enterprise project management, or extreme project management. These are just a few of the many project opportunities that are available to you, which you'll learn more about later in this chapter. Each area of project management has its own requirements—many of which are not standardized—but usually follows a traditional career path from novice to expert project manager.

Your initial career path was to become a professional project manager. During your novice stage, you acquired the know-how to perform project management tasks through learning from preceptors and from your own experience. You followed rules and had little responsibility for the outcomes of your task. As an advanced beginner, you learned more sophisticated rules and you were able to prioritize tasks based on importance. You formed the foundation for making project management decisions and accepted responsibility for those decisions. You probably made those decisions with little assistance from more experienced colleagues.

Next, you became a proficient project manager using the wealth of experience as the basis of your project management intuition. You made calculated decisions

https://doi.org/10.1515/9781501506222-007

that produced an effective result. You finally became an expert project manager, able to perform all project manager duties fluidly, with most actions performed unconsciously based on your broad library of experience. You respond to most situations—including those with critical outcomes—as routine.

Transitioning from a novice to an expert project manager provides the framework for your career path. Set your goal, such as becoming a professional project manager. Explore requirements—education and experience—to attain the goal, then develop and execute a career path. Once you've completed the basic educational and certification requirements, your focus should change to the novice to expert project manager framework. Regardless of your management experience, you'll start off as a novice when you enter an area of project management that is new to you, and you'll need to work through each stage before becoming an expert project manager. You may move quickly through each stage if you are an expert project manager in a complementary field of management, such as going from information technology application projects to information technology networking projects. However, expect a slower transition if you are moving to a different type of project management—such as enterprise project management or extreme project management—where your skills are not directly transferable.

Consider developing an end-game career path. Do you really want to continue managing routine projects when you are in your fifties or sixties? Routine projects take a toll on your body as you grow older, especially if you find yourself on the road most weekdays. There will likely be a time when you can no longer provide quality project management. This doesn't mean you need to give up on project management. Bedside routine project management gives you a wealth of skills that can be transferred to many other areas of project management, as you'll see later in this chapter. Developing an end-game career path helps you build the experience and educational requirements to move to other areas of project management.

Obstacle to Change

Remember the first time you took over a project. You had butterflies in your stomach. There was a sense of excitement of unknown challenges that lay before you. You probably were on your "A" game. That spark and excitement probably left you years ago when you became the expert project manager. You know what to expect each day and even the unknowns become routine. There is little excitement and no butterflies in your stomach. Changing to a new career path in project management rekindles the spark that makes project management exciting again—there are new challenges, new learning opportunities, and new ways to bring ideas to fruition.

If there were no obstacles, what different area of project management would you explore? Give an honest answer, and investigate obstacles that really stand between you and your dream. Learn how to eliminate those obstacles by going around them or breaking them down. Begin your investigation by reviewing a general description of the job. You'll find the more common ones in this chapter. Look at actual job postings at firms around your area. You'll notice that what you think might be job requirements are listed as optional and nice to have, but not a requirement. You'll find educational and professional certifications listed as requirements.

Assume you can meet all requirements with a little work on your part, such as returning to school or taking the PMP certification exam. Make a list of requirements. Check off those requirements that you meet. Identify what you need to do to meet the remaining requirements. Finally, develop a strategy for fulfilling these requirements.

Assess Your Current Project Management Career

Managers use SWOT (Strengths, Weaknesses, Opportunities, and Threats) analysis to assess the effectiveness of operations, such as a department or division of the firm. You can use SWOT analysis to assess the current status of your project management career. Begin by dividing a piece of paper into four—upper left, upper right, lower left, and lower right.

List your strengths in the upper-left portion of the paper. Be sure to consider your education, certifications, leadership roles (i.e., serving on committees, preceptor), project management experience, and non-project management experience (i.e., previous career).

List your weaknesses in the upper-right portion of the paper. Be honest and list items that you see as weaknesses. For example, you may have an associate's degree in business but firms in your area may prefer or require a BS or MBA. You might not hold a PMP certificate, which may limit your choices of employers. Distance between your home and firms may also be a weakness, especially if the nearest firm is a two-hour drive one way.

List what you see as opportunities in the lower-left portion of the page. Opportunities might be to transfer to positions within your current firm. Your firm may offer incentives to continue your education. Your family situation (i.e., empty nest, with children who graduated college) may give you the chance to refocus on your career. You may have developed a strong network of former colleagues and friends who can "open doors" to new employment opportunities.

List threats to your project management career in the lower-right portion of the page. For example, firms in your industry may be merging or closing down, placing you at risk for termination. Your firm may be phasing out project managers with associate's degrees in business and may require you to obtain a PMP certificate or BSN within a specific time frame to maintain your employment. Maybe you have new family obligations that place limitations on work performance. You're getting older and traveling is taking a toll on your body. You are the sole supporter of your family and changing jobs is too risky. You and your new boss are not hitting it off well.

Your goal is to take advantage of your strengths and opportunities while strengthening your weaknesses and preparing a strategy for handling threats to your project management career. For example, stay with your present employer while you go back to school for your BS or MBA, taking advantage of your employer's tuition reimbursement policy. Doing so strengthens your weakness and places you in a strong position should your employer phase out employees with associate's degrees or project managers without a PMP certificate. Likewise, if you find yourself in a project management specialty that is in lower demand, you can use your network of colleagues to move to a high-demand project management specialty within your organization.

Changing Project Management Specialty

Time for a change? If so, anxiety is likely holding you back from making the move because change means you'll face new challenges—and the risk that you may not be able to meet those challenges. The risk of failure is a strong roadblock from exploring new areas of project management. An executive once commented, "You know when it is time for a new pair of shoes, but you may not know if the new pair is a fit until you try them for a few weeks." The same is true about changing your project management specialty. Should you give up a job that you've mastered? What happens if you fail at your new specialty? These aren't easy questions to answer.

It is usually best to change specialties within your current firm for a number of reasons. First, you are known quality. You've proven yourself as an excellent, reliable project manager who provides quality management. Even good candidates from outside the organization still must prove to management that they are reliable and provide quality patient care. Next, you can use your network of colleagues to explore the open position before you apply for a transfer. You'll learn what it is really like to work on that unit for that manager. You won't find out this information if you accept a position elsewhere until you're on the job.

Most important, you know from other employees who transferred how Human Resources and management handle situations when the "new shoe" isn't a fit. Human Resources will probably tell you that you are on probation for the first 90 days on your new job. You can be terminated at will any time during that 90-day period. Practically, this may not occur unless you were a marginal employee in your current position or you made grave errors in your new position. Termination of employment would tell all employees, "Don't transfer from your current job." This simply doesn't help the organization. A better approach is to acknowledge that all "new shoes" don't fit. Sometimes you can go back to wearing your "old shoe"—that is, they purposely hold off replacing you until everyone knows that the "new shoe" is a fit. Other times, you might be offered a position that is comparable to your old position—"another pair of old shoes." That position may be in a different department, but a position that is practically the same as your old position. You are unlikely to find such consideration as a new employee in another firm.

You'll need to meet the job requirements for the new specialty even if you are transferring within your organization. One of the toughest requirements to meet is the "three to five years' experience" requirement. You have to solve the chicken-or-the-egg problem. How can you gain experience if you don't have experience in the specialty? Here's a technique that might work for you. You probably have job skills that are transferable to the specialty—managing a project team, estimating budgets, critical thinking, negotiating with vendors, successfully working with stakeholders. Ask the manager in your current organization if you can assist with projects whenever they are short. That is, work outside your current position during a slow period. In this way, you can get a feel for what it is like to work on the specialty project while helping out the manager. Show that you are willing to learn the specialty. The current staff is likely to help you get up to speed. If both you and the manager feel you are a fit, then you become the ideal candidate for the next opening—and the three to five years of experience may no longer be a requirement in your case because you've been crossed-trained already.

Don't become cocky, thinking that you are now an expert project manager in the new specialty—you're not! You have a wealth of experience, but in a different specialty. Some experience is transferable but other experiences will be meaningless in the new specialty. You still must work your way through the novice, advanced beginner, and proficient project manager stages. Don't let your pride get in the way of learning your new specialty.

Realize that changing your specialty is a major lifestyle change that may be stressful. You are moving from an expert to a novice who has to learn the new specialty by going back to school, reading project management books about the specialty, and taking directions from project managers who could be your younger sibling or your child. You may need to ask your colleagues for help—something you don't do often in your present job. This may not come naturally, but there is a high risk for failure if you don't ask them.

Changing specialty is a family decision in many cases—both your work family and your home family. Family members are supportive by helping you objectively explore the pros and cons of the move. Also consult your colleagues about your current or future position. Colleagues can share their knowledge of the department, the manager, and can help set realistic expectations for the transfer. For example, you might be at the top of the ladder. Changing your specialty could place you back on the first rung of the ladder and affect your pay—you may not receive a pay decrease but you may also not receive an expected pay increase until you prove yourself.

Think about changing project specialty when your present position is no longer challenging—when your new project begins to look like the hundreds of projects that you've managed over the years. There is a risk that the quality of your performance may be unintentionally lowered. Don't change specialties to avoid conflicts in your current position. It is always better the leave your position on a positive note because the "new shoe" may not fit and you need the support from your current management to go back your "old shoe."

Is Management for You?

If you've been a leader on a project team but haven't taken full command of a complex project, you need to ask yourself whether management is for you. Management is challenging and involves more than just being the boss. The project manager has total responsibility for the project, which includes estimating needs, planning to meet needs, and executing that plan. The manager must meet the needs of all stakeholders based on standards defined by the firm, the client, the industry, and the project management profession. Some projects must also meet regulatory standards too. The nurse manager must determine resources (personnel and material) and policies and procedures to meet those needs.

Success is usually defined by staying within budget; passing audits by clients, the firm, and possibly regulators; having an excellent customer service rating; and providing a safe and stable working environment for staff. All must be accomplished without you (the project manager) performing the tasks. Your job is to identify needs, bring in the right people, give them the tools, and lead the team toward meeting those needs.

Some experienced project team members see project management as the next logical step in their career because they've already handled the day-to-day challenges of projects. You know the problems of delivering a project, and you have a few solutions to rectify those problems that you can implement if you became the boss.

Other experienced team members see project management as a lose-lose situation. Everything that goes wrong becomes your problem to solve. Upper management usually doesn't want to hear about your problems and your staff simply asks you, "What do you want me to do?" You have to deal with staffing issues—staff who don't show up for work, don't want to follow work rules, or staff who are just waiting to be terminated. Upper management is ordering you to keep with your overtime budget—and some staff members create situations where they get paid overtime. The manager seems to always be the bad guy.

Consider the following before accepting a project manager's position.

- Firms may require managers to hold an MBA degree, although they may accept a project manager with a BS degree who is working toward the MBA degree. Will you recoup the expense of an MBA degree?
- Project managers don't receive overtime pay.

- For the most part, team members can forget about their job once they are off of their shift. Project managers have 24/7 responsibility for their projects.
- Some firms may not permit you to return to a non-management role once you become a manager.
- Project managers usually lose their technical skills as project team members because they don't perform technical tasks anymore. This may limit career opportunities in the future.
- Project managers are usually not part of a bargaining unit. In some firms, members of the project team are bargaining unit positions, and moving into the project manager's slot loses protection of the bargaining unit.
- Project managers are expected to fix all problems on their unit—even those that are nearly impossible to fix.
- Pay increases for project managers may not be as frequent as staff nurses who belong to a bargaining unit.

The project manager is no longer seen as a colleague—you're the boss. You hire new staff and approve transfers. You write annual evaluations. You discipline staff. You're the person who says, "You're fired!"

Project management is a good experience as long as you are a "take charge" person who is well organized, likes dealing with people fairly, doesn't take failure of others personally, and feels a sense of accomplishment when your staff produces a quality project. Understand that there is little glory in being the project manager when compared with the overall responsibility for the project and for your staff.

Successful project managers rise to a middle-level manager position within the firm where you are responsible for managing a major function within the organization, such as a group of projects. A project manager may also become responsible for all projects in the firm by managing the enterprise project management office.

Working for a Project Management Consulting Firm

A project management consulting firm undertakes projects for clients that want the consulting firm instead of having an in-house project management team develop the project. You are employed by the consulting firm (not the client) as a project manager. Depending on the project, you might have offices both at the consulting firm and at the client's site. The client sets expectations, requirements, and limitations in a contract with the consulting firm and you must manage and deliver the project within terms of the contract.

The consulting firm's sole product is to manage projects from conception through implementation. Managing projects for the consulting firm is much different than managing projects for other organizations. Project management is their product—not an auxiliary task to their product as managing a project is an auxiliary to manufacturing automobiles.

There are benefits for working for a consulting firm.

– You have the opportunity to grow and develop project management skills. Consulting firms usually have a wealth of proven procedures for handling any type of situation that may arise during a project, and they train you on how to implement these procedures.
– You'll work on interesting and diverse projects in various industries. Clients bring on a consulting firm for their expertise, not simply to supplement their staff.
– You learn both formally and informally from top project management professionals who are either on staff or brought in by the consulting firm to increase the skills of their staff.
– You are an earner for the consulting firm, not an overhead. Consulting firms tend to invest in their staff—this is investing in their product.
– You have leverage to negotiate your compensation because without you, the consulting firm won't make money.
– Consulting firms are more likely to bring on project managers who are not perfect fits but who can be groomed into becoming star performers. Consulting firms usually have a formal training process and a well-defined career path for staff.
– You will be taught the ins and outs of the consulting—the business side shows you how to identify new needs of clients that will bring in new business for the consulting firm.

There are also drawbacks to being a project manager for a consulting firm.

– There is increased pressure to deliver above and beyond the client's expectation. You are expected to arrive early and stay later—and encourage your team to do the same—to impress the client, even if doing so is not productive.
– You don't have a home. You'll change projects and clients relatively frequently and will usually spend much time at the client's site, which may be far from your home.
– Promotions tend to be revenue oriented. As you move up in rank you are expected to become more of a sales person than a project manager, and continuation of employment may be based on the revenues that you generate.
– Techniques you learn and the tools used to manage projects might be proprietor to the consulting firm. You can't take them when you leave the consulting firm.
– You may be prohibited from becoming an employee of the client without permission of the consulting firm. Some consulting firms encourage certain employees

to join the client's organization, hoping that they will continue to send business their way.

− Your loyalty is to the consulting firm, not the client. No matter how well you fit with the client's staff, you are not one of them. The consulting firm provides your rewards. This becomes problematic sometime when the client's culture and rules are more accommodating to you than the consulting firm.
− Your commute may be long and you may have little choice in clients.

Working for an Agency

There are times when a firm brings on a project manager and other project team members to fill in gaps in staffing. Some refer to these as an agency project manager because the project manager works for an organization that supplies people working temporarily to fill in staffing needs. The agency project manager does not work directly for the firm but performs the same duties as the firm's own project manager.

An agency is different from a consulting firm that specializes in project management. Project management is the consulting firm's product. They deliver the project. The agency's product is personnel. They deliver a hired hand.

An agency typically has a contract with the firm and may or may not have a contract with you. The contract with the firm specifies the hourly or daily rate that the agency is to receive from the firm, which is typically much higher than the firm pays its own staff project managers. However, as an agency project manager you receive a fraction of what the agency receives from the firm.

The agency is responsible for your performance and certifies that you are competent enough to perform the tasks assigned by the firm. The firm is responsible for educating you on the firm's policies and procedures and to orient you to the firm.

You will fill out the traditional employment forms for the agency. It is likely that you'll go through the firm's orientation process. However, you are expected to hit the road running and to take over projects immediately. At any point, the firm can tell your agency that they no longer require your services.

There are benefits for working for an agency.

− You have the opportunity to work for different firms, depending on the agency.
− You get exposed to different types of projects and industries.
− You don't get involved in the politics of firms.
− You are an earner for the agency, not an overhead. Agency project managers bring in revenue for the agency whereas staff project managers are seen as a necessary expense for the firm. You have leverage to negotiate your compensation with the agency because without you—and the other agency project managers—the agency won't make money.

- You may be able to create your own schedule, depending on the agency.
- At times you receive a higher pay than if you were an employee at the firm. However, the higher pay may reflect the fact that the agency isn't providing you with benefits.

And there are drawbacks to being an agency project manager.

- There are usually no paid sick days or holidays. If you don't work, then you don't get paid.
- Work may or may not be consistent, depending on the agency's contract with the firm. There are contracts where the agency supplies full time project managers for a period of time (e.g., three to six months). Other contracts are on an as-needed basis. That is, you get called only if there is a project and the regular staff is unavailable. Agencies usually don't pay you to stand by.
- Agencies usually don't offer any benefits. Any benefits that are offered to you are likely at a higher amount than if you worked for a firm.
- You're considered an outsider in the firm. You don't get the same treatment by the firm as they treat their own employees (e.g., no parking discount, training).
- You may be prohibited from being an employee of the firm for six months to a year after you leave employment of the agency even if you don't have a contract with the agency. The firm's contract with the agency usually specifies terms under which the firm can convert the agency project manager to becoming their employee. In some cases, the agency wants the firm to pay the agency an amount equal to one year's salary of the agency project manager. This makes it too expensive for the firm to hire you. And some agencies don't tell you about this clause in the contract until you apply for a position at the firm.
- You're always starting over unless your agency places you in the same firm for a long time period. You have to continually prove yourself to the staff and management.
- You are often unappreciated as a hired hand and there are no rewards (promotions, bonuses) even if you are a star performer.
- Some agencies may send you out on jobs that are outside your experience in an effort to bring in revenue for the agency.
- Your commute may be long and you may have little choice in clients.

It is critical that you are totally honest with the agency about your experience and skills, because the agency places you on assignments based on what you tell the agency. You always want to be placed in a position where there are no surprises. An agency project manager is considered experienced and able to provide quality project management with little orientation and no project management guidance from the firm. You'll need to be told where things are, not how to perform the job.

Agency project manager isn't for new project managers or those looking to change specialties. There is little opportunity for training and nurturing. Agency project managers are expected to hit the ground running, otherwise the firm may tell the agency that you are not right for their position. The agency may then place you in a more appropriate position in another firm or not call you for any assignments.

Agile Project Management

Not every project is complicated requiring weeks to develop elaborate detail plans. More common projects are relatively small and require less planning than more complex projects. Work breakdown structure, tasks, subtasks, duration, dependencies, and resource allocation are all components of traditional project management. However, for a typical business project, the project is completed by the time a formal project plan is created.

Small business projects are managed using agile project management techniques where the focus is on self-management by a team that has expertise to know what needs to be done and when and how to do it with little direction from a project manager. The project manager is a facilitator (rather than a manager) whose job it is to keep the team focused and remove barriers using agile project management techniques.

There are advantages of managing an agile project.

- You don't need to master traditional project management techniques and tools (e.g., work breakdown structure, project planning applications).
- You don't need to direct every detail of the project because your team handles the details.
- Projects are typically quick turnaround.
- Projects make an impact on business operations immediately.
- You bond with stakeholders because they are directly involved in the project.
- There is immediate satisfaction from the business unit.

There are disadvantages of managing an agile project.

- You can lose your project management skills over time because you don't use them.
- You'll need to learn agile project management skills—skills that you may not have learned in school or may not have experienced on other projects.
- You feel that you lost control of the project since the project team works relatively independently.
- Other project managers may consider you as having less than professional project management skills since it might appear that anyone can manage a small project.

- Stakeholders may question your value to the project and the firm since it appears that the project team works relatively independently.
- It may be challenging for you to be seen as someone who can manage complex projects.

Enterprise Project Management

Enterprise project management focuses on how all projects are managed within a firm—not overseeing projects but making sure all projects are good investments. This is much different from other forms of project management since there is no direct project management occurring, at least in the traditional sense.

The project management office (PMO) is at the heart of enterprise project management, working toward ensuring that each project is a worthwhile venture for the firm when proposed and continues to be worthwhile throughout development. The PMO usually has a very small staff that is managed by a project manager trained in enterprise project management.

The PMO is responsible for setting project management standards for the firm; facilitating the section of projects; overseeing projects that are underway; ensuring that all project teams use an appropriate project management methodology; ensuring that an enterprise project management application is used for project planning, management, and reporting; and coordinating project management resources (such as staff); and assigning resources to project teams. The firm's executives decide which project is a good investment and continues to be a good investment during development. The PMO facilitates this process.

There are advantages of being a project manager of the PMO:

- You strongly influence project management standards adopted by the firm.
- You manage the framework for deciding which projects are good investments for the firm.
- You help guide project managers in implementing project management standards.
- You implement the tools for project planning and reporting throughout the firm.
- You are an advocate for project managers to all levels of the firm's management.
- You can greatly influence how the firm approaches projects.
- You are seen as a leader within the firm.
- You work with all disciplines within the firm.
- You greatly influence how resources are managed throughout the firm, especially resources that are shared among projects.
- You widely use your interpersonal skills.

There are disadvantages of being a project manager of the PMO:

- Some project managers resent you because of your influence over their projects without your being in the trenches with them.
- You are looked upon as a facilitator rather than a project manager because others in the firm (i.e., executives, committees) make decisions, not you.
- You will lose your project management skills since you no longer manage any type of project.
- You are exposed to upper management who has the power to quickly terminate the PMO (and you) if they feel your efforts are no longer beneficial to the firm.
- Your role is as an advisor, not a manager. Others can accept or reject your advice.
- You are focused on cost versus benefits and project management effectiveness, not on creating projects that enhance operations of the firm.
- There are lots of politics in project management.

Extreme Project Management

An extreme project is one where at least one aspect of the project has never been done before, requiring the project team to break new ground during the project's development. Going to the moon is an example of an extreme project, but any project where something has to be invented by the project team is also considered an extreme project. Although there are few extreme projects, projects that are considered extreme usually have an unmovable timeline. Think of Apollo 13.

Managing an extreme project requires a unique set of management skills where specifications are fluid and determined by high-level members of the project team— each having the autonomy to identify needs, prioritize those needs, and acquire resources to fulfill those needs, all without the project manager's input and approval. The formal approval process takes time that is not available in an extreme project.

The extreme project manager is responsible for assembling the right high-level project team; give them the power to identify and solve problems; remove barriers preventing them from doing their job; and making sure that everyone is focused on each prioritized problem. The project manager is more of a facilitator than a project manager.

There are many advantages of becoming a project manager of an extreme project:

- You have autonomy because it is your job to solve this mission critical problem facing the firm.
- You use unique management skills to lead a high-level project team.
- You create an environment that fosters the project team to make quick decisions that have serious implications on project deliverables.
- You are one of few project managers who have ever managed an extreme project.

There are also drawbacks of becoming a project manager of an extreme project:

- Managing an extreme project is highly stressful and time consuming because the project must be completed within an unmovable deadline.
- You are responsible for solving problems that no one knows how to solve.
- You must manage without knowing all the details of the project and having no detailed plan to follow.
- You never know if the project will conclude successfully.
- You will lose your traditional project management skills.
- It may be difficult to return to a traditional project after managing an extreme project. Sponsors who select a project manager may feel a traditional project is beneath your skills.

Construction Project Management

Construction projects can range from the renovation of a kitchen to building a skyscraper. Small construction projects can use the agile project management methodology in which a general contractor brings in an electrician, plumber, and other trades who decide what needs to be done, when it needs to be done, and then they perform the necessary tasks. Large construction projects use more formal project management methodology such as the Waterfall methodology where the project manager plans each step of the construction process.

Construction projects are complex. An architect designs the building and provides detailed construction plans for every aspect of construction. There are what seems to be countless regulations and government approvals needed before, during, and after construction. There are many parts that need to be ordered—some customized—and brought to the site just in time to assemble by one of the many trades who are involved in the construction process. And then there are logistics. You need to schedule workers, equipment, and construction materials to arrive on the work site when they are needed for the building. This can be a monumental scheduling task.

For example, scheduling the stone façade must include the time when the stone is cut in the quarry; the prep time for the stone; the staff to cut and prep it; the truck driver and the truck to deliver the stone; travel time for the delivery; arrival time; where to park the truck while waiting to load and when unloading; construction equipment to unload the truck and deliver stone to the assembly location on the building; trades needed to unload and install the stone just at the time when the stone must be installed.

There are challenges. Getting the truck carrying the stone to arrive—especially if the construction site is in a large, congested city—is a nightmare. If traffic delays the truck, causing it to arrive late to the construction site, then the project falls behind schedule. Trade workers who unload and install the stone are waiting and getting paid for doing nothing. Arrivals of other materials and equipment and the staff to operate and install them must be rescheduled, if possible. If it is impossible to reschedule them, then the nightmare continues. There will be no place to store materials and equipment on the site. There is the high risk that materials will be damaged when lying around the construction site. Traffic backs up around the site—which is worse if the construction site is in the middle of a big city because it can cause gridlock—as trucks carrying construction materials search for parking.

Don't expect to become a project manager for a construction project without having construction project management experience. However, formal training and experience in managing non-construction projects may provide an in-road to joining a construction project management team where you can gain the experience to eventually move into the role of project manager.

There are advantages of being a construction project manager:

- You learn how to apply critical thinking daily to address the forever-changing variables in the project plan.
- You manage a large project team (large construction projects).
- You learn about regulations and inspections required by government agencies that oversee construction projects.
- You learn to work with many subcontractors.
- You learn to work with the trades and trade unions.
- You have the satisfaction that you led the team that constructed a building that everyone will see and use for years to come.

There are disadvantages of being a construction project manager:

- Construction projects are time-sensitive. There is very little wiggle room to miss the delivery date.
- The developer is constantly watching progress and can become anxious about any missed schedule dates. Typically the developer has taken out a building loan and is paying a daily interest rate. Any extension of the delivery date translates into additional interest payments.
- Coordinating subcontractors, tradesmen, equipment suppliers, material manufacturers, and logistics on the site each day can be nerve-racking. Rarely does everything work as scheduled.
- It is a high-stress environment. Every problem is costly and falls on the project manager to resolve in the most economical way.
- No construction project is like a previous construction project.
- There are many contracts each that specify work rules of how vendors, tradesmen, and others participate in the project. Your planning and decision making must comply with those terms.

Information Technology Project Management

Information technology projects are probably the most common type of project in firms as organizations continue to automate and improve already automated processes. All information technology projects begin with the idea of transforming a manual system into a computer automated system or to adapt an existing system. The computer automated system requires computer hardware (computers), software (computer program), networking (connecting together computers), cybersecurity (preventing unauthorized access), and training (how to use the system).

Small information technology projects may not require formal project management, such as using Excel to automate a process. Front office staff familiar with Excel can develop the project with the assistance of the information technology department since the project is likely departmentally focused rather than used firmwide. In essence, this is a one-person project.

Firm-wide information technology projects are more complicated and can involve systems analysts (who identify details for the business process), programmers (technicians who write computer applications), software vendors (firms that supply pre-built computer applications), computer technicians (make sure desktop computers can run the application), network technicians (make sure computers can share information), database technicians (make sure information can be electronically stored and distributed throughout the firm), and cybersecurity technicians (protect the application and data from unauthorized access). These are all part of the project team led by a project manager.

There are advantages of being an information technology project manager.

– You understand every aspect of the business operation that is being computerized. You might be the only one in the firm who knows the details.
– You become the go-to person who increases the efficiency of a business process. You assemble the pickings of the minds of others involved in the process, and then deliver the computerized solution.
– You use your critical thinking skills and interpersonal skills to coordinate the team and business stakeholders.
– You can implement your own ideas to streamline workflows.
– You become directly involved with all levels of administration and staff in the firm.
– You make computer applications work for the facility.

There are disadvantages of being an information technology project manager.

– You must translate tedious requirements into workflows that are incorporated into the computer application.

- You tend to get blamed by the administration and everyone else who uses the computer application when the computer application doesn't work as they expect it to work.
- You are expected to fix all problems with the computer application—problems that only the vendor who supplied the computer application can fix (if the application was purchased off-the-shelf). The vendor can take months or years to make fixes.
- You will perform hours and days of tedious testing prior to releasing updates to the computer application.
- You are blamed for delays in implementation that are beyond your control.
- You are likely to have difficulty explaining what causes problems with the computer application because few members of the administration who use the computer application understand the technical aspects of the system.

Engineering Project Management

Engineering projects can run the gamut of projects that build something. A construction project and an information technology project can be considered an engineering project. More common engineering projects are projects in which the project team builds a machine or machines that are used in manufacturing. For example, an engineering project creates a computer chip that is assembled onto a circuit board (another project) that is installed in a robot (another project) that is used in the assembly of construction equipment (another project) that will be used to construct a building (another project).

The project manager of an engineering project leads a project team that consists of engineers and technicians that are problem solvers. They see a challenge and then use their skills to devise a clever way to meet the challenge and produce a product that at times revolutionizes an industry and society. The project manager doesn't have to be an engineer but needs to have solid skills in project management. Project planning and management is done with the advice—and sometime consent—of engineers on the project team.

There are benefits of being an engineering project manager:

- You make a tangible product.
- You learn various aspects of engineering that might be outside your current knowledge.
- You implement the latest technology as part of the engineering project.
- You develop knowledge and skills that are easily transferable to other engineering projects.
- You become the go-to person in the firm for improving operations through implementing technology.

There are disadvantages of being an engineering project manager:

- You are required to manage a team of engineers who are experts in their field of engineering, and you're not an expert.
- You must rely on your project team to identify tasks, durations, dependencies, and other aspects of project planning because there is a need to fully understand engineering details within each specialty of the project.
- At times you may feel like you're the project leader but lack full control because of your dependence on the project team for direction and advice.
- You are to blame even for unexpected problems that occur out of your control.
- Deadlines are easily missed because engineering is a science and there is no cookie-cutter approach to developing and implementing new technology.
- There is a high risk of burnout.

Project Management Educator

A project management educator is an experienced project manager who is responsible for developing curriculum and educating potential and current project managers on project management related subjects. Education takes place online, in the classroom, using computer-based simulation, and on the job. Colleges and universities employ project manager educators as faculty members in degree programs and professional education programs. Degree programs such as engineering or business degrees usually have a project management course(s) that focuses on project management skills. Professional education programs focus on continuing education, including courses that prepare for a PMP certificate. Firms, especially consulting firms, employ project management educators to develop and implement project management in-service training programs for their staff.

You'll be updating curriculum based on current regulatory and PMP certification requirements and translating the curriculum into training material, online courses, classroom presentations, and in-service training—and you'll be teaching in the classroom and on the job. You'll implement testing procedures that identify whether students understand and implement curriculum. You'll also develop remediation for students who fail.

A project management educator typically requires a master's degree in business or engineering for degree courses and at least a BS degree along with professional project management experience for professional courses. A PMP certificate is highly desirable. You must be a leader and be comfortable speaking in front of groups of strangers. Good presentation skills are critical to the success of a project management educator. You should be well-versed in the use of presentation software since you are expected to create your own presentations.

In consulting firms, you may be responsible for project management education for the firm. You'll be expected to make sure that the staff has completed all necessary training, and you must provide documentation to support your findings.

Colleges and universities usually offer part-time teaching positions, referred to as an adjunct, that are worth exploring as a way to see if you like teaching. You'll be responsible to teach either a course or a class or two. Pay is minimum. There are usually no benefits. If you like teaching, then you may want to consider working as an adjunct and keep your full-time project manager's job.

There are advantages of being a project management educator:

- You mentor new and current project managers.
- You keep your project management skills current and provide training that keeps other project managers current.
- You help correct project management related job problems.
- College and universities require a minimum of classes to teach (e.g., 24 credit hours), specific office hours, and committee assignments. You typically work during the academic year (10 months).
- Project management educators for a consulting firm typically have broad responsibilities to create and maintain training for all staff (including managers) and advise on facility-wide policies and procedures.
- You have autonomy both at colleges and universities and in a consulting firm as a project manager educator.

There are disadvantages of being a project management educator:

- Colleges and universities may offer lower salaries compared to working as a project manager.
- Colleges and universities may require faculty members to perform research and publish frequently to maintain employment. Expect to work during school breaks and vacations without additional compensation.
- Your assessment may determine if a project management student becomes a project manager or a current project manager continues employment due to incompetence.
- You'll be expected to manage multiple assessments simultaneously.
- Minimal project management opportunities can lead to you losing your project management skills.
- Lots of pre-work.

Project Management Auditing

Auditing is a review process to determine if policies and procedures of the firm are being followed. Projects of a specific size set by the firm are audited regularly to assess if the project manager and the project team are following the firm's rules. Project size is determined by the budget for the project and by the critical nature of the project to the firm. Small projects are not audited unless they cross the auditing threshold.

The auditor usually has a background in project management and is likely to have been a project manager at one point in their career, which gives the auditor a unique background to conduct the audit. The auditor's job is to know policies and procedures that govern projects within the firm and then carefully look through documentation of the project (i.e., project plans or invoices) and interview the project manager, members of the project team, and stakeholders to determine if those policies and procedures were reasonably followed.

The auditor looks for a paper trail that describes the planning and execution of the project and builds a timeline of events. The project manager and others on the team help assemble the information and assist the auditor with interpreting what took place. The auditor then writes an audit report that is sent to the chief auditor of the firm and is likely shared with the audit committee of the board of directors and executives of the firm.

The audit report describes the methodology used for the audit and lists facts that the auditor found. Most facts support the finding that the project was managed by reasonably following the firm's policies and procedures. Other facts may indicate that the project deviated from the firm's policies and procedures Each deviation usually has a rationale for why the project manager did not follow the rules. Sometimes the rules didn't address the problem, causing the project manager to use their professional judgment to address the problem. Other times, there was an error. The audit report states how the project manager will mitigate the issue in the future.

You'll need several years of project management experience leading various types of projects to become a project management auditor. In addition, you'll need excellent verbal and written communications skills, be comfortable with using electronic documentation, and be detail oriented. You'll need to interact with project managers, the project team, executives at all levels of the firm, and stakeholders that may be customers and vendors.

There are advantages of being a project management auditor:

- You are on the first line to ensure that projects are being run according to policies and procedures of the firm.
- You recommend changes to ensure that policies and procedures reflect the realities of managing projects and ensure that project managers adhere to policies and procedures.
- You are the person who provides information to convince project managers that policies and procedures are designed to protect staff and the firm.

- Your project management skills are transferable to any organization who performs audits.
- You are able to work independently.

There are disadvantages of being a project management auditor:

- Staff may feel you are a "spy" for the firm and not a colleague.
- You review documentation all day. There are no project management opportunities.
- You lose your project management skills.
- You must learn details, policies, and procedures of the firm—information that usually doesn't increase your knowledge of project management.
- There is a potentially heavy workload. Usually there are not many project management auditors in a firm—however, there are usually lots of projects to be audited. You are always under deadlines to complete complex audits.

Chapter 7
Prepping for the Interview

Whether you are a new graduate looking for your first job or a seasoned professional seeking to move on to a different firm, you'll need to prep for the pre-employment interviews, which can be challenging since you have no idea what you'll be asked. It is safe to say that the recruiter will try to discover if you fit the firm's culture; if you meet all requirements for the position; and if there is anything in your work history that might imply you are not a good worker.

Ask your colleagues and friends if they know what it is like to work for your prospective employer. You might see a trend in their replies that gives you a hint as to the culture within the firm. Sometimes you'll hear that the pay is above average but the workload is also above average. Take comments with a grain of salt since opinions are based on perceptions and misperceptions. Aside from asking around, there is little you can do to prepare for questions that explore whether you fit the firm's culture, primarily because you may not know much about the culture.

Questions about job requirements are something you can prepare to answer. Make two columns—one containing job requirements and the other containing evidence that proves you meet each requirement. The goal is to help the recruiter match your background to the position. Don't be concerned if you are unable to match every job requirement—few candidates meet all requirements. Take time before the interview to match as many requirements as you can and come up with a way that you might be able to meet missing requirements in the near future. Keep in mind that the recruiter believes you meet enough of the requirements to invite you in for an interview.

Your resume presents your work history. The ideal candidate will have stayed for five or six years with each employer and show signs of increased responsibilities such as membership in committees. There are few ideal candidates. The reality is that sometimes jobs don't work out the way you and the manager anticipated. It's like walking around in a new pair of shoes and you discovered they don't fit, so you change shoes. The recruiter understands that work histories may not be pristine. Prepare a reasonable response to potential questions related to any employment gaps or short-term employment. Be honest and consider bringing up these situations even before the nurse recruiter asks the question. This shows that you're not hiding any information.

Preparing Your "Script"

Become a good sales representative for yourself by anticipating probable and possible questions that might be asked during your interviews. Later on we'll focus on

https://doi.org/10.1515/9781501506222-008

technical questions, but before any technique questions come your way, the recruiter and the manager need to get to know you by asking some probing questions. No one knows the questions that will be asked—sometimes the interviewer comes up with the question on the spot. However, you can anticipate typical questions asked during interviews and anticipate questions that your background might generate, such as gaps in employment or short periods of employment.

Prepare a response to each anticipated question similar to how politicians prepare for questions posed by the media or are asked at public events. Prepared responses are commonly referred to as a script. The script is carefully written with words and phrases that convey a response that will satisfy the audience's curiosity. Politicians memorize and "stay on script" (recite the script) and avoid "going off script" (ad-libbing) when answering questions. You should do the same so you won't be flustered and appear confused at the time of the interview. Instead, you'll come off appearing confident and honest. The script should be a few short sentences that clearly answer the question. The goal is to deliver a succinct response.

Here are likely questions that you'll be asked. Write a script for each one.

- Tell me about yourself.
- What do you know about our firm?
- Why do you want to work here?
- What makes you feel you are qualified for the position?
- Why did you become a project manager?
- Where do you see yourself in five years?
- What do you like and dislike about project management?
- What are your strengths and weaknesses?
- Why should we hire you?
- What is your most important accomplishment?
- What failures have you encountered and what would you have done differently?
- Describe your ideal position.
- What motivates you?
- How would you resolve a conflict with your manager?
- What is your strategy for multitasking?
- Why should you be hired for this position?
- Why are you leaving your present position?
- What do you like and dislike about your present position?
- How do you keep your project management skills current?

Make a list of questions based on the job requirements listed in the job posting. The recruiter will probably walk you through each job requirement to determine if you meet the requirement. You should have a script prepared for each requirement that clearly links your background to the requirement. Be forthright if you don't meet the requirement. Your script should acknowledge that you're lacking the requirement. However, show how something in your background is similar to the requirement or how you plan to meet the requirement in the near future. For example, "I'm not PMP certified; however, I'm scheduled to take the PMP course in four weeks." But if you don't meet or will not meet the requirements, state so. The recruiter will decide if that's a dealbreaker or not.

Here are considerations that might need to be addressed:

- Work schedule – five-day week, working from home, working holidays, mandated to work
- Assignments – assigned to a division, floating to projects throughout the firm, project staffing, support staff availability, management expectations
- Commuting – travel distance from home, travel time during rush hour, public transportation availability and schedules, parking (employee parking, parking fees, location)
- Employment – pay period, probation period, transfer to another position, education benefits, pay increases, time off (vacation, personal days, and sick days), non-compensated time (required online training on your own time)
- Travel – travel required, number of travel days, where you will be required to travel, how much notice is given, can you refuse to travel if there are family conflicts, travel arrangements, travel expenses.

Create an opening "script" for the initial meeting with the recruiter that includes the greeting and small talk such as "This was an easy place to find" or about the weather—something to set the stage for the interview. Keep everything upbeat. Speak with confidence. Be yourself. The worst that can happen is that you're not invited back to the next interview, but you might be surprised.

Scripts have stage directions that tell you what you should be doing. Some project managers include stage directions in their interview "script." Active listening is the stage direction found in many "scripts." You stop, listen, and process what the interviewer is saying to you. This is the most important action you take during an interview. You learn by listening, an instructor once said.

Remember that the recruiter leads the interview, not you. The recruiter can take any number of directions once the small talk is over. Some recruiters begin with an open-ended statement such as, "Tell me about yourself." Others recruiters may step through your resume, quizzing your experience, such as, "I see you are a project manager at ABC Company. Tell me about what you do." In a rare situation, the recruiter—who may be new to the job—may seem a little disorganized. You can help get the interview back on track by asking, "Would you like me to tell you about myself?"

Be prepared to follow the recruiter in any direction that they take the interview. Anticipate questions similar to those mentioned in this chapter and then prepare a "script" to respond to each question. "Scripts" help you speak with confidence about anything in your background and about project management. You'll come across as a professional, especially when the recruiter compares you to other candidates who applied for the same position.

The Game Plan

You know that you can do the job successfully but you still must make it through the pre-employment gauntlet before you'll get a chance to prove your skills to the manager. This can be a frustrating period but you must put aside those frustrations and perform every task requested of you as if each task were an exciting new challenge. Leave the "attitude" at the door, especially if you feel that your experience and training should exempt you from some pre-employment activities (e.g., testing). You are being carefully observed during all phases of the pre-employment and probation period if you are offered the job. Typically the recruiter and the manager will stop the pre-employment process if the candidate appears to have an "attitude." They would rather cut their losses sooner than be saddled with a problem employee for the long haul.

There are probably situations that you prefer the recruiter to gloss over rather than explore in detail. For example, you might have had a position that didn't work as well as you had hoped and it clearly appears on your resume. Expect that the recruiter will bring this up during the interview; however, your response determines how much time is spent exploring the situation. Here's a strategy that may help you deal with uncomfortable situations in your background.

- Don't try to hide the situation. It is best to bring this out during the interview rather than have the recruiter learn about the situation as a result of a background check.
- Be consistent on your resume and in your responses to recruiter's questions. If a position didn't work out, still list the employer, position, dates of employment, and a brief description of your duties on your resume in the same format used to describe your other positions.
- Limit details both on your resume and in your responses about the potentially negative situation. Be specific but light on details. Try to satisfy the most obvious concerns without dwelling on the problem. Be prepared to give a brief reason why a position didn't work out, such as the position required a more experienced project manager.
- Don't blame others for the situation. That is, the position didn't work out because you lack the required experience. It wasn't that "they" didn't train you or didn't give you time to prove yourself. This demonstrates that you objectively assessed the problem and accepted responsibility. It isn't that you are a bad project manager, but simply that the "shoe didn't fit."
- Keep your response short and to the point. The recruiter wants the headline, not the full story. If the headline conveys sufficient information, then the recruiter is not interested in the whole story.
- Acknowledge the negative situation and then try to refocus the interview on positive situations. After explaining that the position didn't work out because you lacked experience, mention that you found a more appropriate position at ABC Company where you were successful and now have experience.

- Use a three-part structure to respond to questions. Describe the situation succinctly and then describe the action you took to deal with the situation. Follow with the outcome of your action. Don't elaborate! The recruiter will ask for more information about the situation, if necessary.
- Speak about yourself, not the team. The recruiter wants to know what you can do and how you do it, not the team.
- Time is on your side, not the recruiter's. You have about an hour to convince the recruiter that you are a viable candidate. The recruiter has the same amount of time to decide if you are. Spending unnecessary time explaining negative situations reduces the time available to talk about your positive attributes. Briefly explain negative situations and then refocus the conversation on positive situations.

It's a Wrap

Plan your closing as the interview winds down—prepare a "script" for your closing act. Leave on a positive note and imply that you want to remain a candidate for the position, even if you don't want that position. You don't want to bring closure to your candidacy during the interviewing process. Wait until they offer you the position before telling the recruiter that you are no longer interested in the position.

Rarely will you be offered the position on the spot—although that might happen if the hiring manager conducts the interview. Be cautious if you get such an offer. Have a "script" prepared that politely probes why the offer is being made on the spot ("I wasn't expecting such a quick decision"). This opens the door for the manager to explain the situation. You might have been the last candidate interviewed and you surpassed the qualifications of the other candidates. On the other hand, it might also be that not many other candidates applied for the position—you're the first one who wanted the position since the job was posted months ago and they're desperate to hire someone. This may not be a good sign for you. Why didn't others apply for the position? Did they know something you don't know about the manager, the department, or the firm that would make the position undesirable?

Even if you're "hired on the spot," it is not official. The manager needs to process the hiring decision with the recruiter. Typically the recruiter formally reviews the job requirements and compensation with you. You must verbally agree before the recruiter sends you the official offer letter in writing. The offer letter states the terms of employment and supersedes all verbal and written communication about the job. Any arrangements you made with the manager that are not contained in the terms of employment might not be enforceable. For example, if the manager agreed to let you work from home once a week but this is not stated in the offer letter, then you may not be working at home.

Interviews tend to end either as you're not a fit for the position or you are still a viable candidate. The recruiter is usually straightforward and will tell you if you are no longer a viable candidate. Don't take the rejection personally. The recruiter knows the culture and personalities of the department, plus performance expectations and feelings for whatever reason that you won't be successful in the position. Prepare a "script" on how you are going to respond to the rejection—you could respond, "I appreciate your being up front. Are there other open positions that might be a better fit?"

You might be asked to meet with the hiring manager if you're still in the running for the position. Be accommodating. Try to meet with the manager immediately following your interview with the recruiter if offered. You're already warmed up for the interview with the manager, and you don't have to come back. You finish the interviews in one day. If the manager is unavailable, then schedule an interview sooner rather than later.

Don't become overly optimistic. A good recruiter always gives candidates the feeling that everything is on track for a job offer. This is not necessarily true. The recruiter usually hedges bets if the top candidate turns down the job. Prepare a "script" that you can use if you're still a viable candidate. You could say, "Thanks for the opportunity to explore the position. I'd like to continue our discussions. Do you have any timeframe when I might hear from you?"

Some Thorny Questions

There are questions that are illegal to ask during a pre-employment interview, and some questions that might be asked that are simply inappropriate. The recruiter probably knows what questions cannot be asked during the interview; however, some managers may be inexperienced interviewing potential employees and may deviate into illegal or inappropriate questions during the interview.

Areas off-limits to pre-employment questions are:
- Age
- Birth place
- Disability
- Marital and family status, including if you are pregnant
- National origin
- Race
- Religion
- Gender

Be aware that the interviewer may intentionally or inadvertently touch upon these areas indirectly during the conversation. Rarely will you be asked questions directly. For example, "We live in the same town. My daughter is a junior at the high school." This may lead you to continue the conversation that reveals "do not ask" information, such as, "My daughter is in the first grade." This reveals your family status. Although your response may seem inconsequential, the interviewer may extrapolate situations that may interfere with your employment—a young child at home raises childcare issues during working hours.

The recruiter and experienced managers may use carefully worded questions that may appear to explore "do not ask" information but are perfectly legal because the question focuses on whether or not you are able to perform the job function. For example, you might be asked if you can travel for three or more weeks at a time. You can be asked if you are willing to travel but you can't be asked questions about your family status that may interfere with your job, such as childcare issues.

The interviewer can't ask about your age or cunningly ask the year you graduated from high school to estimate your age. You can be asked if you are over the age of 18, which is the legal age to work in most states. Likewise, you can't be asked if you are a United States citizen but you can be asked if you are authorized to work in the United States.

If you are asked directly or indirectly a "do not ask" question, then politely ask for clarification ("I'm a little puzzled by your question. Can clarify it for me?"). Hopefully the interviewer picks up your hint that the "do not ask" line has been crossed. If not, then you can restate the question in a way that focuses on whether or not you can perform the job. You can state, "I'm not sure I understand the question but if you're asking if I'm available to travel, I am, as long as it is not every day."

Some questions may probe how you would respond to a realistic situation where there is no easy answer. Simply think through the question and respond reasonably. Don't try to give an answer that you think the interviewer wants to hear. Here is one of those questions.

The business unit manager gives you a direct verbal order to add a new feature to the project. The firm's policy requires that proposed changes to a project come before the project's change management committee, who will approve or disapprove. What would you do?

Bring a List of Questions to Ask

You need to decide if the job is a fit for you and the best way to make your assessment is by gathering information that might influence your decision. Listing factors that you are looking for in a job is a good way to begin your assessment. Focus on the obvious (and the not so obvious) that will affect your quality of life, both at work and during off hours.

Write a "script" using wording that doesn't imply the importance of the question to you accepting the position. For example, instead of asking, "Is there adequate parking on campus?" you may want to rephrase the question as, "What is the parking situation for employees?"

The recruiter is likely to be forthright in responding to the question. Always respond positively even if the recruiter's response is a possible dealbreaker for you. Let's say that the recruiter tells you that employees park in remote parking areas off-campus and are bussed to the campus and that employees are responsible for arriving at work on time. This could end up being a quality of life issue for you since your arrival time must consider time to go to the remote parking area and the shuttle bus schedule during change of shift. The same consideration must be given at the end of shift. You may not want this hassle, but don't give the recruit any hint that this is a problem at this time. Make a list of pros and cons about the job if you are invited back for another round of interviews—or are offered the position—and then decide if any dealbreakers are really dealbreakers. You'll be in a better mindset to make this decision than during the interview when the potential dealbreaker appears.

Here are a few questions that you may want to consider.

- How many projects will the position manage simultaneously?
- How are project teams formed?
- Can a project team member be floated to another project?
- Under what conditions, if any, are you mandated to travel?
- How are vacation and holiday requests approved?
- Will there be an orientation period?
- What are the benefits (i.e., health insurance, educational benefits, 401K)?
- What is the annual review process?
- What opportunities are there to increase compensation (i.e., annual increases, meeting/exceeding goals, bonuses, longevity increases, shift differential, certification, degree)?
- What is the parking situation (i.e., remote parking areas, parking fees, designated parking for employees, and adequate parking)?
- Is there any non-compensated time (i.e., online training at home)?
- How are sick days handled (i.e., doctor's note, length of time before required to go on disability, disability pay)?
- What is orientation like?
- What are the manager's expectations and what should you expect during the first six months of the job?
- Is this a new position? If so, why was the new position created?
- Why did the previous person leave the position?
- How long was the previous person in the position before they left?
- How long has this position been available?
- Can you tell me about performance reviews (i.e., annually, goal-setting, basis for evaluation)?
- Why should I work here?
- What is the compensation?
- Are there special incentives for accepting the position (i.e., a signing bonus)?

And If the Interview Doesn't Go Well

You will have to face the reality that something may not go well during the interview. What you said might be taken the wrong way or there may be a misunderstanding of what the recruiter is saying. Whatever the case, the temperature of the interview might change from warm and cozy to chilly. You'll notice this right away when the upbeat tone switches to uncertainty, focusing on mismatches to job requirements rather than matches.

You may not experience this, but be prepared for this unexpected turn of events. A good strategy is to acknowledge the concern immediately when you detect the change in direction. You might say, "It seems that you have some concerns." The recruiter will likely appreciate your observation because there is an issue that the recruiter needs to resolve and you'll be able to get the interview back on course.

Plan to ask the recruiter to tell you about their concerns. Listen carefully to the response. The recruiter's response may indicate that your original choice of words might have been misleading, or words used by the recruiter may have misled you. Clarify the issue using different words. Better yet, plan to describe a scenario that illustrates the situation in conflict and how you would handle that situation.

There might be dealbreakers for you or the recruiter that make it impossible to continue the pre-employment process. You'll probably know which of your qualifications are weak when you compare your background to the job requirements. The recruiter might have noticed these weaknesses for the first time during the interview, which dampens the upbeat tone of the interview. Write "scripts" to address each potential issue. Don't hide the mismatch. Explain how your plan to meet those requirements shortly after being hired or why your other qualifications weigh more than your deficiencies. Write another "script" that you can use if this truly turns into a dealbreaker. Thank the recruiter for taking the time to chat with you about the position, and ask if you would be considered for future positions in the firm.

Be Prepared to Walk Away

Prepare to negotiate. The initial interview with the recruiter is probably not the time to enter into negotiations unless you are offered the position on the spot. However, you should do your homework to prepare to negotiate if and when that time comes. Senior management negotiates a contract that has a start and end date and contains specific expectations of both the firm and the senior manager. Employment terminates at the end of the contract period. Both parties need to sign a new contract to continue employment.

Most employees are not at the senior level and will not be offered a contract. In place of a contract, you receive an offer of employment letter that states the terms of employment. The letter contains your title, where you are going to work, shift, wages, and when to report to work. Terms of employment generally reflect the firm's policies.

You and the recruiter may have some wiggle room to modify the standard terms of employment. Depending on your position and the firm's policies, the wiggle room may not exist or is very narrow. Assume that the wiggle room exists and prepare to negotiate terms of employment at the appropriate time during the pre-employment process. You might be surprised that a barrier to employment for you isn't one for the recruiter who can remove that barrier.

Decide the minimum terms of employment that you will accept, and list them before meeting with the recruiter. Also create a list of ideal terms of employment for the perfect job. For example, in the perfect world, there would be no travel on weekends; however, you are willing to travel late Sunday. No weekend travel at all would be an ideal term. Traveling late Sunday is a minimum term.

Minimum terms of employment are the "line in the sand" that you won't cross. This is your "walking away" point. The recruiter also has minimum terms of employment that won't be crossed and a "walking away" point. Don't waver on your minimum terms of employment and feel that you'll figure something out when the conflict occurs. The pre-employment period is where you identify and resolve conflicts, not after you begin work.

Ask the recruiter toward the end of the initial interview to walk you through details of the pre-employment, orientation, and probation periods and the remainder of the work year. Take good notes and refer to them when developing your minimum and ideal terms of employment.

Be assertive if your minimum terms of employment cannot be met or if the job isn't a fit for your current situation. Your situation may change in the future and a similar position in the firm might be a fit, so you don't want to burn bridges. Plan to point out the conflict to the recruiter at the appropriate time during the pre-employment process. Bring up the conflict sooner rather than later because the recruiter doesn't want to spend time and money continuing with your pre-employment process if you already know there is a conflict that prevents you from accepting a job offer.

Prep for the Technical Interview

You'll need to prepare for technical interviews by the hiring managers and other staff who want to learn the level of your project management knowledge. Technical interviews are informal. Questions may not be formally vetted for clarity and accuracy. You can be asked anything about project management, and your response to questions may be subjectively evaluated. You don't know what is passing—the interviewer may not have defined a passing grade. Passing might be the overall impression that you leave with the interviewer.

Challenging as a technical interview may seem, you still have to prepare to answer questions to the best of your abilities—and your best may not be adequate to pass the technical interview, especially if you are an experienced project manager. You are probably an excellent project manager but it might have been a while since you've been quizzed on details (by the book) of project management. You likely take shortcuts that pose no harm to the project but wouldn't pass if your project management professor were watching you.

Furthermore, you have no clue as to what you might be asked. The remaining chapters of this book will help you prep for technical interviews. Questions tend to focus on critical thinking skills. You probably know the answers—at least the answers are somewhere in your head. You might simply need something to jog your memory. In the rest of the book, you'll find those memory joggers that provide an in-depth review of project management that will help you on technical interviews and tests.

Chapter 8
Prepping for Project Manager Questions

You Don't Need to Be a Genius

Be prepared to be asked questions about project management during interviews with the manager and other staff. A few facilities may require that you pass an online project management test even before you meet with the manager. One thing is for sure—there are no standards when it comes to quizzing you about projects. In fact, you may be lucky and no one may challenge your knowledge about projects until you begin orientation for your job.

There may be general questions about project management and then there may be questions that focus on project management in a specialty area, if that is a requirement for your job. The format of the questions may range from simple questions formulated by the manager to more complex (PMP certification exam) online questions supplied by a vendor.

Don't panic! You probably know the answer. Managers tend to ask questions related to practical project management rather than ones that require knowledge of obscure facts about project management. For example, the manager may ask you about how you approach a new project. The manager is looking for more than just making sure you that you know the scope of the project. That's a given. Think about process. The manager is probably hoping you'll say that you'll explore whether or not the project is feasible and then work with the project sponsor to develop an acceptable project charter. You'll then be expected to walk through an overview of the project management process.

Listen carefully to the question asked by the manager. The question may not be as carefully worded as a PMP certification question. Ask the manager if they can restate the question if you don't understand it. You also can restate the question before answering to ensure that you understood the question.

Rather than give a brief textbook answer, walk through a real situation that you experienced, highlighting the problem mentioned in the question, and then explain how you handled the situation. For example, you might say that you once had a project sponsor whose expectations were unrealistic. You realized this during the initial conversation regarding the project. Agreeing with the project sponsor would set up the project for failure. Disagreeing with the project sponsor might be seen as being disrespectful. You then state that you restated in your own words what the project sponsor said. In doing so, you rephrased each expectation clearly, identifying advantages and disadvantages. This gave the project sponsor information to determine that their expectations were unrealistic. Walking through a real situation when answering a question gives you an opportunity to share your critical thinking abilities with the manager.

https://doi.org/10.1515/9781501506222-009

Walking through a real scenario is also a good approach to take when you are unsure of what the manager is looking for in the answer. The walkthrough may satisfy the manager, because somewhere during the walkthrough you've answered the manager's question. Even if you don't specifically answer the question, the walkthrough may provide the manager with sufficient insights into your project management skills.

Each manager establishes their own criteria when selecting the ideal candidate for the position. You don't know what questions, if any, will be asked. You don't know how the manager will evaluate your problem-solving ability. You don't know the passing grade except on a project management online test.

The manager is likely evaluating how you approach solving the question and is less concerned about your using the perfect language or reciting policies and procedures. Can you think on your feet? Are you focused on effectively managing a project? How do you compare with other candidates who might have been asked the same questions?

Expect that some questions may be vague or difficult to answer. As a result, you might give the wrong answer. Typically, the manager may give you additional information or hints that help your thoughts get back on track. Don't take this as a negative. Other candidates may have also needed help answering the question. What is important is how you handle incorrect questions. That is, how many hints do you need before you answer correctly?

Also expect that you'll answer questions incorrectly. That's OK too. Rarely does anyone answer all questions correctly. Be honest and tell the manager that you are unsure of the answer. However, also state how you would find the answer if you were faced with this problem during a project. This shows how you would solve problems in real life. Doing so changes an incorrect response (not knowing the answer) to a correct response (how you would find the answer).

Online Project Management Tests

You may have to take an online project management test prior to employment as a way for the facility to remove unqualified candidates from the mix before time and money is spent on the interview process. Online project management tests are more structured and predictable than questions asked during interviews because typically online tests are provided by a vendor.

The pre-employment online project management test is likely to have elements of the PMP certification exam. This is a good thing if you have recently passed the PMP certification exam because you have recent testing skills and the content is fresh in your mind. However, the test might be a challenge for experienced project managers who are PMP certified but who haven't prepped for a PMP certification exam in years.

Don't assume that you can whiz through the online project management test because you administer hundreds of projects. It is not that you are asked about strange aspects of project management—nearly all questions are on basic project management. The problem is that experienced project managers don't prep for the test.

Vendors tend to use the PMP certification exam-type multiple-choice questions in which two answers are wrong and two answers are correct—one more correct than the other. Although vendors provide firms with project management tests, the firm determines the passing grade. There are a number of philosophies used to establish the passing grade. The firm may base the passing grade on what local project management training schools use as the passing grade. The firm may follow the lead of the project management training schools but then lower the passing grade if they find an insufficient pool of applicants who can pass the test.

Always ask a recruiter if they have a review sheet available—many do if they require a pre-employment project management test. Sometimes the review sheet simply lists general information about project management. If the firm prepares the review sheet, this is likely. Other times, the review sheet is prepared with assistance from the vendor who prepared the test and hopefully reflects project management concepts that are on the test. If a review sheet isn't available, then review Chapter 8, which covers areas that are found on the PMP certification exam and possibly a pre-employment project management test.

A Project Management Review

Let's review basic information about project management that you are bound to be asked somewhere along the interviewing process. The project begins with the project sponsor having an idea that will improve the firm in some way. The project manager and the project sponsor decide on a scope statement and project charter before the project manager sets out to develop the project plan.

The *scope statement* summarizes the project into a few words, or sometimes it can be a slogan. Use the scope statement to help the project sponsor, stakeholders, and the project team to refocus on the project goals. Some project managers post the scope statement in clear sight at every meeting. Others use words from the scope statement as a slogan that appears at the top of all emails and project documents, making it difficult for anyone to lose sight of the goal.

The *project charter* is another tool used to manage the project. Think of the project charter as the contract between the project manager and the project sponsor. It contains the project sponsor's expectations, goals, constraints, limitations, timelines, and costs. The project manager refers to the project charter throughout the project to make sure that the project is being managed according to the terms of the contract.

The project charter specifies the following about the project:
- Project Overview: Summary of the project
- Purpose of the Project: Business reason for the project
- Project Objective: Outcome of the project
- Project Scope: Limits within which to complete the project.
- Major Milestones: Visible markers of progress towards the project objective
- Major Deliverables: Significant parts of the outcome of the project that is presented to the project sponsor.
- Assumptions: Assumptions that the project manager, project sponsor, and stakeholders make when the project gets underway.
- Constraints: Restrictions within which the project is developed.
- Preliminary Cost of the Project: The estimate price of the project.
- Project Charter Acceptances: Names, titles, and signatures of the project sponsor, project manager, and other stakeholders who have to agree to terms of the project.

The *project plan* is the step-by-step guide that tells the project team how to meet the project's goal. There is an old saying: plan to work, and then work the plan. Follow your project plan once the project is launched. However, you might need to change the project plan to meet the challenges of the project such as deadlines and budgets or new requirements. Remember to plan to work—that is, change the project plan first before working on the changes.

From an Idea to a Work Package

A project begins as the project sponsor's idea, such as an order entry system. Think of the idea as a whole thing—that is, the project's deliverable. The project manager must devise a plan to make the idea a reality. As described later in this chapter, there are several approaches that can be used to manage a project. For now, let's use the traditional approach where the project manager uses the *work breakdown structure*. The work breakdown structure uses the 100-percent rule to define the all the work necessary to complete the project.

The project manager takes the whole (the idea) and divides it into pieces, and those pieces into further pieces. The final piece is called a *work package*. The work package consists of a set of temporary activities that produce a portion of the project's deliverable. In smaller projects, there is one work package, but there can be many work packages in larger projects. For example, building a data entry screen is a work package.

Next the project manager breaks down the work package into tasks that must be performed to produce the deliverable. This process is like looking at the cover of a jigsaw puzzle box to see what the puzzle looks like when completed, and then identifying pieces before you decide how you are going to assemble the puzzle.

Work Breakdown Structure

Here is an example of the work breakdown structure for an order entry application (see Figure 8.1). Each step in the breakdown is identified as a level. The whole is the completed order entry application and is the first level of the work breakdown structure. Ask yourself what the major components of the order entry system are. Let's say the following are those components that are each considered at the second level:
- Product display
- Order entry
- Order processing
- Order inquiry
- Management reporting

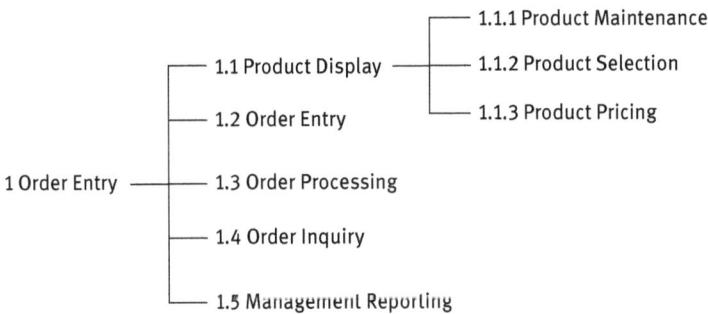

```
                                              ┌── 1.1.1 Product Maintenance
                         ┌── 1.1 Product Display ──┼── 1.1.2 Product Selection
                         │                    └── 1.1.3 Product Pricing
                         ├── 1.2 Order Entry
1 Order Entry ───────────┼── 1.3 Order Processing
                         ├── 1.4 Order Inquiry
                         └── 1.5 Management Reporting
```

Figure 8.1: The work breakdown structure for an order entry application identifies each breakdown level by numbers that show a relationship.

Notice the numbering sequence used to identify levels. The first level is 1 and represents the whole. Second-level components are identified by a whole number and a decimal number. The first component, called product display, is numbered 1.1, which shows the relationship of the product display to the order entry application. The same process is used to identify all second-level components.

The work breakdown process continues by identifying the third level of components. For product display, let's say the following are third-level components:
- Product maintenance – products are added, modified, or removed
- Product selection – customer browses the product offering
- Product pricing – pricing rules for each product

You can probably come up with more subdivisions.

Each third-level component is identified by a number that relates it to previous divisions. Here, product maintenance is numbered 1.1.1. This is the first level of product display, which is the first level of the order entry application. This process continues until you have completed the smallest division of the work (a work package) and it is identified. At this point in the process, the project manager identifies tasks required to complete the work package.

Stop Already!

The obvious question is when to stop breaking down the work. There is no easy answer. You can use the 80-hour rule. You stop breaking down work when the group of activities will take 80 hours to complete. That is, the last subdivision of each branch of the work breakdown structure—a work package—takes approximately 80 hours to build. The 80-hour rule tries to establish a uniform duration of each work package. A drawback is that not every work package fits nicely into an 80-hour work effort.

An alternative is to use a *reporting period* as a guide. A reporting period may be a quarter, half a year, or a full year, depending on your organization. That is, completion of a work package must not exceed a reporting period. This makes marking progress straightforward, since one or more work packages will be complete in time for the reporting period. However, work packages may not neatly fit into a reporting period.

Many project managers use the common sense rule and stop breaking down work when a logical work package can be identified. For example, you might stop at product maintenance as the work package, and then build a product plan to add, modify, and remove products. Another project manager may break down product maintenance further into subdivisions—add, modify, remove. Each becomes a work package. A work package is then broken into tasks. When all tasks are completed, the work package is completed, and when all work packages are completed, the project is completed.

Tasks and Subtasks

Once the work package is clearly defined, the focus moves to identifying tasks that are necessary to be performed to complete the work package. This can be a tricky process because the project manager may not know the work needed to complete the work package. The project manager is an expert in managing the project, not performing the work. Sometimes the project manager can logically arrive at tasks and other times, someone more knowledgeable about building the work package is consulted. Regardless of whether an expert is consulted, the project manager is responsible for identifying tasks.

A task is an action that has a beginning, an end, and produces a result. This seems obvious, but it is important to remember. If an action doesn't have a result, then it is not a task. Think of a task as a piece of the puzzle. You are asking a member of your project team to deliver a completed piece of the puzzle—a result—within a specific time frame. The result must be clearly defined—otherwise, you won't receive a completed piece of the puzzle.

For example, designing a way to add a product to the product offering is a task. When the task is completed, you'll have a process designed about how to add a product. The next task might be to build the software to add a product to the product offering.

A subtask is an action that has a beginning, an end, and the result is used as an action of a task. For example, a systems analyst needs to assess how products are described as a step toward designing how to add a product to the product offering. This is a subtask that, when completed, becomes part of the design task. There can be many subtasks for each task.

Task Relationships

Performing a task may be dependent on one or more tasks. These are referred to as task relationships or dependencies. For example, you must sit behind the wheel of a car before you can drive the car. Sitting behind the wheel is one task and driving the car is another task. These tasks are related.

There are several types of task relationships (Figure 8.2). The finish-to-start relationship is where Task B cannot begin until Task A is finished. That is, you can't drive the car until you sit behind the wheel.

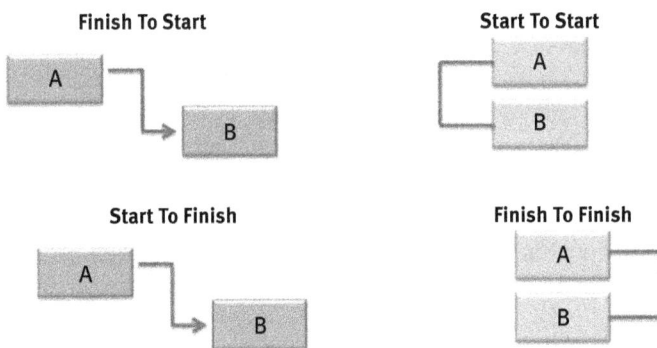

Figure 8.2: Lines connect tasks to show dependencies among tasks. Here are common dependencies found among tasks in a project.

Some tasks must begin at the same time. This is referred to as a start-to-start relationship. For example, in some cars you must step on the brake while moving the gearshift into drive.

The finish-to-finish relationship is when two tasks must be finished at the same time. For example, the driver and the passenger must be seated in the car before driving the car.

The start-to-finish relationship is when the start time of Task A determines the finish time of Task B. For example, if you are driving to a destination, the time you start to sit behind the wheel of the car determines the time when you stop driving the car.

Let's say it takes 5 minutes to sit behind the wheel of your car and 20 minutes to drive to your destination—this is when you end Task B, driving the car. You start to sit behind the wheel of the car at 5:00. You start driving at 5:05 and stop driving—arriving at your destination—at 5:25. That is, Task B ends at 5:25. If you started to sit behind the wheel of your car at 5:10 then Task B ends at 5:30, which is when you stop driving.

Sequencing and Duration

Sequencing is the process that determines the order in which tasks and subtasks are performed based on the needs of the work package and relationships among tasks. The project manager may alter the sequence during the project to keep the project on time and on budget—more on this later.

The length of time to complete a task is referred to as the *duration* of the task. Duration is the time spent working on a task plus elapsed time. Elapsed time is an important component when estimating duration. For example, a task might take 1 week to complete; however, the resource to complete the task might not be available to begin work for 1 week. Therefore, the duration is 2 weeks—that is, 1 week of wait time and 1 week of actual work on the task.

Duration is estimated in a unit of time such as workdays, work hours, or, in rare circumstances, work minutes. The unit depends on the nature of the work package and policy of the firm. The most commonly used unit is a workday, as defined by the organization's policy. Some organizations work a 7-hour day and others an 8-hour day.

Although the smallest duration unit could be an hour, project managers tend to use a half-day as the smallest duration unit. A 1-hour duration is seen on labor in-tense projects where a person may take on more than one role and each role has a different hourly rate. For example, a worker may spend 3 hours as a packer and then 5 hours as a delivery driver. Each position has a different hourly wage therefore it is critical that the unit is 1 hour when measuring duration.

Avoid micromanaging the project by setting the duration to an hour, unless the project calls for it. Always give members of the project team flexibility to manage their own time. Put yourself into the team member's position. Would you want someone telling you what to do each minute of your workday, or would you want to be allotted a reasonable amount of time to do your work?

The project manager must balance the performance needs with a team member's freedom to work. UPS, for example, specifies tasks for drivers that include pre-trip vehicle inspection, where to park if there are multiple deliveries on the same street, and the best way to deliver a package. Being specific can have a financial benefit. Designating delivery routes where only right turns are made resulted in saving UPS 2.5 million gallons of fuel each year.

Setting duration for a task is challenging even if you know how to perform the task because each of us works differently. Here are several methods that can be used when estimating duration.

- Prior experience
- Historic statistical relationships
- Call in an expert to give you an estimate
- The bottoms-up method of estimating duration
- PERT—determine duration by calculating three estimates
- The three-point estimate

A common approach to setting duration is based on the project manager's prior experience. Let's say that it took four days to design an order entry screen in your last project, so you estimate it will take someone else the same amount of time to design an order entry screen for your current project. This sounds reasonable, but there is a problem. No two order entry screens are alike, and no two designers are alike either. The designer of your current order entry screen may require a longer or shorter time to design the screen, making your estimate wrong.

You can take the historic approach to estimating, called the historic statistical relationship. Look at previous project plans to see how long it actually took to perform a similar task, then use that duration for your current task. This also sounds reasonable, but there is also a problem. History may not repeat itself. The task was performed by different staff under conditions that are likely different from the conditions specified in your project. You might be misled using the historic statistical relationship.

You can ask an expert to give you an estimated duration for a task. The expert's opinion should take into consideration the needs of your project. However, there are a number of challenges to using this method. How do you know the person is really an expert? You are looking for a person who has performed nearly the same task several times in the past. Is this person qualified to give you an estimate? And then there is this overriding concern: The expert is faced with no consequences if the estimate is wrong. The expert has no "skin in the game." The expert may say it will take 10 days to complete the task. The expert isn't penalized if the task actually takes 30 days.

The bottoms-up method is another way of estimating duration. This is where you decompose and analyze how long it takes to complete each step in the task. This is a common practice in manufacturing. A stopwatch is used to time a person who performs steps of the task. The time is recorded and totaled to estimate the duration for the task. The bottoms-up method is time consuming and not practical for estimating most tasks.

Program Evaluation Review Technique (PERT) can be used to estimate duration by using three estimates: optimistic, most likely, and pessimistic. Each estimate is given a weight, with more weight being given to the most likely estimate. The three-point estimate is similar to PERT except the average of the optimistic, most likely, and pessimistic estimated are used to estimate the duration for the task.

Another approach is a variation of the expert method. Ask an expert for the estimate and assign that expert to the task. The expert is now faced with consequences if the task is not performed within the duration.

Whatever method you choose to estimate duration, make sure that you document any assumptions you make related to the task. Let's say that a person who is experienced in designing an order entry screen will take four days to design the order entry screen for your project. Document this as an assumption made when estimating duration for this task. If you later assign this task to a less experienced designer, then you may want to revisit your duration estimate because a critical assumption has changed.

Analyze a task to determine if the task is effort-driven or duration-driven. An effort-driven task is one where the duration is determined by the number of resources working on the task. The more resources, the shorter duration. A duration-driven task is one where duration isn't affected by the number of resources working on the task—it will take the same duration to complete the task whether one or ten people work on the task. Remember that whatever method you use to set a duration, you are held responsible for meeting that timeline.

Resources

A resource is a thing or person required to complete a task or a subtask. Identifying resources seems straightforward because we tend to think of a resource as a person. To design a screen for the order entry application, you need a person: a screen designer. However, we tend to overlook the resources that the person needs to perform the task, and missing such resources is a problem—picture the person sitting at the desk but being unable to work because they are missing tools. Analyze each task to identify resources. Ask what human resource is needed to perform the task, and what resources that person needs to complete the task.

Project management tools such as Project Libre (open source) and Microsoft Project have a *resource list* where you can identify resources and key information about the resource. Add each resource to the list of resources for your project.

Resources are listed using unique titles such as Business Analyst 1 and System Analyst 1. Avoid using a person's name because the person may leave the project. You can then slot a person into the role identified by the unique title. For example, Mary Smith is assigned the role of Business Analyst 1.

A key piece of information about the resource is the maximum amount of the resource's time that can be allocated to the project. Many times, the person spends 100 percent of the workday on the project (the max time is 100 percent), however, shared resources may be available 50 percent of the shared resource's time. The maximum time is then 50 percent. Financial information related to the resource is also identified in the resource list. This includes an hourly rate to use the resource, an overtime rate for the resource, and the cost to use the resource, such as licensing the application.

Let's walk through the process of identifying resources. The task is to list data requirements for the application. The task consists of several subtasks—we will focus on identifying resources for each subtask.

Analyzing and some brainstorming will produce this partial resource list. The list is in random order. The next step is to prioritize resources. In which order should resources be acquired? You need to logically think through the order in which resources are needed. Notice that the business analyst and systems analyst are not the first resources to acquire. Strange as this may seem, the first resource is office space, followed by furnishings. This will give the analysts a place to work.

Determine how long it will take to acquire each resource. This is a factor easily overlooked. Don't assume that resources are readily available. Here, we estimate that it takes 180 days to acquire office space (Figure 8.3). The process begins when the project manager requests space from the facilities department and ends when

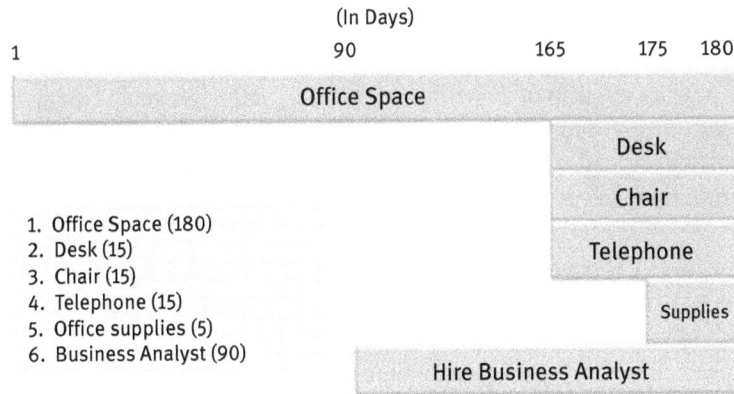

Figure 8.3: Always consider the time to acquire resources as part of the project plan. Here, we show that 180 days are needed to acquire office space before the project begins.

the space is ready to be occupied. The facilities department may have to locate and negotiate a lease for space outside the existing facility.

Likewise, it may take three months before a new employee is hired and up to speed to work on the task. This includes acquiring the head count, settling on title and compensation with HR, sifting through resumes and interviewing candidates, and waiting several weeks before you know if the new employee is competent. The process begins again if the employee doesn't work out.

Always consider approval times, approval processing, delivery time, and time before the resource is fully operational. You have a start date for your project, but you must add tasks for acquiring resources to your project plan. Tasks to acquire resources must all end on the same date: the date that your project starts.

Notice that the task to acquire office space must begin 180 days before the start date of your project. Likewise, you must begin your search for the business analyst 90 days before the start date. Any delay in acquiring resources will delay the start of the project.

Resources are assigned from the resource list to tasks or subtasks in the project plan. The project management tool uses the duration of the task, resource availability, and the cost to perform several useful calculations that can help you manage the project. Resource allocation is one of those calculations. Resource allocation graphically depicts the percentage of the resource availability that has been allocated to tasks.

Here is the resource allocation for the business analyst (Figure 8.4). Light grey indicates over-allocation. That is, the project manager assigned the business analyst to two times the number of tasks that can be completed in one day. This is like asking the business analyst to do three things at the same time.

You can identify over-allocation problems by reviewing the resource allocation after assigning resources to tasks. This enables you to identify and fix allocation problems before giving assignments to resources. The goal is to minimize over-allocation to 110 percent. The extra 10 percent might be achieved by asking the business analyst to work a few hours overtime or come in on the weekend.

The project management tools can generate a work schedule for each resource that shows all tasks assigned to the resource along with the start and end dates. Resource utilization involves managing resources based on the changing needs of the project.

- If a task becomes too expensive, then you could assign a less expensive resource to the task, but there are risks—the quality may decrease or the duration of the task could increase.
- If a task is taking too long to complete, you may increase productivity by using a more experienced resource, but there is a risk that the cost to perform the task could increase.
- If tasks are falling behind schedule, you can ask the resource to work overtime or outsource the task to consultants, also at an increased cost.

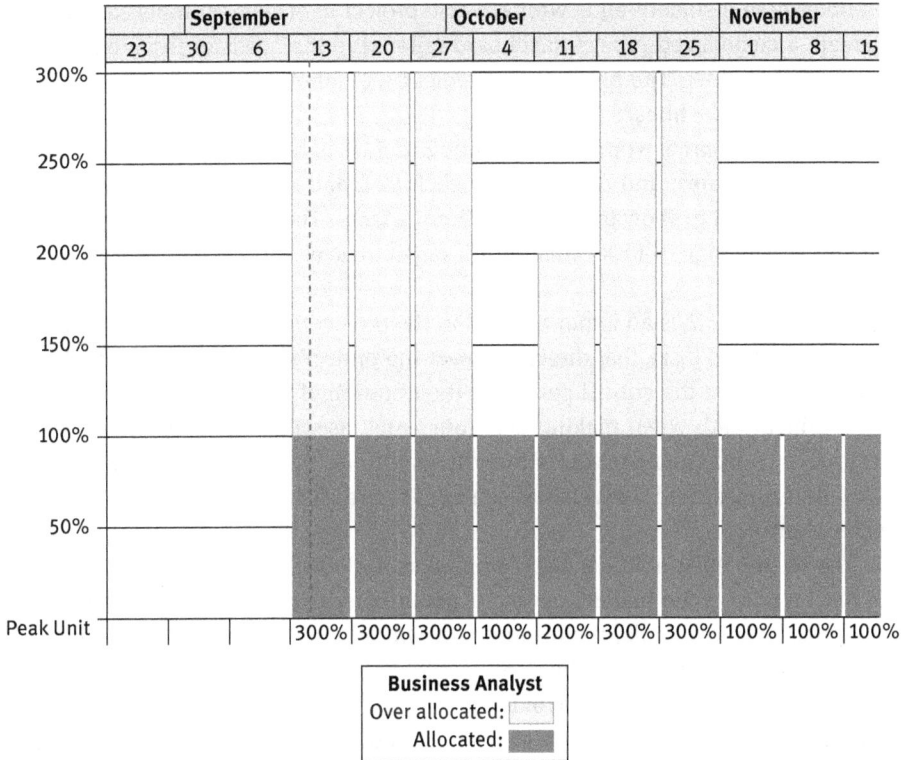

Figure 8.4: The resource allocation graph shows in light grey when a resource is over-allocated. The project manager is asking the resource to do two things at the same time, which is impossible.

You can also reassign resources to tasks that are on the critical path to make sure that the tasks are completed on time—however, that works only if the task is effort-driven. More resources reduce duration.

Reporting Progress

Project sponsors, stakeholders, and the project team all want to be kept apprised of the progress of the project. The best way to do this is by using status reports. A good approach is to ask what information the project sponsor or stakeholder wants to see in the report and how frequently they want the report. Ask first— don't assume—because you don't want to provide too much or too little informa- tion. Some project sponsors want a weekly email stating whether the project is on budget and on time and any variance—no details.

A best practice is to create a *dashboard* for your project. This is like the dash- board on your car. A quick glance enables you to see all the performance indicators and determine if something is wrong. Some project management tools can be used to create a customized project dashboard tailored to the needs of the project sponsor and stakeholder. The project management tool automatically displays the project status in the dashboard.

The *Gantt Chart* is your main planning tool. It is here where you enter tasks, subtasks, start dates, and durations for each task and subtask. The Gantt Chart is also the tool used to show relationships among tasks. The Gantt Chart automatically displays a calendar of tasks that shows dependencies and resources assigned to tasks.

The *critical path* is an important tool in the project manager's toolbox. The critical path identifies tasks that directly impact the project's deadline. Increase the duration of a task on the critical path, and the duration of the project increases. Refer to the critical path when making decisions, such as when to approve time off for the project team. Calendars are a friendly way to let the project team know about tasks, milestones, and deliverables. Calendars are easier than the Gantt Chart to read and print.

The resource list is like a roster of players and available tools. Always refer to the resource list when making decisions about personnel and resources needed for your project. For example, the resource list will tell you if there is a less expensive resource available, which can be used to reduce the cost of performing a task.

Resource allocation helps avoid headaches when assigning resources to tasks. It shows at a glance if you over-allocated a resource—that is, asked the resource to do more than one thing at a time. Knowing about problems in advance provides the opportunity to reallocate resources and prevent conflicts.

The Acceptance Process

Once the project team is satisfied that the finished project meets requirements, the project sponsor and stakeholders move in to examine and test the system to verify that requirements have been met. This is referred to as the *acceptance process*. The goal is for the project sponsor and stakeholders to ensure themselves that the systems satisfy the terms in the project charter. There should be no surprises at this stage of the project life cycle.

The acceptance test is the focus of the acceptance process. It is an objective test that the project manager, project sponsor, and stakeholders develop at the beginning of the project. The acceptance test contains the acceptance criteria for the system that is quantitative and measurable, removing subjectivity from the results.

For example, the order entry system must:
– Handle all types of orders
– Process 1000 orders an hour
– Make the order available to the fulfillment department within one minute

- Place orders in priority order
- Be accessible 24/7

The acceptance test must:
- Test all types of orders
- Test that at least 1,000 orders can be processed in one hour
- Test that the fulfillment department receives the order within one minute from the time the order is entered
- Test that orders are placed in priority order
- Test the accessibility of the system

There should be no surprises during the acceptance test because during development, the project team makes sure that the system can pass the test. It is like having the answers to the test before taking the test. The project sponsor and stakeholders approve the acceptance test. The test is usually developed by the project manager with input from the project sponsor and stakeholders.

The project sponsor and stakeholders conduct the test. The project team observes and provides assistance when necessary. There is no simulation. Real orders are entered and processed. It is important that the acceptance test be conducted at all sites within the organization. A site may have an environment where the system doesn't work. For example, there may be a dead spot in the Wi-Fi network.

Problems may arise during the acceptance test. However, it is important that the project sponsor and stakeholder distinguish between a requirement not met and a function that wasn't in the scope of the project. Problems are noted and the project returns to development. A full acceptance is conducted once problems are addressed by the project team.

Migration

Once the system passes the acceptance test, the focus is on making the system live. This is referred to as *migration*—commonly called moving the project into production. *Production* is a term used to describe the live computer environment. Migration requires its own plan that consists of tasks, durations, resources, and costs. The plan identifies all stakeholders and systems affected by the new system.

The migration plan also addresses:
- Existing data: Will existing orders and customer records be converted to the new system before the system goes live? If so, how does this happen?
- Operational constraints and limitations of workflows in the organization: Do you go live with all areas or selected areas? What day and time of day do you go live? There are many questions that need to be addressed before the system is live.

With the migration plan in place, the moment of truth has arrived, and another group of questions must be answered.

- Who decides when to cut over to the new system?
- Who manages the cut-over process?
- How do you determine if the cut-over was successful?
- How are you going to recover if the cut-over fails?

The project manager working the project sponsor and stakeholders answer these questions. In many organizations, the cut-over occurs late Friday and into Saturday. The system is run with indicative test data and the results are analyzed for accuracy. By mid Saturday, it should be known if the cut-over is successful, and the new system should be ready for start of business on Monday. If the cut-over is unsuccessful, then the project team has from mid-Saturday to very early Monday morning to return to the old system.

The project manager—working with the project sponsor, stakeholders, and the administration—must develop a migration strategy. The migration strategy must answer the following questions.

- What is the acceptable level of business disruption? How long can the workflow be disrupted?
- Is there a drop-dead date for cutting over to the new system? Regulatory requirements may set a deadline.
- Will everyone be onboard and willing to use the new system, even if they oppose the system?

There are two frequently used migration strategies:

- The old system can be immediately replaced with the new system—a turn-off/turn-on strategy.
- Both systems can run in parallel—the old system is live and the new system processes live data. Processing results are compared and cut-over to the new system occurs when the project sponsor and stakeholders are comfortable with the new system.

Managing People

Communicating with the stakeholders can be a major challenge for the project manager because some stakeholders have leadership roles within the firm, functioning with autonomy. Many stakeholders work in stressful situations responsible for a portion of the business operations. They've developed a workflow that produces results—the last thing they want is someone dramatically changing how they work.

Your goal as project manager is to change behavior, get stakeholders to take action, and persuade stakeholders that change is good for them while ensuring they fully understand the purpose of the change. Above all, your goal is to manage information—that you communicate with stakeholders, ensuring that you achieve your goal and change from a reliable workflow to something new, such as introducing a new approach that makes a process less burdensome while lowering cost and increasing security.

Don't underestimate the challenge of changing workflow and behavior, especially if the change involves technology. One of the underlying and unmentioned challenges is computer literacy among some (not all) of the staff. Some don't know how to type efficiently. Others are uncomfortable using technology. Compounding the problem is the fact that some staff who are seen as experts don't want others to see their technological weakness.

The following examples are objections raised by some of the staff.
- "The old way works fine."
- "Don't tell me how to manage my business."
- "I don't have time."
- "I only listen to my boss."
- "I'm retiring soon. I'm really not paying attention."
- "Save time for whom?"
- "I can squeeze in 30 minutes of training."
- "I can write a better program than this one."
- "I cooperated with all five of your predecessors."

Your job is to overcome these objections. As you try to engage some staff, maybe you are cut off in mid-sentence, yelled at, or told to speed up your presentation. You may be speaking with staff who don't have the desire to listen to you. They may make you feel it's your fault that they are not cooperating with changes. You return to your office in frustration. Your well-thought-out strategy and polite, respectful presentation falls on deaf ears, and you need staff cooperation to make the project successful.

Begin the process of effectively communicating by analyzing the following needs of stakeholders.
- What are the stakeholder's goals?
- How can your message help the stakeholder reach the goals?
- Determine how much information the stakeholder needs to accept change.
- Determine how the stakeholder wants to receive your information—maybe through a staff meeting, or a five-minute, one-on-one meeting.
- How much influence does the stakeholder have over other stakeholders? Winning over one stakeholder might win over others.

Next, analyze your needs.
- Clearly define your objectives for communicating with the stakeholder.
- Decide how to position your message and the amount of information you want and need to share with the stakeholder.
- Most important is to know what you want the stakeholder to do.

Don Hewitt, creator of "60 Minutes" for CBS, developed a formula for successful communication. Tell them something they don't know and why they should know it. You can use this formula to communicate with staff.

Your tools for communication are phone calls, meetings, e-mails, reports, texting, one-on-one conversation, and techniques for resolving conflicts.

Face-to-Face Meetings and Presentations

Here are important factors to consider with face-to-face meetings. Your body language communicates most of your message, followed by the tone in your voice—your words alone are least effective. When speaking, your tone conveys most of your message, not your words.

Read the listener's body language to determine if your message is being received. Ask open-ended questions. The response will let you know if your message was received as intended.

Interest is the most important factor in written messages. Your presentation and words count little if there is no interest in what you have to say.

Use headlines to tell the reader why they should read further—this is the way newspapers and magazines get the reader's attention. The fewer pages and less dense text, the better.

Written communication has inherent problems:
- You don't know if the message was read and understood.
- You have no immediate feedback so there is no opportunity for clarification.
- To ensure the best possible communication you must fine-tune each phase of the communication: the delivery, the sender, the message, the channel, and the recipient.
- Are you really communicating when you give a presentation?

You're presenting a new workflow. Staff might be thinking:
- "Who needs this? Things work fine now."
- "I don't have time for this."
- "What do you know about my job?"
- "When will you finish?"

Staff size up the situation almost immediately.

When it comes to change, some staff draw on experiences and intuition rather than systematically comparing all available options. Some learn more about you by observing body language and facial expressions than by asking questions.

In theory . . .

- No one should judge by appearance, but we do.
- We should not prejudge, but we do.
- We should not jump to conclusions, but we do.
- We should not stop thinking after our first impression, but we do.

Ask yourself what signal you are sending. Are you conveying that you are confident, knowledgeable, and trusting? You should prepare your audience before making your presentation. In the entertainment business, this is commonly referred to as warming up the audience before the main act goes on.

Prime your audience by providing favorable information about your topic before the meeting. This influences their unconscious decision making. If the audience has a good impression about you, then they are likely to have a good impression about the change that you want to implement. This is called *sensation transference* and is used by consumer product companies. They create packaging that leaves consumers with a good impression, and consumers subconsciously transfer that impression to the product.

Staff often react based on memory. The new and unusual make them nervous—they need time to understand the change. You can influence their first impression by relating the change to what they already do. Show today's process and then focus on the changes to the process.

Create an environment for your discussion. Don't present unless stakeholders are receptive to receiving your message. An angry or frightened stakeholder is not going to listen attentively. A stakeholder with a time constraint is unlikely to give you their full attention. Find a time and place when stakeholders can give you their full attention.

Give the stakeholder time to buy into your change by helping work through the stages of adoption. While you and the project sponsor are convinced that your solution improves workflow, stakeholders have yet to arrive at the same conclusion. Stakeholder acceptance follows a process. Your job is to help stakeholders process each stage of adoption, referred to as the *stages of adoption*:

1. First, stakeholders have to be aware that a problem exists and that a solution exists.
2. Next, stakeholders take a superficial look at the solution to see if it really solves the problem.
3. If so, they take a closer look and examine the situation in detail, trying to uncover reasons why it won't work.
4. If you can resolve their concerns, they then test the solution under various scenarios, using critical thinking or playing with a demo.
5. Good test results usually mean stakeholders adopt the solution.

Communications Plan

Devise a plan for communicating your message. First, identify what you want to say. Remember, tell your audience something they don't know and why they should know it. Next, identify your audience. Who are the stakeholders? Are they for, against, or neutral to change? If they are against change, why? If you can address their objections, you may win them over. Next, select the delivery method: personal meeting, group meeting, phone, email, or a combination.

Formulate your message. What points do you want to make? Consider using the SBAR approach. Present the *situation, background, assessment*, and *recommendation*.

Also consider using the inverted pyramid style, which is common to newspaper writing. Start with the most important information first and then provide supporting information, additional facts, and background.

Then write your message. Be sure to:
- Define words that may be misunderstood
- Select words that the audience will understand
- Use simple language and avoid jargon—some people pretend to understand, but really haven't a clue as to what you are saying.
- Be clear and precise
- Stay on point and avoid negative stories
- Avoid words that are difficult to pronounce—this distracts from the message. The listener changes the focus to pronouncing the word rather than under-standing the word.

Test your message in the following ways:
- Have someone read and critique it. Ask the person to explain what they read. This is a way to find out if your message was received as intended.
- Read the message to someone, especially if you plan to present the message personally. Ask for honest feedback and suggestions.
- Refine your message.
- Finally, deliver your message and watch the audience's facial expressions and body language to pick up clues on whether or not your message is being received.

Ask for feedback either during or after the presentation. Then listen carefully to what they say—make eye contact and concentrate on what the person is saying. Let the person finish their comment, even if their remarks are off-base. Focus on the message and not the speaker—keep an open mind and suspend judgment until you gather all the facts. Put yourself in the other person's position so you can under-stand their viewpoint. They may identify a flaw in your message. Always let the speaker save face even if their remarks are outrageous.

The winning strategy is to be well-organized and prepared to respond to stake-holder questions. Be professional, calm, efficient, persistent, and assertive. Don't feel intimidated, rushed, or emotionally involved. Strike a balance between asser-tiveness and respect and understanding.

Working with Groups

A group is a collection of people who are gathered together to achieve a collective goal. The goal might be to develop policies and procedures, to perform root cause analysis, or to review a system.

The group can meet formally such as in a conference room or as an impromptu gathering in the hallway. Groups can be a small work group or an auditorium filled with staff. The group's goal can be focused on one issue, such as root cause analy-sis of an incident, or can be broad, such as a kickoff meeting for the annual budget review. The group can consist of selected members such as executives or can be open to any employee, such as planning for a holiday party.

A lot happens when a group gets together. This is referred to as *group development*.

1. The group forms, during which time members accept and trust each other.
2. Next is *storming*. This is when some members vie for power and control over the group. Many times, one person is designated the leader prior to the meet-ing. Other times, a de facto leader emerges.
3. *Norming* is when the group formally or informally develops standards of accep-tance. This is when members agree to follow the leader and agree to the group's goals.
4. Next is *performing*. This is when the group begins working toward the goal.
5. And then the meeting is adjourned.

You must give the group time to work through the group development process; oth-erwise, members of the group won't be receptive to your presentation. Although we tend to speak of a group as one uniform collection of people, it isn't.

A group is fluid, with many personalities and personal agendas trying to influence members of the group. This is referred to as *group dynamics*. Knowing the dynamics of a group helps you to make sure your message is clearly being received by the group.

Each group member may take on one or multiple roles within the group.

−   The *information giver* provides factual information to the group.
−   The *opinion giver* suggests a direction for the group.
−   The *information seeker* ensures that the group has all information needed to reach its goal.
−   The *opinion seeker* makes sure each member voices an opinion.
−   The *energizer* motivates the group to take action.
−   The *evaluator* is the sounding board for the group and makes sure that the group's action is reasonable.

- The *recorder* takes notes for the group.
- The *orienter* periodically summarizes what has been said and actions that the group plans to take.
- The *elaborator* builds on ideas and explores the consequences of proposed actions.
- The *coordinator* pulls opinions and ideas into a cohesive action plan.
- The *procedural technician* works out the logistics of the meeting.
- The *initiator* proposes ideas.

Some roles within a group help the group work toward its goal. These are referred to as positive group functions.

- The *compromiser* changes their opinion in order to help the group develop a cohesive plan.
- The *observer* provides feedback on the group's progress, keeping everyone focused on the objective.
- The *follower* summarizes accomplishments of the group.
- The *evaluator* is a listener and does not contribute to the group's decision. The evaluator goes along with whatever the group decides.
- The *gatekeeper* makes sure every member of the group contributes to the conversation, and limits members who try to dominate the conversation.
- The *harmonizer* reduces tension by reconciling differences within the group.
- The *encourager* is the cheerleader, encouraging members to continue to work toward the goal.

Some members take on roles that disrupt the cohesiveness of the group. These are referred to as *disruptive* group functions.

- The *special interest pleader* makes suggestions based on what they think others would like to hear but is careful not to reveal their own opinion.
- The *blocker* opposes every idea but refuses to make a suggestion.
- The *dominator* exaggerates their knowledge and controls the conversation, telling the group what they should do.
- The *aggressor* personally attacks other group members by insulting or belittling them.
- The *help seeker* acts as if they are helpless.
- The *recognition seeker* draws attention to themselves and away from the group's task.
- The *disrupter* uses the meeting as a way to get out of work.
- The *self-confessor* focuses on disclosing personal feelings and issues that are unrelated to the group.

In the ideal world, the meeting has one item on the agenda, and that item is addressed by the end of the meeting. Only those who can make decisions should attend the meeting. The meeting lasts no longer than 15 minutes. All information needed to make the decision is distributed with sufficient time before the meeting, giving decision makers time to review and question the information. Decision makers actually read the information prior to the meeting. The presenter follows the SBAR guidelines.

Informally meet with each group member before the meeting to discuss key features of your presentation. You'll receive feedback, enabling you to refine your plan before the presentation. You'll identify your supporters, detractors, and those who have no opinion. Make sure you find out why they are against your idea so you can be prepared with a counterargument for the presentation.

Be sure to identify the person who has the power to make decisions—usually a group recommends an action to the person who actually has the authority to make the decision. Also be sure to help each group member walk through the stages of adoption.

Clearly state your expectations at the beginning of your presentation, then present your ideas and allow time for group members to digest and react to your message. Invite questions. You may find others with opinions that you haven't considered. Be open and don't jump to conclusions. Keep the meeting on the focus. At the end of the meeting, summarize your message and acknowledge areas where group members agree and disagree. Identify unanswered questions that still need to be answered. Lastly, state the next action for the group.

Barriers to Communication

Be aware of barriers that prevent your messages from being received. Here are some examples.
- Don't use vocabulary that others don't understand and won't ask you to define.
- Your message may pass through too many hands before it is received.
- There is a personality clash that prevents others from listening to your message.
- Some people may lack basic reading, writing, and listening skills and go to great lengths to hide this weakness.
- Your message may place the other person in a defensive position. They may be focused on protecting themselves rather than listening to your message.

There are several things that can distort your message. You can avoid these by:
- Asking everyone to turn off their cell phones and no cross-talking. Stop the presentation if you see these distractions. The group member will get the message.
- Speaking clearly at a reasonable pace. Use words that are comfortable for you to pronounce.
- Testing your presentation with colleagues before the meeting to ensure your presentation is clear, complete, and accurate.

- Being conscious of cultural differences among members of the group. Your ges-
  tures and phrases may be misunderstood.
- Not using subjective terms. For example, your definition of expensive might
  differ from those of group members.

Conflicts and Conflict Mediation

A conflict occurs when two parties disagree in principle or disagree over an issue. A
principle is a deep-rooted fundamental belief, such as maintaining that no one
should tell the manager how to manage their business. A conflict in principle is not
related to the issue at hand and is very difficult to resolve because the party has to
change a long-standing belief. A conflict arising from an issue relates to the immediate situation, not a deep-rooted principle, and therefore is easier to resolve because both parties are inclined to resolve the issue.

The best way to resolve a conflict is to minimize opportunity for conflict. Conflicts
frequently occur because of a lack of communication. If stakeholders had the same
information and time to explore the problem and all options, there is a good chance
they would generally agree to the solution if there wasn't a conflict in principle.

Meeting regularly with stakeholders in one-on-one conversations provides an
opportunity to share points of view. Encourage all stakeholders to participate in the
decision process. Stakeholders should be brought onboard well before changes are
recommended and implemented. This instills the feeling of ownership in the
change—they then become willing to champion the change to colleagues.

Change should be implemented gradually—small changes are quickly adopted.
Above all, be honest—some changes will have an adverse effect on workflow. Be
upfront and acknowledge this fact—don't minimize it—then focus on the benefit of
the change.

Not all conflicts can be avoided. Mediate the conflict when it arises. First, give
parties a period to cool down their emotions and then create a meeting environment
that is conductive to exploring the conflict. This is usually in a neutral conference
room away from where parties normally work, such as a conference room on the
other side of the building. No one has a home field advantage.

The *mediator* defines the mediation process and the mediator's role. Mediation
is the process of identifying facts—those in agreement and those in dispute—and
attempting to have both parties resolve the disagreement. The mediator is a facilitator and does not have an opinion on the issue. The mediator is not an advocate for
either side. The job of a mediator is to help both parties resolve the disagreement.

Make a long list of facts that are in agreement. This should be easy because we
tend to agree with each other more than we disagree. Write the list on a legal pad or
on a whiteboard. Make a visual statement—show the long list of facts that are in
agreement.

Next, do the same with facts in dispute. This will be visually a much shorter list. Write this list alongside the list of facts in agreement so both parties can see that their disagreement is relatively small.

Break down each fact in dispute into elements that are in agreement and elements in dispute. List each alongside the existing list so it is obvious that elements in dispute are very minimal compared to all the facts related to the issue. In the end, it should be obvious that the conflicts center on a few elements and not the entire issue.

Let each party explain their position on elements in dispute. Listen carefully and list each position. Restate what you heard and give them the opportunity to clarify their position. Summarize both positions and then conduct a reality check. Is each position feasible?

Ask each party for possible solutions. Rarely is either proposal perfect, yet some proposal must be enacted. Try to find common ground, or at least a position where parties can live with the proposal.

During mediation, parties have time to cool down. The mediation process enables them to clearly see the reality of the situation and of their positions. They are usually able to resolve their conflict.

Arguments

An argument is a series of statements that present the rationale for a position with the goal of persuading others to adopt the position. However, some argue to avoid accepting the other position, such as not wanting to change from the current process to the new process.

Here are some types of arguments that are less likely to persuade and more likely to avoid change.

- Changing the subject
- Moving the goal post when you are winning the argument
- Half-truth
- Uninformed opinion
- Selective observation
- False compromise, or splitting the difference even if the difference isn't a solution
- Ambiguous assertion that leaves room for the speaker to backtrack
- Drawing a broad conclusion from a small number of facts
- Saying something often enough that people believe it as fact
- False authority
- Being loud and pounding the table
- Discrediting the source used by the opponent
- Inflating the conflict

Here are more arguments commonly used to avoid change.

- Attacking the person instead of the argument.
- Attacking by innuendo
- Delaying tactic, such as needling to make the person angry without addressing the argument
- Pretending that there are only two alternatives when there are more
- Scare tactics
- Oversimplification
- Not invented here – change only occurs if the stakeholder comes up with the change.
- Halo effect (e.g., the person must be right if they are a doctor)
- If you can't prove it false, then it must be true
- Dismissal (being rejected without saying why)
- Using jargon or complicated words, making the person seem to be an expert
- Weasel-wording—using carefully chosen words to mislead the underlying intent.

Be aware of the half-truth argument. This is where only one side of the issue is presented, making it obvious that you should support the position, but there is no mention about opposing alternatives that makes the position less attractive.

Strategic Planning

Strategic planning defines a direction and a method to achieve a strategic goal. Strategic planning begins by gathering information about processes involved in your project. To do this, you need to speak with the right people. Corporate leadership can provide information about policies, procedures, and how decisions are made within the organization. The *process manager* is the expert in overall process operations. The process supervisor is the expert on how a process operates on a detailed, day-to-day basis. And the staff can tell you how a process is actually performed.

Introduce change at the highest levels of the organization. Executives can anticipate barriers to change and can help you develop a strategic plan. Use critical thinking to develop your strategic plan for implementing change. Critical thinking results in making judgments that are logical and well thought-out. Identify stakeholders who are critical to developing and implementing your project and anticipate how much information they need to make a decision.

Reduce their concerns to simple elements and then provide them with basic information that helps them participate in the project. Stakeholders don't need to get involved in details. Next, size up stakeholders by asking questions. The answers become the foundation for your strategic plan.

- Who makes the actual decision?
- Who is in favor of the project?
- Who is against it?
- Who doesn't have an opinion?

It is time to prepare the strategic plan once you gather information. Review all documents associated with the project and review the positions of stakeholders. Identify influential stakeholders and their positions. Clearly identify each stakeholder's expectation. Brainstorm and create a list of potential problems and develop potential solutions.

You must develop the right attitude to manage the project. Take control—right or wrong, you're in charge. Stay objective and don't become emotionally involved. Don't take anything to heart. Listen and fact-find.

Stay flexible and change direction if needed. Avoid talking until you have a plan. Make yourself appear different from others and remember that you're in charge. Plan your moves carefully. Decide on your breakpoint. A breakpoint is the least terms you will accept. For example, you may agree to postpone the project a few days, but your breakpoint is one month. The project cannot be postponed more than one month.

Know the value of the change that you are implementing. For example, implementing the change is highly valuable to the executive leadership team because it affects revenue. The change is less valuable to staff who can live without the process. Knowing the value of the change to each stakeholder helps you identify leverage to persuade the stakeholder to accept the change.

Plan your moves. Don't change your position quickly. Give the impression that you are making a big effort to modify your plans to accommodate the stakeholder, even if that isn't true. This gives a strong sense of compromise.

Open with the ideal plan for change even if you don't expect anyone to adopt this plan. Basically, ask for what you want. The ideal plan gives you room to maneuver when stakeholders counter the offer. Research each stakeholder's situation. This enables you to estimate their bargaining room. For example, the staff has very little bargaining room if executive leadership needs to implement the process. Find out what is of value to each stakeholder. That is, what will it take for the stakeholder to embrace the project?

Provide stakeholders with proof that the project is an improvement over the existing system. Show staff how the change improves their workflow. Make sure that you always have something else to offer to close the deal with stakeholders. For example, tell the staff that they no longer have to do an element of the process. Always speak with authority and use a firm tone even when you are unsure of yourself. Be prepared whenever you discuss anything. Never discuss anything until you are ready to discuss it. Open discussions on an upbeat and avoid all discussions if the other person is totally unreasonable. You will have to deal with difficult stakeholders at some point in the project.

Here are a few points to consider.

Typically, their behavior is habitually inappropriate and they look for you to challenge them. Stand up to a difficult stakeholder. Present the situation. Don't appease the inappropriate behavior. You can't change their behavior, but there is no justification for the behavior, so don't seek to rationalize it.

Cranky stakeholders usually have internal problems and they use their cranky behavior to get their way. Your job is to determine what the cranky stakeholder is trying to tell you. Ask the stakeholder to speak in a calmer voice. Agree only with true statements made by the stakeholder—don't agree just to appease the stakeholder.

An *aggressive stakeholder* expects you to run away from them or react with rage. Your job is to stand up to the stakeholder without arguing. Wait for the stakeholder to run out of steam. Call the stakeholder by name and voice your opinion with confidence. The *subtle sniper* stakeholder gives disapproving looks and uses a sarcastic tone when voicing humorous put-downs.

Your job is to provide feedback on how you are receiving the stakeholder's message. Ask if you understood correctly. Don't overlook this inappropriate behavior. Some stakeholders seem to always complain, primarily because they focus on the negative effects of the change. Your job is to speak with optimism. Acknowledge the stakeholder's concerns but balance those concerns with a sense of reality.

And then there are the *silent stakeholders* who avoid conflicts and responsibility. Your job is to ask questions that require a full response. Wait for the response—don't permit the stakeholder to remain silent.

Say that your goal is to implement a web-based ordering system, moving from paper to electronic documentation.

Define the problem first.

– Accuracy of orders and convenience are a consideration, but money tends to be the motivation.
– The new system will reduce costs associated with entering and processing paper orders.

Prime your message to stakeholders. This is like the warm-up act that prepares the audience for the main act in a concert. Informally make decision makers and influential managers aware of the situation. Explain how the business will be affected. Then allow time for them to explore how to address the problem without your help.

Follow up with one-to-one meetings and hint there is an MIS solution. Explore how other businesses are addressing the situation. Don't sell your idea—just listen to their concerns. Ask them to recommend the next step—give a hint, if they hesitate. Ask the key decision maker to call a *leadership meeting*.

You should create the agenda, informally lead the meeting, and present the situation. Position yourself as the reporter or investigator, someone watching out for the business. Ask for a committee of key staff members to be formed to work with you on coming up with a way to solve the problem. Help each decision maker work through the stages of adoption—don't force the issue. Let them discover the solution with your help.

The solution should be obvious: web-based order entry. Let committee members draw the conclusion and propose the solution. Manage concerns during the adoption process. Understand the staff's concerns. Show empathy even if the concern cannot be addressed. Ask the staff for possible solutions. Take action immediately and follow up with the staff to resolve the concern before moving on.

No project is perfect and no application is perfect. State facts and have evidence available to support your position, Acknowledge limitations of the application and your expertise. Don't dismiss any rationale options and don't be quick to put down other ideas. Instead, explore the pros and cons of each option with the decision maker and let the decision maker draw their own conclusion.

If emotions—yours or the stakeholders—are running high then change the messenger. Adjourn the meeting and let another representative of the project lead the next meeting. Force a decision to be made at every meeting. Create a one- or two-item agenda that clearly identifies the decision. Make sure all options are open to discussion. List concerns and the likelihood that those concerns will occur. Focus on reality. Ask for a go- or no-go decision.

Leadership

A project manager is a skillful leader who—with the assistance of the project team, project sponsor, and stakeholders—makes decisions through the course of the project. However, not all decisions are made by the project manager. The project team and others involved in the project make decisions independently. The project manager must develop a culture that influences how decisions are made.

A project plan defines tasks that must be performed to achieve a desired outcome. However, not everything is defined in a project plan. There are countless decisions that each member of the project team makes during the course of the project that aren't defined in the project planning documents. The project manager may not be consulted in these decisions.

Think of a project plan as a strategic plan or an overall way to achieve the goal. There are many small plans that each project team member develops to enact the strategic plan. These are referred to as *tactical plans*. The project manager develops and implements the strategic plan, not the tactical plans—tactical plans are left up to the project team to develop and implement. Members of the project team make important decisions for the project at the tactical level. The project manager cannot make these decisions. The project manager has no time or expertise to do this.

The project manager can influence decisions by setting values for the project and for the project team. A *value* is a principle that defines what is important. Values are usually fairly stable, but don't have strict limits. For example, a team

member should spend no more than a few hours attempting to solve a problem before sharing the problem with other team members. The value is that sharing a
problem is more effective and efficient than one person spending an endless
amount of time attempting to solve a problem in isolation.

Values guide team members when making decisions to ensure that the decision
adheres to principles set by the project manager or the organization. Here are common values useful to many projects.

- Participatory – All stakeholders should have meaningful participation in the
  project.
- Proactive – The project team should be creative and proactive when solving
  problems.
- Open – All information is shared openly with stakeholders and the project team.
- Outward-oriented – The project manager is focused on the outcome of the proj-
  ect and meeting stakeholder's needs.
- Trusting – Members of the project team and stakeholders must be trusted.

An important value for a project is celebrating failure. This sounds strange, but failure is as valuable as success in a project. There can be multiple options for solving a
problem. Not all will work, but you don't know which one will work. You try option 1
and it fails, which is a good thing because the project team learned not to attempt
option 1 again. The project team learned from failure. Learning what doesn't work is
just as important as learning what works—both should be celebrated equally.

The makeup of your project teams is critical to the success of the project, particularly because team members will be making tactical decisions. To help form your
team, categorize prospective team members as:

- Expert – Able to intuitively grasp the situation based on tacit understanding
  with a vision of what is possible. The expert is able to transcend reliance on
  rules and guidelines to make successful tactical decisions.
- Proficient – Sees a holistic view of the situation and is able to prioritize, but
  may lack the insight to see what is possible beyond the rules and guidelines.
- Competent – Can achieve the outcome with oversight but may lack a holistic
  view of the project.
- Advanced Beginner – Has a good view of the current task but treats all work
  with equal importance.
- Novice – Rigidly adheres to taught rules and the plan—no exercise of discretionary judgment.

Place a team member in a category based on skills, not based on years of service or
perceived expertise. For example, someone who has been with an organization for
15 years and has programmed many of the organization's mission critical systems
may have little experience programming mobile applications. This person is really
a novice or advanced beginner when it comes to programming mobile applications.

Likewise, a highly competent systems analyst may fit the proficient category but lacks the insight and tactical understanding to know what is possible and how to make it happen.

As the project manager, you need to ensure that team members who make tactical decisions have the skillset to do so. For example, an expert in programming a mobile application is capable of making tactical programming decisions. There is an old saying that it is who you know, not what you know, that influences success. And this is somewhat true in a project.

Relationship Capital

Who you know is referred to as *relationship capital*. Consider two project managers. One has successfully completed many projects for the division and is well respected by stakeholders. The other has done the same for another company but is new to your company.

If a stakeholder makes a reasonable request (at least for the stakeholder) and the new project manager says it can't be done, would the stakeholder doubt the new project manager? The new project manager lacks relationship capital with the stakeholder.

It takes time to build relationship capital. However, you can enlist those who have relationship capital with stakeholders to join your project team or become an advocate for your project. You are using that person's relationship capital to positively influence stakeholder opinion.

This is similar to companies hiring a lobbyist to deliver their message to a senator. The lobbyist may have developed relationship capital by once being on the senator's staff or being a colleague or personal friend of the senator. When there is little time to form an opinion, a stakeholder is likely to adopt the opinion of the person who has the relationship capital with the stakeholder.

Relationship capital also is an effective tool to gather information about tactical situations. A stakeholder may be more willing to informally share information with someone they have a relationship with rather than with a new person. For example, the stakeholder shares some other stakeholders' concerns that have not been made known to the project manager. This gives the project manager and the project team an opportunity to be proactive to address those concerns.

Real-Time Planning

There are countless decisions made once a project is launched. Some decisions are straightforward, such as determining if a project can get back on schedule by reassigning staff. You review the critical path, tasks that are off the critical path, and staff skillsets, and then decide if staff can be reassigned.

Other tasks may be more challenging and time sensitive. You may be unsure if your choice is the right choice. Think of this as arriving at a fork in the road. You can go left or right; however, you don't know which is the right road to travel. You simply don't have enough information to make the decision, but you need to make one.

A *real-time planning model* is the perfect method to help make those decisions. In real-time planning, you modify the plan to accommodate changes that occur during the execution of the plan. Stormin' Norman Schwartzkopf, Jr., the general who led Desert Storm, is credited with developing real-time planning.

You don't know what lies down either fork in the road. You can't predict with certainty what lies ahead, so don't put your next series of tasks in a schedule. Instead, use the OODA loop decision model to plan in real-time. The OODA loop decision model supports quick, effective, and proactive decision making. There are four points, called stages.

The first stage is to *observe the situation* by collecting information from as many sources as is practically possible—you don't have time to conduct extensive data gathering. The more information you can take in here, the more accurate your perception will be.

Next is the *orient stage*. Analyze the data and update your current understanding of reality.
- One of the main problems with decision making is we all view events in a way that's filtered through our own experiences and perceptions.
- Be aware of your perceptions. By speeding up your ability to orient to reality, you can then move through the decision loop quickly and effectively.
- You need to process it quickly and revise your orientation.

The *decide stage* is where you determine what to do next based on updated data.
- Decisions are your best guesses, based on the observations and the orientation you're using.
- They should be considered to be fluid works in progress.
- New suggestions keep arriving; these can trigger changes to your decisions and subsequent actions.

The *act stage* is where you follow through on your decision.
- Choose one road.
- Collect as much information about the road from what you can see and hear.
- Analyze this information to help you understand if you made the correct choice.
- Decide what you will do next—either continue down the road a little or return to the fork in the road.
- Make a decision.

Repeat the OODA loop when you either go further down the road or when you return to the fork in the road.

Virtual Team and Rapid Planning Session

At times, decisions must be made quickly but effectively in order the keep the project on time. *Rapid planning* is the planning technique to use. A virtual team comes together in a rapid planning session, referred to as a *RAP session*. A RAP session is two to four hours, during which the virtual team focuses on making a decision by the end of the meeting.

Only stakeholders who can contribute to the decision-making process should attend. All information about the problem is shared with the virtual team. A facilitative meeting format is used where all stakeholders interact. Ideas and solutions are shared and openly challenged to find weaknesses. In the end, a decision is made based on the best information available.

A virtual team is formed to address a specific issue. The team disbands once the issue is solved. Virtual teams can consist of employees, outside experts, and anyone who is needed to address the issue. Some team members can join the team for a few minutes via telecommunications to provide advice. Other members remain with the team until the problem is solved.

Delegate

Realize that the project manager cannot make every decision about the project. There are times that you must delegate decision-making responsibilities. Consider the time that is necessary for you to make every decision and consider the value that you add to the decision-making process. You simply don't have time to listen to recommendations for every decision that needs to be made during the project. Doing so delays the decision process and delays tasks from being performed.

Project team members are experts in their field—you're not. Who is the better person to make a tactical decision: the expert or you? Your decision is to either trust your team or replace them with someone you trust. When delegating, you are relinquishing all control but keeping the liability. You remain accountable for decisions made by the project team.

A middle-level project manager for a major Wall Street firm once said, "I'm waiting for the next disaster to happen. I know my project managers are telling me half-truths and what I want to hear, but it is beyond my scope to delve into details of these projects." This is like sitting in the back of the plane going through turbulence in a storm and the pilot telling you everything is well and apologizing for a bumpy ride.

Here are techniques for delegating.
- Establish standards and values that are used to guide decision makers on your team.
- Clearly define what needs to be done and the range of discretion that the team member can use when performing a task.

- Make sure that the outcome of every task can be measured objectively.
- Be sure that the team member is comfortable making the decision.
- Delegate to team members who are competent in making decisions.
- Trust your project team to make decisions that deliver quality results.

For decisions that you deem critical to the project, ask the project team to notify you prior to acting and after implementing the decision. This alerts you to a potential fail point in the project and if the decision was successfully implemented.

Always monitor the effectiveness of delegating decision making. Keep in mind that it is the other person's decision, not your decision. You might have made a different decision. Avoid arguing about the decision—you delegated making it. As long as the decision is reasonably effective, then support it.

If the decision did not bring about the desired results, then assess the rationale the team member used for making the decision. Given the circumstance, this might have been the best possible decision. If the rationale was flawed, then coach the team member and show other factors that should have been considered. The decision was made, so focus on improving the process for the next decision.

Project Management Models

A project management model is the framework within which you manage the project. Choosing the right project management model for your project is critical to the success of the project. Think of selecting the project management model as selecting the right tool for the job. Sometimes the selection is challenging because the most obvious choice is not necessarily the most efficient choice.

Let's say that the operations manager of your company needs a new payroll system. The current payroll system runs on a mainframe. The obvious choice is to replace the payroll system with a web-based system using relational database technology and then use the traditional project management model to build the system.

However, the most effective method is to call one of the leading payroll service companies. They already have a robust payroll system. The project is really meant to send data feeds to their payroll system. Traditional project management methodology is probably overkill for this project.

There are many types of project management models. Here are three of the more commonly used models.

Waterfall Project Management

The traditional project management method sometimes referred to as the *waterfall* method has strong central leadership in the form of the project manager.

The project manager negotiates an agreement with the project sponsor that is formalized in a charter.

The project charter is a formal agreement between the project sponsor and the project manager that sets the project's objectives and constraints, within which the project has to be built. Think of a project charter as a contract—signed by both the project sponsor and the project manager—laying out the terms of the project.

The project sponsor comes up with the idea as a whole thing, such as the need for an order entry system. The project manager takes that idea and breaks it into pieces using the technique called the *work breakdown structure*. The project manager takes the whole and divides the whole into pieces and those pieces into further pieces. The final piece is called a *work package*.

The project manager then identifies tasks that are necessary to create the work package. This is like looking at the cover of a jigsaw puzzle box to see what the puzzle looks like when completed. The project manager then identifies pieces before they decide how you are going to assemble the puzzle.

The project manager also determines the length of time to complete a task. This is referred to as the duration of the task. *Duration* is the time spent working on a task plus elapsed time. Elapsed time is an important component when estimating duration.

The project manager also determines resources. A *resource* is a thing or person required to complete a task or a subtask. Identifying resources seems straightforward because we tend to think of a resource as a person. For example, to design a screen for the application, you need a person—a screen designer. However, we tend to overlook resources that the person needs to perform the task, and missing such a resource is a problem. Picture the person sitting at the desk but being unable to work because they are missing tools.

Agile Project Management

Agile project management is a methodology used to manage relatively small, routine projects that don't lend themselves to traditional project management methodology. Agile project management focuses on customer value and delivering quality results fast. The focus is on small batches of work by virtual teams. Virtual teams are self-organizing, self-managed, and are well integrated with disciplines needed to address the issue at hand. There is intense collaboration with face-to-face communication.

The goal is to achieve small, continuous improvements toward the solution while learning and adapting to change. There is light-touch leadership in agile project management. The virtual project team is empowered to learn what must be done, plan to do it, and then execute the plan. Stakeholders define their needs as *stories*. Think of a story as the stakeholder telling you what is needed. There are many stories. Stories are also issues that need to be resolved.

The virtual team creates a focus board that contains a list of user stories. The focus board is left in a common area so team members can frequently review the status of the project. The virtual team works from the list of user stories, resolving one small aspect of the issue at a time and producing a result. The goal is to maintain a sustainable pace.

The makeup of the virtual team changes as new and revised issues are recognized. The virtual team is responsible for resolving the issue, but new team members with expertise missing from the virtual team may join the team to resolve the issue.

There are core roles on an agile project management team.

- The *product owner* is a member of the team that speaks for stakeholders and writes user stories called *churn*. Think of a churn as a stakeholder requirement. The product owner also manages the order in which user stories are addressed.
- The *development team* addresses each user story—that is, they fulfill the stakeholder requirements. For example, the engineering manager needs to fix the leaking valve located three miles below the water surface—this is a user story. The development team must fix the valve and stop the leak.
- The *scrum master* facilitates the *scrum*—the gathering (meeting) of the team following a period of activity. The *scrum master* is not the team leader. Instead, the scrum master makes sure the team is focused and has no impediments to working on the issue. The scrum master also makes sure that the team follows the agile project management methodology.

The Scrum

The daily *scrum* is a daily stand-up meeting lasting no longer than 15 minutes. Each team member must answer:

- What have you done since yesterday?
- What are you planning to do today?
- Are there any impediments preventing you from accomplishing what you plan to do today?

The Sprint

A *sprint* is a basic unit of development that focuses on an item from the product backlog. The product backlog is lower priority user stories. A sprint is performed within a specific duration. The goal is to keep a sustainable pace. The goal of a sprint is to resolve a portion of the issue.

The sprint sequence begins with a sprint planning meeting, during which tasks are identified and commitments are made by the team. Next is the sprint followed by the retrospective, a review identifying lessons learned that can be used for the next sprint.

Extreme Project Management

Extreme project management is used to manage a complex project that needs to be completed rapidly. Variables in the project are constantly changing. There is high uncertainty and high stress because problems associated with the project may have never been solved before. The project team may find itself doing research to solve the problem. The project is highly visible and there is no cookie-cutter approach to the management of the project.

Extreme project management is focused on reality, not theory. Usually there is no precedent for an extreme project—there is no book that is going to show the proven path to managing the project. Therefore, the project team must devise new ideas and test them. The team must also throw those ideas away if they don't work and start over—this is planning, deplanning, and re-planning.

Managing an extreme project requires radical concepts—concepts that are not common to managing other types of projects. Decisions are made at lower levels (not by the project manager) because many decisions must be made rapidly—there may not be time to consult the project manager on every decision. The project manager is the facilitator and integrator. Team members identify and address problems. The project manager makes sure they have everything needed to do the job.

Planning is done in real-time—called *scenario planning*—rather than centralized planning (before a project begins). The team that is charged with addressing a problem develops its own plan—this is referred to as *participative rapid planning*. Plans are made quickly based on the existing circumstances.

Virtual teams come together to address a problem and then move on once the problem is resolved. An extreme project is going to the moon. No one knew if it could be achieved. There was no book that told you how to go to the moon. You might say that they were writing the book during the moon project. There are unknowns in an extreme project—for example, part of science that has yet to be explored—but they must be explored as part of the project.

Rebuilding the World Trade Center is an example of an extreme project. At first glance, the rebuilding effort seems like any massive high-rise construction project in Manhattan—large, complex, but nothing really new. There are plenty of books and courses that describe how to manage such a project. The extreme element is the politics surrounding the project. The New York New Jersey Port Authority—a bi-state agency that reports to the governors of New York and New Jersey—owns the site. The site was leased to a private organization that has the building rights. The site was also hallowed ground. Federal, state, and local officials and the surviving families all wanted a say in the design and rebuilding of the World Trade Center, and they had competing desires.

Imagine managing a project where there were countless influential and powerful stakeholders wanting to tell you how to manage the project. This degree of influence probably hadn't been seen prior to the rebuilding of the World Trade Center.

Enterprise Project Management

Enterprise project management is not really a way to manage a project. Enterprise project management is a branch of project management that focuses on treating all projects as an investment for the organization.

A key element of enterprise project management is to create a portfolio of projects, much like a portfolio of stocks, bonds, and other investments, and manage the project portfolio as one would an investment portfolio. Project sponsors now have to convince a committee of executives who manage the portfolio that the investment in the project is a better investment than other investment opportunities.

Enterprise project management is housed in a project management office called a PMO. The PMO oversees all projects in the enterprise, but not necessarily in the way you may think. They don't manage projects—instead, the PMO develops a process for creating and managing a portfolio of projects. Think of the PMO as a facilitator—key executives (not the PMO) decide which projects are included in the project portfolio and which projects continue to be a good investment.

The PMO also establishes project management standards throughout the organization. For example, they define when to use traditional project management methodology and when to use agile project management methodology. The PMO decides which project management software to use and provides super-user support for project managers. The PMO manages shared resources and some PMOs also manage all project managers. PMOs don't tell project managers how to manage their project. Many times, project managers report to the project sponsor, not the PMO.

Choosing the Project Management Method

There is no definitive rule to deciding which project management methodologies to use. If a project is routine and requires a limited skillset, then consider agile project management. Let's say that the project sponsor wants a relatively straightforward client contact system. You need one person to identify the requirements, one person to design and develop the interface, one person to program the web side of the application, and one person to develop the database. Each member of the team has built similar systems and needs little direction.

Let's say the project sponsor requests an e-commerce system that includes a nationwide distribution system. You need a variety of skillset developers, web programmers, interface designers, and systems analysts. Traditional project management methodology is a good choice. Extreme project management is best if the project is fast-moving, mission critical, and if there are tasks that no one has ever performed. With this method, you're writing the book as you develop the project.

Inspiring the Project Team

Not all projects are exciting to work on and have a dramatic impact on the mission of the organization. Some projects are long, tedious, and receive little or no recognition. Even projects that are exciting to work on, have a material impact on the organization, and are widely recognized can become tedious and never-ending to a point where the project team loses interest in the project. The project becomes simply a job and a paycheck.

One of your jobs as a project manager is to get the project team excited about the project. Motivate them so the project isn't simply another job. You're the coach that gives the pre-game pep talk in the locker room and rekindles the spirit when the team becomes discouraged.

You do this by keeping everyone involved in the project (including stakeholders) and giving them a sense of ownership. If the project fails, then they feel a sense of failure too.

Tap into the fact that people want to make a difference. Make the project a mission, like going to the moon, not a project. The team will see the project as a cause. Show each team member and stakeholder how their job contributes to the bigger picture. For example, everyone in the operating room isn't a surgeon yet they all know how their job will make the surgery a success. People support what they create. Let team members determine how to do their job and influence the outcome of the project.

Don't micromanage. Focus on the strategic plan. Set values for the project. Assemble the best project team and then let the project team handle tactical planning and execution of the tactical plan. Be results-oriented—focus on resolving the issue, not justifying time spent on trying resolving the issue. Trust and confidence in the team is vital. Henry Ford is quoted as saying, "If you think you can, you can. If you think you can't, you can't. In either case you are right." Your job as project manager is to instill the confidence that your team can, and then trust that they can.

There has to be a free-flow of information constantly between stakeholders and the project team. Everyone involved in the project must be forthright with honest communication, regardless of the message. There are no reprisals.

People first. Focus on what the team needs and eliminate barriers so your team can produce quality work and not simply the process of doing something. The process has to help, not hinder, the team. Keep everyone focused on the purpose of the project—use slogans, banners, hats, and other visible means to remind everyone of the goal.

Quality of life is a critical value—make sure each team member balances work and personal life. A project is time-sensitive, but your project team needs time away from the job too. Develop a friendly culture that embraces change. It is important that the project team sees change as a friend. Change represents an opportunity to improve the chances of resolving the issues. Change also brings about fear. Instill courage—everyone involved in the project must face the fear of unknowns in a project and act on what they believe is the right thing to do.

Lead by commitment to the team. Create an environment that motivates the team to succeed. Where possible, keep the structure flexible—use a light control on the team—and allow the team the freedom to innovate and get the work done. Keep communication in real-time—remove all roadblocks that inhibit the free-flow of information.

In long projects, rekindle spirits by having periodic meetings or more of small celebrations with the project team, project sponsor, and stakeholders. Show a timeline of accomplishments and project the future accomplishments.

In the ideal world, a project should be developed as planned—on time and on budget. Resources are ready and capable of performing the assigned tasks and perform them perfectly within the duration set by the project manager.

Risk Management

Unfortunately, your project is being developed in the real world, where the unexpected can occur at any time to disrupt your perfect project plan. Maybe that perfect project plan isn't as perfect as you thought.

There is a saying that projects are rarely on time and on budget—not so. The success of a project is measured by the project plan—you know a task is late because the project plan tells you the duration for the task. The question rarely asked is: Is the project plan wrong?

Let's say there is a room with five light fixtures. The project is to change all the light bulbs. The duration according to the project plan is 10 minutes. An employee takes 20 minutes to replace the light bulb. Is the employee to blame for taking 10 minutes more than was planned to change the light bulb, or could it actually take 20 minutes to change the light bulb and the project manager's estimate was wrong?

The initial step is to assess how much risk the organization can tolerate. Is it worth the effort and money to mitigate the risk, or should the risk be accepted? Each time you drive, you risk the chance of becoming involved in an accident. Most times, you accept that risk and there is no accident. However, would you drive when there are snow flurries, heavy snow, sleet, or a blizzard? At some point you decide that the risk of an accident is too great.

A project is complex and rarely goes according to the original plan—you need to develop a risk management plan to address problems that occur during the execution of the project plan. Problems can occur, such as:

- A lack of support from the project sponsor or senior staff.
- Stakeholders refusing to become involved in the decision-making process.
- The project manager may lack the skills to manage the project.

- No one is clear on the project's scope.
- Communication among the project manager, project sponsor, stakeholders, and the project team may be poor.
- Estimates are unreliable and unrealistic.
- Business needs change.
- The technology is outdated before the project is implemented.
- The project team is incompetent or unmotivated.
- Directions received from the project sponsor or stakeholders are in conflict with the organization's policies.
- Vendors fail to live up to their obligations.

Many of these problems can be addressed by a risk management plan. The project manager must identify potential risk events that can occur during the execution of the project. A risk event is something that changes the course of the project. There are two types of risks events:

- A negative risk event is an event that may impede the project. These include performance failures, delays, underestimating cost, shortages, litigation, and labor action. The event occurs and the project may stop.
- A positive risk event is an event that may enhance the project, such as completing work sooner and reducing cost.

A positive risk event may not be positive for the project manager. The organization tries to coordinate projects so that project teams are always busy. Completing the work sooner may result in the project team idling until the next project begins. Likewise, bringing the project in under-budget should be rewarded, but the project being too under-budget might reflect poorly on the project manager's estimating skills.

Steps should be taken to avoid a risk event. Dependency on one resource is a potential risk event because the resource (a member of the project team or a tool) may not be available, placing the entire project at risk. The project manager can avoid this risk by having two or more of the same resources—two or more team members with the same skillset or duplicate tools. The project manager can also cross-train the project team so team members can back each other up.

Not all risk events can be avoided. You may experience a risk event during the course of the project. You need a risk management plan that tells everyone what to do should a specific risk event occur. Think of a risk management plan as Plan B, enacted when your original plan stops working. Risk management plans include:

- Contingency plans
- Fallback plans
- Contingency reserves

A *contingency plan* consists of predefined actions that will be taken if an anticipated risk occurs. Let's say that a key member of your project team gives you two weeks' notice and is moving out of state. Your initial reaction determines that they are working on a series of tasks that are on the critical path. Their leaving will affect the duration of the project. Replacing them will take 90 days. However, your contingency plan calls for outsourcing those tasks to a firm who has frequently worked with your company. Prior to the project, you made contingency arrangements with the firm—the firm can begin work within two weeks.

The *fallback plan* is the contingency plan of last resort and is put into effect if contingency plans are not available or don't mitigate the risk. For example, the vendor may not be able to accept the outsource assignment, leaving your contingency plan unworkable for the loss of the resource. The fallback plan is to reorder tasks to free up staff to work on tasks that are on the critical path while beginning the recruitment process. If the project is critical to the organization, staff might be reassigned from other projects to work on your project.

Contingency reserves are funds used to mitigate unanticipated risks. These are budgeted amounts that can be used to keep the project on track. For example, contingency reserves will be used to pay for outsource services.

Vendor Management

As a project manager, you manage stakeholders, the project team, and vendors who supplement your project team. A vendor is a person or company that offers sales or services to your organization. Think of a vendor as someone who provides something that is not provided by your project team but is needed for the project. Let's say that you need a database designer. You have one database to design. Your project team can implement the design. It doesn't make sense to hire a database designer because you have nothing for them to do once the design is completed. The best alternative is to hire a vendor to design the database.

What the vendor will do and how the vendor will do it is contained in a written agreement called the contract, which specifies the services that will be provided and the compensation (usually money) that you'll provide for the services. Always refer to terms of the contract when managing the vendor. The terms of the contract define the binding promises of the vendor and your organization. Any activities not listed in the contract are not performed unless added to the contract. You can't expect the database designer to build the database if the contract only calls for them to design the database. They may be willing to build the database but the terms must be negotiated and added to the contract.

Vendors are an option for a number of reasons:
- Risk associated with a task is shifted from your organization to the vendor. The vendor is liable for damages if the task is improperly performed. Say that you outsource website hosting to a vendor and the vendor's servers crash, causing

you to lose orders. The vendor is liable for the missed orders and any impact it has on your customers, depending on the terms of the contract.

- Vendors are also used because the vendor has competencies (such as designing a database) that you lack within your organization.

Your organization has a procurement process used to acquire the services of vendors. Initially, the organization pre-qualifies vendors to assure that the vendor is financially sound and has the capability to deliver quality services.

Pre-qualified vendors are placed on a master vendor list. Project managers can select vendors who appear on the list. Project managers can also propose vendors who will then be pre-qualified.

A procurement process is designed to receive the best possible service for a reasonable price. Some procurement processes require competitive bids from at least three pre-qualified vendors. A procurement process also ensures there is no conflict of interest between vendors and anyone in the organization.

You begin the procurement process by writing a request for information, commonly referred to as RFI. The RFI is sent to prospective vendors from the vendor master list, describing the services you seek and asking if they are capable of providing the services. The result is a list of possible vendors for your project. Next, you write and send either a request for quotation, called RFQ, or a request for proposal, referred to as RFP.

A request for quotation is used for standard services. Each vendor then submits a quotation that contains the price per item, terms of payment, quality level per item, and other information that helps you select the vendor.

A request for proposal is used to request a vendor to provide a service, such as designing a database. The request for proposal contains a problem statement, expectations, constraints, and timeline. There will likely be meetings with vendors to further discuss the problem. The vendor is expected to send a proposal that restates requirements and how the vendor will solve the problem. The proposal will also provide a price for the service.

There are pitfalls when selecting and managing vendors.

- The organization may be using a vendor too frequently. If the vendor fails, many projects within the organization will also fail.
- The organization may become too dependent on the vendor. The vendor may say, "Do it my way or I won't do the job." This may even happen in the middle of the job.
- An unclear statement of work is a common pitfall of working with a vendor. Maybe your original specifications are incomplete and you don't realize it until the job is underway. You have no alternative but to negotiate with the vendor to provide the missing elements. You might pay a premium for this work since you are at a disadvantage.

– Objective measurement of work (or lack thereof) is another contention in vendor relations. How do you and the vendor know that the vendor fulfilled terms of the contract? Let's say that you want a 2x4 board. This is 2 inches by 4 inches. The vendor delivers a board that is 1.25 inches by 3.5 inches. You might say that the vendor did not live up to the terms of the contract, but that's not true. It meets industry standards.

It is critical that at the beginning of the contract, you and the vendor come to terms on how to objectively measure the work. This avoids many conflicts.

You will likely have to negotiate either at the beginning of the relationship or during the relationship with the vendor. Before negotiating, decide on your breakpoint, or the least terms you will accept. Be ready to walk away if negotiations go beyond the breakpoint.

Know what you're worth to the vendor. The vendor may use your job as a selling point to potential customers. This gives you leverage because the vendor benefits by delivering a high-quality job to you.

Never negotiate until you are ready to negotiate. Don't negotiate if the vendor is totally unreasonable. Open negotiations with your maximum sustainable position—ask for what you want and then some. If your opening offer is too close to your breakpoint, then you will not have enough bargaining range. The vendor can always counteroffer. *Bargaining range* is the negotiable area between your opening position and your breakpoint.

Think along the lines of bartering when negotiating. There are things that are low-value to you and high-value to the vendor, and things that are high-value to you and low-value to the vendor. Sometimes these are referred to as sweeteners. The vendor is paying the laborer for a day's pay. The extra work won't cost the vendor any additional money, since there is probably time in which the employees don't have tasks to perform.

Another sweetener is when the vendor is paid. Vendors are usually paid at the end of the job. The vendor must send an invoice, which is usually aged by the organization. Aging is an accounts payable method in which invoices are paid when they are due and not when they are received. Typically, an invoice may not be paid for up to 90 days. A sweetener by the project manager is to have the vendor paid within five days. A sweetener by the vendor is to reduce the invoice amount by 1 percent if the invoice is paid within ten days.

Depending on the nature of the project, the project manager may authorize progressive payments. A *progressive payment* is made after each fully functional deliverable is made by the vendor. In this way, the project manager is ensuring that the vendor can pay its bills on time.

When managing a vendor, remember:

– Read the terms of the contract. The vendor is only obligated to adhere to those terms.
– Don't ask the vendor to do something outside the terms of the contract. The vendor will expect to be paid beyond what is stated in the contract.
– Be prepared to renegotiate with the vendor if specifications were missing from the contract.
– Look for signs that the vendor is unable to complete the job. Missed deadlines, avoiding contact, partial deliverables, poor-quality work, and changes in employees are all clear signs.
– Know the industry standards for your job. Vendors need to meet industry standards unless otherwise specified in the contract.

Chapter 9
Prepping for Test Questions

A Test?! You Gotta Be Kidding

You won't know if a firm will ask you to take a pre-employment test on your project management knowledge until you're a promising candidate for the recruiter. Don't panic if you hear the surprising words, "Do you mind taking our project management test?" The recruiter and the hiring manager may be in a position to waive the test if your years of similar project management experience clearly demonstrate your in-depth understanding on how to effectively manage a project. Having a PMP certification usually trumps the need to take a test. However, taking the test may be a requirement for the position. Answer no and you'll probably kiss that project management opportunity goodbye.

You probably won't, but if asked, respond by inquiring more about the test. Be upfront and ask if all candidates are required to take the test or whether there is something in your background that raises doubt about your project management ability. The answer implies whether the test is required or not. If your background is an issue, you'll have an opportunity to verbally bolster your resume. If everyone takes the test, be positive and agree.

Follow up by gathering as much information as possible about the test. You'll probably learn that the test focuses on topics from the PMP exam and that questions resemble the PMP exam format, in which you are expected to use critical thinking skills and apply the Project Management Book of Knowledge (PMBOK) to respond to a test scenario. Expect to have multiple choice answers where at least two are correct. Your job is to select the one that is more correct than the other.

You might get lucky and the recruiter may provide you with a study guide, but don't count on it. If not, don't worry—this chapter reviews PMBOK concepts to give you a leg-up on any pre-employment project management test. No one knows what will be asked on a test if there is a test. However, focusing on terms and concepts will provide the foundation for responding to questions.

Domains, Process Groups, and Knowledge Areas of PMP

The PMBOK organizes projects into five basic domains, also referred to as process groups. A *process group* consists of project management processes used to reach a specific project objective. It is important to understand that a process group is not a project phase and is not linear but is iterative, repeating throughout phases of the project. Each process group has one or more of the 47 processes used to manage a project. Here are the process groups:

https://doi.org/10.1515/9781501506222-010

- Initiating
- Planning
- Executing
- Monitoring
- Closing

The PMBOK breaks down the project manager skills into ten *knowledge areas*, each of which is necessary to master in order to professionally manage a project. Each knowledge area describes processes, inputs, tools and techniques, and outputs for processes used to manage a project. Simply, the project manager applies tools and techniques to input (i.e., information and results of other processes) and produce a specific output to achieve a project goal.

Knowledge areas are:
- Integration management
- Scope management
- Time management
- Cost management
- Quality management
- Human resource management
- Communications management
- Risk management
- Procurement management
- Stakeholder management

Down to Basics

Now that you have the PMBOK framework, let's focus on terms and concepts that are fundamental to PMP knowledge. It would be surprising if the test questions directly test your knowledge of project management terms and concepts, because this doesn't test your critical thinking skills. It is more likely that you'll be presented with scenarios containing information you need to know (and misleading information called a *distractor*) so you can apply project management terms and concepts to respond to the scenario. You need to know how to apply terms and concepts.

Here are terms and concepts that you'll need to know that are part of the framework and will be used later in the chapter.

Term	Definition
	Project
Project	A temporary set of activities that has a beginning, and ends when a unique objective is met.
Operation	An ongoing set of activities that repeats when a non-unique objective is met.
Why are projects undertaken?	To achieve a goal that meets market demand, customer requests, organization needs, and/or legal requirements.
	Project Management
Project management	Applying processes, knowledge, and experience to reach the project objective.
Project manager	A person who has the knowledge and experience to lead a project team to achieve the project's objectives.
Project manager competencies	Leadership, technical project management, strategic planning, and business management.
Project deliverable	A measurable, verifiable work product.
Project phase	A group of related activities that result in one or more deliverables.
Project constraints	Limitations within which the project is managed that include scope, risk, quality, and/or resources.
Corrective action	An action that realigns work with the project plan.
Preventive action	An action that ensures that the future work aligns with the project plan.
Defect repair	An action that modifies a non-conforming activity to conform with the project plan.
Updates	An action that modifies or adds ideas to the content of a project plan.
Tailoring	Modifying project management processes to the project needs.
Integration	Merging the knowledge areas into a strategy for managing a project.
Integrator	The person, usually the project manager, who is responsible for integration.
Enterprise environmental factors (EEF)	Factors not in control of the project team that influence the project. These include: infrastructure, organizational culture and structure, risk tolerance, and market conditions.
Organizational process assets (OPA)	Processes, standards and procedures used by the organization. These include processes to escalate decisions, define span of control, accountability, responsibility assignments, delegations, lessons learned, and alignment of the project with organizational objectives.

(continued)

Term	Definition
	Project Management
The PMI Talent Triangle	Technical PM, strategic and business management, leadership.
Assumption log	A list of agreed-upon assumptions with the project sponsor about the execution of the project.
	Program and Portfolio
Program	A group of related projects or subsidiary programs that are coordinated to achieve a common object and could not be achieved by managing each project individually.
Focus of program management	Maintain the interdependencies of projects while using the best approach to achieve program objectives.
Portfolio	A collection of projects, programs, and subsidiary portfolios managed collectively to reach strategic objectives.
	Project Management Office (PMO)
Project Management Office	A centralized activity that facilitates the selection and management of projects within an area of a firm or across the entire firm.
PMO Supportive Type	Acts in a consultative role identifying and developing project management methodology, best practices and standards. Supplies templates, best practices, training, access to information and lessons learned from other projects. No direct project management responsibilities.
PMO Controlling Type	Ensuring projects are compliant with the firm's policies and procedures. Monitoring compliance through audits, and comparing practices to standards, policies, and procedures. Moderate direct project management responsibilities overseeing compliance.
PMO Directive Type	Acts in a direct role managing all projects by supervising project managers.
	Work Performance
Work Performance Data	Raw observations and measurements taken during activities of the project.
Work Performance Information	Work performance data that is analyzed in context (such as duration of tasks) that is used to determine when the project will be completed.
Work Performance Reports	Work performance information compiled in project documents used for status monitoring and decision making on staffing, resources, and activities associated with the project.

Affinity diagrams	A diagram that groups related ideas together into logical groups.
Context diagram	A diagram that identifies flows of information between processes.
Requirement traceability matrix (RTM)	A document that traces user requirements with test cases and statuses.
Mind mapping	A graphical method to represent and analyze ideas.
Enterprise environmental factors	Any internal or external factors that influence the success of the project including regulations, market conditions, and any other factors that are out of the project manager's control.
Level of accuracy	The precision required by a stakeholder in a project deliverable.
Control thresholds	The metric used to maintain acceptable control of the project.
Defined activities	An activity has a start, end, and deliverable.
Project schedule network diagrams	A diagram that displays activities and logical dependencies in chronological order.
Precedence diagramming method (PDM)	A diagram that illustrates the precedence of project activities.
Critical path method	The sequence of tasks that form the longest duration that determine the duration of the project.
Schedule compression	A technique used to shorten an existing project schedule.
Inspection planning	A method used to determine the inspection operations used in a project to ensure that activities are performed correctly.
Matrix diagrams	A diagram that shows relationships between or among items related to the project.
Team charter	A document that explains the team's objectives and boundaries that guide the team through the development of the project.
Responsibility assignment matrix (RAM, RACI)	Defines roles and participation expectations for the activities of a project.
Analogous estimating	The method of estimating activities based on similar projects.
Communication models	A structure within which the project manager, project sponsor, project team, and stakeholders communicate within each other during a project.
Communication requirement analysis	A tool that determines the need of each stakeholder for project information.
Organizational process assets (OPA)	Anything that is acquired that can be used to manage the project.
Claims administration	A process of contract procurement and administration that handles claims, disputes, and appeals related to conflicts of a contract.

(continued)

Closed procurements	A process that occurs when a contract is terminated either before or after the contract is completed.
Change control tools	A process that ensures any proposed change to the project specification is evaluated and approved by the project sponsor and the project plan is revised to reflect the approved changes.
Variance analysis	A quantitative assessment of differences between an actual activity and a planned activity to understand why the plan was inaccurate.
Agile release planning	A method of summarizing a high-level timeline of the release schedule. This is also used to determine the number of iterations (sprints) in a release.

In the remainder of this chapter, we will review the project process in detail. You will see that there are numerous tables that offer the specifics of each step in the process. You may wish to read through the chapter first to review the entire process and then go through the chapter again, reviewing the detail in the tables in a second pass. This chapter walks through the process in order. We will begin with initiating the project.

We list groups—these are groups of activities required to complete the project. Each group has activities or general tasks that need to be performed. Each activity requires input and tools and techniques required by resources to perform the activity. Each activity has a defined output—the results of the activity. You'll find these represented in tables within this chapter.

Initiating the Project

The Project Charter Process

The project begins with an idea of how to meet a need. The need is part of a strategy to achieve a goal, such as returning profit to shareholders by meeting the needs of the marketplace, fulfilling customer requests, and adhering to legal and regulatory requirements. The *project sponsor* is the person who identifies the need, sets the goal, and builds the business case to gain support of stakeholders to finance and launch the project.

Once approved, the project sponsor selects a *project manager* who, along with stakeholders, establishes the project charter. The *project charter* is a formal document authorizing the existence of the project and establishes the framework within which the project manager will produce the deliverable, fulfilling the need. The project charter gives the project manager the authority to acquire and manage resources to deliver expected results and specifies the scope of the project.

Consider the project charter (Figure 9.1) an internal contract between the project manager and the project sponsor in that the project charter specifies details of the agreement, including the amount the project sponsor expects to pay for the deliverable. The project charter is a formal contract if the project is undertaken by a vendor. Attorneys will be involved in drawing up the contract.

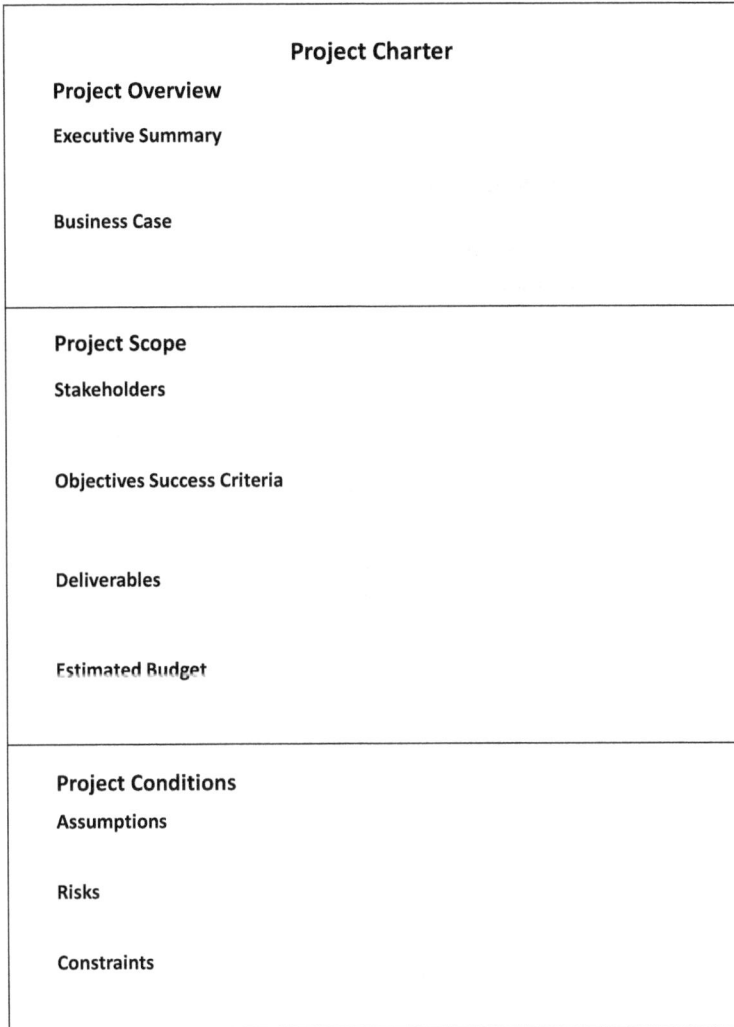

Project Charter

Project Overview

Executive Summary

Business Case

Project Scope

Stakeholders

Objectives Success Criteria

Deliverables

Estimated Budget

Project Conditions

Assumptions

Risks

Constraints

Figure 9.1: The *project charter* is an internal contract between the project manager and the project sponsor that specifies the terms of the project.

The project charter provides the:
- Authority given to a specified project manager to undertake the project

- Selection of the project sponsor
- Purpose of the project
- Business justification
- Project description
- Project requirements
- Legal and regulatory requirements
- Acceptance criteria
- Expected milestones
- Deliverable date
- Funding source
- High-level budget
- Constraints within which the project is conducted
- Agreement on possible risks
- Assumptions within which the project is managed
- Enterprise environmental factors

Initiating Process Group	Develop Project Charter	
Inputs	Tools and Techniques	Outputs
- Agreements - Benefits management plan - Business case - Business documents - Enterprise environmental factors - Organizational process assets	- Brainstorming - Conflict management - Data gathering - Expert judgment - Facilitation - Focus groups - Interpersonal and team skills - Interview - Meetings	- Assumption log - Project charter

Collecting Requirements Process

Collecting requirements is the process of identifying and documenting requirements to meet the objectives of the project. A context diagram (Figure 9.3) is used by a systems analyst to identify the business flow requirements. The project manager engages all stakeholders with the goal of identifying both their needs and wants from the project. A *need* is an element that is necessary to meet requirements of the marketplace, customers, and legal and regulatory authorities. A *want* is an element that improves an operation without necessarily being required. Think of a need as a must-have and a want as a nice-to-have.

All requirements gathered are documents and reviewed with the project sponsor and stakeholders, who collectively decide if each requirement becomes a requirement of the project. Requirements are entered into the Requirements Traceability Matrix

(Figure 9.2). Some will be outside the scope and be rejected or placed on a waitlist to be reconsidered in a later phase of the project. Once requirements are identified, the project manager can begin to develop the project plan.

Requirements Traceability Matrix			
Business Requirement	Process	Stakeholder	Description

Figure 9.2: The *requirement traceability matrix* is a diagram that illustrates project requirements and the stakeholder who is responsible for the requirement.

Context Diagram

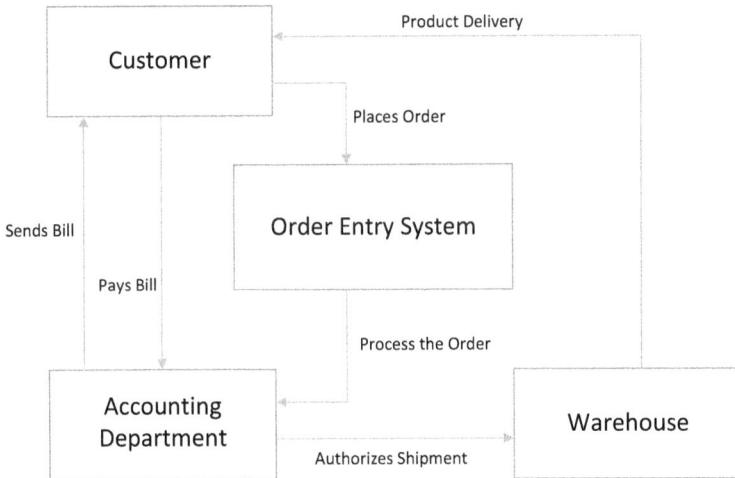

Figure 9.3: The *context diagram* illustrates relationships among processes within a project.

Initiating Process Group		Collection Requirements	
Inputs	Tools and Techniques	Outputs	
− Agreements	− Affinity diagrams	− Acceptance	
− Business documents that contain the business case that describes the business needs	− Agreements	criteria	
− Enterprise environmental factors	− Brainstorming	− Functional	
− Lessons learned register that provides information on effective requirements collection techniques	− Business plans	requirements	
− Organizational process assets	− Business processes	− Nonfunctional	
− Project charter	− Context diagram that show the boundaries of the project scope	requirements	
− Project documents	− Data analysis	− Quality	
− Project management plan	− Data gathering	requirements	
− Requirements management plan, which dictates how requirements will be collected and analyzed	− Data representation	− Requirement	
− Scope management plan	− Decision making	traceability matrix	
− Stakeholder plan, explaining how to work with stakeholders	− Expert judgment in how to collect requirements	used to trace the	
− Stakeholder register, used to identify stakeholders who can provide information on the requirements	− Focus groups	source of col-	
	− Interpersonal and team skills	lected	
	− Interviews	requirements	
	− Mind mapping	− Requirements	
	− Prototypes used to obtain early feedback before actually building it	documentation	
	− Questionnaires	− Business needs	

Scope Definition Process

The *scope definition* is a detailed description of the project (and the deliverable) that contains elements to be included and excluded from the project. In essence, the scope definition sets the boundaries within which the project manager and the project sponsor operate during the development of the project. The project scope becomes the foundation used to create the project plan and manage the project.

The project manager continually refers to the project scope whenever a stakeholder asks for elements that are not included in the project plan and are outside the scope of the project. The stakeholder must work through the change management process to have a new element incorporated into the project, resulting in a revision to the project scope. The project scope sets expectations for stakeholders, the project sponsor, and the project team.

Initiating Process Group	Develop Scope	
Inputs	**Tools and Techniques**	**Outputs**
– Enterprise environmental factors – Organizational process assets – Project charter – Project documents – Project management plan – Requirements documentation – Scope management plan	– Data analysis alternatives analysis used to evaluate ways to meet the requirements – Decision making – Expert advice – Interpersonal and team skills to form a common understanding of the project deliverables and project boundaries – Product analysis describing characteristics of elements of the project	– Product acceptance criteria – Project constraints and assumptions – Project deliverables – Project document updates – Project exclusions – Project scope description – Project scope statement defining work included and excluded in the project

Project Management Plan Process

Developing the *project management plan* is unique to each project, but typically explains how the project will be managed. Included are ways that the project will be executed and monitored throughout the process and how risk and quality will be managed by the project team. The project management plan also identifies performance measurements and how the project manager and stakeholders will communicate with the project manager and the project team.

Think of the project management plan as setting the ground rules for how the project is managed and setting expectations for everyone involved in the project. Throughout the project, the project management plan is referenced at the first instance of a conflict so that everyone can review the process agreed upon when the project was initiated. The project management plan—along with other early documents used in the initiation of the project—help to refocus on guidelines for meeting the project goals.

Initiating Process Group	Develop Project Management Plan	
Inputs	**Tools and Techniques**	**Outputs**
– Enterprise environmental factors – Organizational process assets – Project charter	– Data gathering – Expert judgment – Interpersonal and team skills – Meetings	– Basic plans – Cost baselines – Project management plan – Scope baselines – Scope management plan – Stakeholder management plan – Time baselines

Plan Schedule Management Process

Plan schedule management is the process that creates policies and procedures along with elements of how the project will be planned, developed, managed, and controlled. This process gives the project sponsor and stakeholders clear directions on how the project manager will go about planning the project. It is also used to help the project manager flesh out the details of the planning process.

The plan schedule management process contains:
- Control thresholds
- Level of accuracy required
- Performance measurements
- Project schedule model development software
- Project schedule model maintenance
- Units of measurement

Initiating Process Group	Plan Schedule Management	
Inputs	Tools and Techniques	Outputs
– Enterprise environmental factors – Organizational process assets – Project charter – Project management plan	– Data alternatives analysis – Expert judgment – Meetings	– Schedule management plan

Identify Stakeholder Process

A *stakeholder* is anyone who is directly involved in a project or who can be directly or indirectly impacted by the project. The project sponsor, project manager, and the project team are stakeholders. Workers in a department who supply information to the project or use the deliverable are also stakeholders. So are customers and vendors who might be indirectly influenced by the deliverable. All are considered stakeholders and need to be identified during the *identify stakeholder process*. The outcome of this process is a *stakeholder register* that lists and describes all stakeholders and a *stakeholder engagement plan* that states how the project manager and project team interact with each stakeholder.

The process creates a power and interest grid to map stakeholders by level of authority and interest in the project outcome. This helps the project manager define the stakeholder's expectations and roles in the project. The project manager also classifies each stakeholder based on direction of influence. Classifications are:

- Upward (senior management)
- Downward (the project team)
- Outward (stakeholder outside the project)
- Sideward (the peers of the project manager)

Stakeholders are also classified using the *salience model*, which groups stakeholders by:

- Power (ability to impose their will on the project)
- Urgency (need for immediate attention)
- Legitimacy (their purpose for involvement in the project)

Initiating Process Group	Identify Stakeholders	
Inputs	Tools and Techniques	Outputs

– Agreements
– Business documents
– Communications and
  stakeholder engagement
  plan
– Enterprise environmental
  factors
– Organizational process
  assets
– Project charter
– Project documents
– Project management plan
	– Data analysis
	– Data gathering
	– Data representation
	– Document analysis
	– Expert judgment
	– Meetings
	– Stakeholder analysis
		– Change requests
		– Project documents updates
		– Project management plan
		  updates
		– Stakeholder engagement
		  plan
		– Stakeholder register

Validate Scope Process

The validate scope process is used by the project manager to ensure that the project sponsor and stakeholders agree to the project scope. The validated scope process is also used by the project manager, the project sponsor, and stakeholders during the acceptance process, in which the project sponsor and stakeholders accepts the project deliverable. The validated scope is also used by the project manager, the project sponsor, and stakeholders at the end of each phase of the project when a major portion of the project deliverable is completed. This ensures that the project deliverable aligns with the project sponsor's and stakeholders' expectations.

Initiating Process Group	Validate Scope	
Inputs	Tools and Techniques	Outputs
– Project document – Project management plan – Verified deliverables – Work performance data	– Decision making – Inspection	– Accepted deliverables – Change requests – Project document updates – Work performance information

Planning the Project

Work Breakdown Structure Process

The project sponsor has an idea that is sketched during the initiating process. The project manager then uses the *work breakdown structure* to plan how make the idea a reality. The work breakdown structure segments the work into small, manageable work packages, each becoming the focus of the project team. Work packages are assembled to create the deliverable once each work package is completed by the project team.

The project manager uses five core processes in the work breakdown structure:
– Cost estimating
– Cost budgeting
– Resource planning
– Activity definition
– Risk planning

Planning Process Group	Create Work Breakdown Structure (WBS)	
Inputs	Tools and Techniques	Outputs
– Enterprise environmental factors – Organizational process assets – Project documents – Project management plan – Project scope statement – Requirements documentation – Scope management plan	– Decomposition – Expert judgment	– Assumption log – Project documents updates – Requirements documents – Scope baseline, which is the approved version of a scope statement – Scope statement: outlines deliverables, constraints, assumptions, and key success metrics – Work breakdown structure dictionary contains definitions of terms used in the work breakdown structure – Work breakdown structure shows the work packages for the project

Define Activities Process

The work breakdown structure identifies work packages each necessary to be completed in order to produce the project deliverable. The *define activities* decompose each work package into activities that must be performed to create the work package deliverable. These activities are called *scheduled activities*. Scheduled activities are then used by the project manager as the basis for estimating the duration and cost of the project, identifying resources needed to perform each activity, and scheduling work.

The project manager uses *rolling-wave planning* to define activities. Rolling-wave planning is an ongoing process of planning. The initial plan called the *baseline plan* is created based on activities that are known at the beginning of the project. Additional activities become apparent as the project is underway and need to be incorporated into the project plan for appropriate work packages.

Planning Process Group		Define Activities	
Inputs	Tools and Techniques	Outputs	
– Project management plan – Schedule management plan – Scope baseline	– Decomposition – Expert judgment – Meetings – Rolling-wave planning	– Activity attributes describe characteristics of each activity – Activity list contains the name and description of activities – Change requests – The milestone shows when important achievements in a project are expected to occur – Project management plan updates	

Sequence Activities Process

Activities are listed on the activity list and need to be organized in a sequence of when the project team needs to perform each activity. The project manager identifies the sequence of activities by using a *precedence diagram* (Figure 9.4). Each activity is represented by a node on the precedence diagram. Nodes are connected with arrows that picture dependencies among activities, referred to as *activity on node* (AON).

A dependency determines when an activity can be performed. Some activities must wait until a previous activity is completed, while others can be performed simultaneously with other activities. Dependencies are identified as follows.

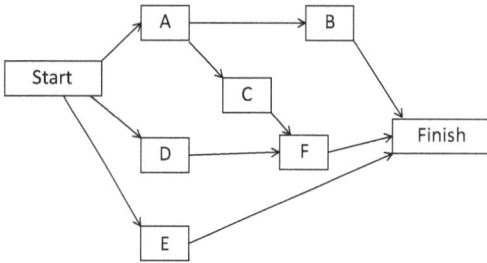

Figure 9.4: The *precedence diagramming method* is used to identify dependencies of project activities. Each activity is shown in relation to other activities of the project.

- *Discretionary dependency* is based on the preferences of the project manager based on best practices and experience. This is also sometimes referred to as a *soft-logic dependency*.
- *External dependency* is where a non-project activity determines when a project activity is scheduled.
- *Internal dependency* is where the project team controls the dependency.
- *Mandatory dependency* is where the nature of the work determines the order in which the activity is performed. This is based on physical limitations and contractual and legal limitations. Sometimes this is referred to as a *hard dependency* or *hard-logic dependency*.

Dependencies are also identified by when the activity can start related to another activity.
- *Finish-to-finish* is where two activities must finish at the same time.
- *Finish-to-start* is where an activity must finish before the next activity can start.
- *Start-to-finish* is where one activity must start before the dependent activity can finish.
- *Start-to-start* is where two activities must start at the same time.

Planning Process Group	Sequence Activities	
Inputs	**Tools and Techniques**	**Outputs**
– Activity list, activity attributes, milestone list	– Dependency determination and integration	– Project documents update
– Enterprise environmental factors	– Precedence diagramming method (PDM)	– Project schedule network diagrams
– Organizational process assets		
– Project documents	– Project management information system	
– Project management plan		

Estimate Activity Durations Process

The time necessary to perform an activity is called its *duration* and is measured in work periods defined by the project manager (for example, an hour, half a day, or a whole day). The *estimate activity duration process* is used by the project manager to estimate the duration for each activity using a specific number of resources, which can be challenging since the project manager may have never performed the activity. The project schedule network diagram in Figure 9.5 is used to estimate duration. However, the estimate is critical to delivering the project. An estimate way off its mark can materially delay the project.

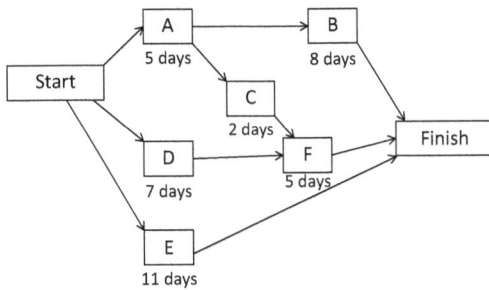

Figure 9.5: The *project schedule network diagram* is similar to the precedence diagramming method, except the duration of each activity is displayed on the network diagram.

Five common methods are used to estimate duration, using top-down estimating and bottom-up estimating.

- *Top-down estimating* assumes that the activity is similar to other activities that were performed during other projects; therefore, the project manager uses the duration from other projects as the duration estimate for the current project. Top-down estimating is sometimes referred to as *analogous estimating*. Top-down estimating is positive only if the same variables (i.e., staff, tools, and environment) exist in both activities — otherwise, the activities are not analogous, resulting in a poor duration estimate.
- *Bottom-up estimating* determines the duration for completing each element of an activity, sometimes by measuring duration during a run-through commonly referred to as a *time-study*. Bottom-up estimating provides a better estimate of duration than other estimating methods, but it is time-consuming and may unnecessarily delay project planning.
- *Expert judgment* is an estimating method that asks an expert to estimate the duration of a particular activity. If the person is truly an expert and the activity is within the expert's expertise, then estimate of duration is acceptable. The challenge is how the project manager knows whether the person is an expert.

- *Parametric estimating* is an estimating method that uses ratio analysis to derive the estimate duration. This is similar to bottom-up estimating in that the project manager measures details of elements that comprise the activity. This is used when there are many of the same element used in the project and the duration of each must be estimated. Instead of estimating the duration of each element, only the duration of one element is measured, and the results are then extrapolated to estimate the duration of the other elements. Let's say the activity is to install a widget. Twenty bolts need to be tightened in each element of the activity. The project manager measures the time necessary to install and tighten one bolt, then multiplies the time by twenty to arrive at the duration. Parametric estimating is good only if the elements are identical.
- *Three-point estimating* is an estimating method that arrives at three estimates for the same activity. These are optimistic, most likely, and pessimistic. The project manager averages these to set the duration for the activity.

Planning Process Group	Estimate Activity Durations	
Inputs	Tools and Techniques	Outputs
– Activity attributes – Activity list – Enterprise environmental factors – Milestone list – Organizational process assets – Project documents – Project management plan – Project team assignments – Resource breakdown structure – Resource calendars – Resource requirements – Risk register	– Alternatives analysis looks at different ways work can be performed – Bottom up estimating – Data analysis – Decision-making is documenting how the project manager decided on duration – Expert judgment – Parametric estimating – Reserve analysis is setting money aside in the budget to be used if estimates are inaccurate – Three-point estimating – Top-down estimating (Analogous estimating)	– Basis of estimates is justification for how duration was estimated – Duration estimates for each activity – Project documents updates

Develop Schedule Process

Once activities are identified, the precedence determined, and the estimated duration calculated, the focus is on developing the project plan. The process of developing the project plan requires the project manager to analyze each activity—reviewing sequencing, duration, and resources to assemble a plan that clearly defines the order that each activity must be performed to produce the project's deliverable. The project manager must consider constraints, which include events that might occur externally to the project.

The result is a baseline schedule that is used by the project sponsor, project manager, and the project team to schedule their activities. A baseline schedule is the project manager's best estimate as to how the project should flow. The baseline schedule is expected to change during the course of the project as the project team deals with the reality of developing the deliverable. New information comes to light, causing stakeholders and the project sponsor to change the expected outcomes of the project and resulting in changes to the project schedule. Changes are approved through a change management process before the change is incorporated into the project plan.

Planning Process Group	Develop Schedule	
Inputs	**Tools and Techniques**	**Outputs**
– Activity attributes	– Agile release planning	– Change
– Activity list	– Critical path method	request
– Agreements	– Data analysis	– Project
– Basis of estimates	– Project management information	calendars
– Duration of estimates	system	– Project docu-
– Enterprise environmental factors	– Resource optimization	ments update
– Milestone list	– Schedule compression is a	– Project man-
– Organizational process assets	technique for reducing the	agement plan
– Project documents	duration of a project	updates
– Project management plan	– Schedule network analysis	– Project
– Project schedule network	– Simulation enables experimenta-	schedule
diagram	tion with how the project sched-	– Schedule
– Project team assignments	ule will function under different	baseline
– Resource calendars	events that could occur during	– Schedule
– Resource requirements	the project	data
– Risk register	– "What-if" scenario analysis de-	
– Schedule management plan	velops a strategy for dealing with	
– Scope baseline	scenarios that could throw the	
	project off course	

Plan Quality Management

The *plan quality management process* identifies how the project manager will conform to quality requirements set forth by the project sponsor. The process begins with a review of the standards required in the project deliverable. Standards and quality requirements are based on market demands, customer requirements, industry standards, regulatory mandates, and stakeholder expectations.

Throughout the project, the project manager plans to benchmark quality comparing elements of the deliverable with requirements as elements are assembled into the deliverable. The goal is to ensure that the deliverable is within tolerance of expectations. The deliverable may not be perfect, but is acceptable to the project sponsor and stakeholders. The plan also specifies roles and responsibilities necessary to maintain quality, metrics that will be used to measure quality, and tests that will be used to determine if the deliverable meets quality requirements.

The project manager also calculates the cost of quality. The total cost of quality is the sum of four cost factors:

- Appraisal costs, which are the costs of inspecting and testing during the project
- External failure cost, which is the financial impact to operations caused by the failure of the deliverable
- Internal failure cost, which is the cost if the deliverable fails, such as repair and replacement costs
- Prevention costs, which is the cost of quality planning and training of staff

Planning Process Group	Plan Quality Management	
Inputs	Tools and Techniques	Outputs
– Assumption log – Enterprise environmental factors – Organizational process assets – Project charter – Project documents – Project management plan – Requirements documentation – Risk register – Stakeholder register	– Benchmarking – Brainstorming – Cost benefit analysis – Cost of quality – Data analysis – Data gathering – Data representation – Decision making – Inspection planning – Interviews – Logical data model is used to identify where data integrity issues can arise – Matrix diagrams identify the strength of relationships among different factors – Meeting and expert judgment – Mind mapping creates visually organized information that helps the rapid gathering of project requirements	– Project documents updates – Quality management plan – Quality metrics

Plan Resource Management Process

The *plan resource management process* specifies how the project manager plans to manage project resources. The plan estimates the type and number of resources required for the project and when each resource needs to be onboard and ready to work. The plan also describes how resources are acquired. Some are existing employees, others are new employees, and others are supplied by vendors. The plan outlines how the project team is organized and managed. At the end of the plan resource management process, there will be a resource management plan and a team charter that establishes values and operating guidelines that direct the project team to develop the deliverable.

A hierarchical organization chart is used to identify human resources for the project and illustrates the lines of authority on the project team. A responsibility assignment matrix shows specific responsibility for each project team member. Basically, which team member will do each activity. Roles and responsibilities are also described in text-based documents as part of the plan resource management process.

The *RACI matrix* (Figure 9.6) is another important tool that is used to plan resources. RACI stands for responsible, accountable, consult, and inform. Each describes the involvement of stakeholders. For example, the project sponsor has overall responsibility for the project; the project manager is accountable for planning, managing and delivering the project. Key stakeholders need to be consulted on major changes in the project, and all stakeholders need to be kept informed on the project status. This is all clearly defined in the RACI matrix.

RACI Matrix

Person

Task	Roberts	Jones	Taylor	Ryan
Acquire Specifications	A	R	C	I
Design Workflow	R	A	I	C
Design Screens	A	C	R	I
Build Screens	R	A	C	I

R = Responsible   A = Accountable   C = Consult   I = Inform

Figure 9.6: The RACI matrix shows stakeholders who are responsible and accountable for project activities and who should be consulted and informed about those activities.

The project manager also adopts organization theories that help manage the project. The most commonly used are:

- Maslow's Hierarchy of Needs, which states that people must have lower needs met before thinking of achieving higher needs. The manager must help the person meet each need:
  - Self-actualization
  - Esteem
  - Belonging
  - Safety

- Physiological
- Herzberg's Theory of Motivation states that after job security, a person's salary, acceptable working conditions, and relationship with the manager can motivate them through opportunity, responsibility, appreciation, and education.
- Theory X and Theory Y are two management theories. Theory X assumes that employees are lazy and hate work. Theory Y assumes employees enjoy physical and mental work.
- Expectancy Theory states that people will behave based on what they expect and will work according to expected reward.

Planning Process Group	Plan Resource Management	
Inputs	Tools and Techniques	Outputs
- Enterprise environmental factors - Organizational process assets - Project charter - Project documents - Project management plan - Project schedule - Requirements documentation - Risk register - Stakeholder register	- Data representation - Expert judgment - Hierarchical charts - Meetings - Organization chart - Organization theory - RACI Matrix - Responsibility assignment matrix - Text in a specific format	- Project documents updates - Resource management plan - Team charter

Estimated Activity Resources Process

The *estimated activity resource process* determines resources required to perform activities to produce the project deliverable. During this process, the project manager specifies the type and quantity of resources for the project. Resources including employees, agency staff, vendors and suppliers, materials and equipment that the project team needs to perform the scheduled work.

It is critical that the project manager doesn't assume resources are available and therefore they do not need to be included in the resource estimate. For example, the project team requires office space, desks, computers, electricity, network access, telephones, copiers, restroom facilities, parking, and the list goes on. There is a tendency to presume that these already exist within the firm, which may be true—however, those resources might be allocated to other operations and may not be available to the project.

The estimate activity resource process produces a basis for estimating resources for the project and resource requirements. In addition, it produces a *resource breakdown structure* that associates activities with specific resources.

Planning Process Group	Estimate Activity Resources	
Inputs	**Tools and Techniques**	**Outputs**
– Activity attributes	– Alternatives analysis	– Basis of esti-
– Activity list	– Analogous estimating	mates for
– Cost estimates	– Bottom-up estimating	resources
– Enterprise environmental factors	– Data analysis	– Project docu-
– Organizational process assets	– Expert judgment	ments
– Project documents	– Meetings	updates
– Project management plan	– Parametric estimating	– Resource
– Resource calendars	– Project management information	breakdown
– Resource management plan	system	structure
– Risk register		– Resource
– Scope baseline		requirements

Communication Management Plan Process

The *communication management plan process* identifies the communication approach used by the project sponsor, stakeholders, project manager, and the project team during the project execution. The outcome is a plan that clearly shows how communications will flow; be controlled; and the format of the communication. The plan describes items to be communicated, the purpose of the communication, frequency (including start and end dates), the format of the communication including the medium used to communicate, and the responsible parties involved in the communication.

The project manager analyzes communication requirements by reviewing organizational charts, the RACI matrix, and relationships among project participants. Communication technology is also part of the analysis. The project manager determines availability of technology and appropriate technology used in situations that occur during the project (i.e., cell phone, text message, intranet project website, email). Technology selection is dependent on the communication model used for the project. These are:

- *Push communication*, where information is sent directly to the project participant.
- *Pull communication*, where project participants are expected to access a project website or a central application to review the latest postings.

Planning Process Group	Communication management plan	
Inputs	Tools and Techniques	Outputs
– Enterprise environmental factors – Organizational process assets – Project charter – Project documents – Project management plan – Requirements documentation – Stakeholder register	– Communication models – Communication requirement analysis – Communication technologies – Data representation – Expert judgment – Interpersonal and team skills – Meetings	– Communication management plan – Project document updates – Project management plan updates

Plan Stakeholder Engagement Process

For each stakeholder, the project manager needs to develop an approach for engaging the stakeholder during project development, which is the purpose of the *plan stakeholder engagement process*. Engagement is based on the stakeholder's needs and expectations along with the stakeholder's potential impact on the project. The result of this process is clear, concise directions on how the project sponsor, project manager, and project team should interact with each stakeholder as described in the *stakeholder engagement plan*.

The program manager uses the stakeholder engagement assessment matrix as a guide to developing the stakeholder engagement plan. The stakeholder engagement assessment matrix classifies the engagement level of each stakeholder based on the stakeholder's expected involvement in the project. Engagement level classifications are:
- *Unaware* of the project
- *Resistant* to the project
- *Neutral*, aware of the project but has no opinion about the project
- *Supportive* of the project
- *Leading support* of the project among colleagues

The stakeholder engagement plan (Figure 9.7) contains key information besides the engagement level classification of each stakeholder. The plan also identifies interrelationships among stakeholders, describing any overlapping interest and each stakeholder's communication requirements during each phase of the project. Also included is the frequency of communication, the level of detail, and the format of communication and the reason for the information to be distributed to the stakeholder. Collectively, this helps the project manager target the needs of each stakeholder, effectively communicating to them during the project.

Stakeholder Engagement Plan				
Stakeholder Category	Goals Interests	Influence	Interest	Strategies Working With Stakeholder

Figure 9.7: The plan stakeholder engagement identifies stakeholders, their role in the project, and a plan on how the project manager and the project team interacts with each stakeholder.

Planning Process Group	Plan Stakeholders Engagement	
Inputs	**Tools and Techniques**	**Outputs**
– Enterprise environmental factors – Organizational process assets – Project charter – Project management plan – Project schedule – Risk register – Stakeholder register	– Benchmarking – Data analysis – Data gathering – Data representation – Decision making – Expert judgment – Meetings – Mind mapping – Stakeholder engagement assessment matrix	– Stakeholder engagement plan

Plan Scope Management Process

The *plan scope management process* is used by the project manager and project sponsor to create the project scope and devise a plan to prevent scope creep where new requirements are undertaken by the project team without officially becoming part of the project plan. This includes a way to incorporate new requirements into the project plan as new elements are uncovered during development of the project.

The outcomes of the plan scope management process are the *scope management plan* and the *requirements management plan*. The scope management plan specifies how changes will be managed once the project is launched by clearly defining the scope statement and the formal acceptance of changes by the *change control board*. The requirements management plan describes how requirements are collected, documented, and analyzed to justify requirements to be included in the project scope. The requirements management plan also creates a requirement log that provides a traceable structure for each requirement.

Planning Process Group	Plan Scope Management	
Inputs	Tools and Techniques	Outputs
– Project management plan – Project charter – Enterprise environmental factors – Organizational process assets	– Expert judgment – Meetings – Data analysis – Alternative analysis	– Scope management plan – Requirements management plan

Project Quality Management Process

The *project quality management process* is used by the project manager to identify quality standards that guide the project team throughout the development of the project deliverable. The outcome of the process is the *quality management plan* that will be implemented during the project. The quality management plan is then translated into project activities that adhere to quality standards and implements quality control procedures to assure each phase of the project meets expected quality.

A goal of the project quality management process is to make the project manager and project team responsible for providing stakeholder satisfaction. This is done by continually improving the project management process to prevent occurrence of defects that would result in repeating an activity.

The project manager can employ one or more strategies for providing quality management.

- The *fitness for use* philosophy focuses on meeting stakeholder expectations by conforming to project specifications.
- *Kaizen process* is a strategy of ensuring consistency by applying continuous, small improvements that reduce the cost of an activity.
- *Marginal analysis* is a quality measurement that compares the cost of incremental improvement with the benefits from the improvement.
- *Total quality management* is that quality improvement is a continuous way of performing activities and must be managed each step of the process.
- *Zero defects* is a quality strategy in which preventing defects ensures a quality outcome. This is the "do it right the first time" philosophy.

Planning Process Group	Project Quality Management	
Inputs	Tools and Techniques	Outputs
− Lessons learned register − Organizational process assets (OPA) − Policy compliance and auditing procedures − Project documents − Project management plan − Quality metrics − Risk report − Stakeholder engagement − Standards and regulatory compliance requirements	− Audits − Checklists − Data analysis − Data gathering − Data representation − Decision making − Problem solving − Quality improvement methods	− Policy compliance and auditing plan − Quality management plan

Plan Risk Management Process

The *plan risk management process* is used by the project manager to identify risks that might impact the project and to define approaches to add risks. A risk is an unplanned event that could have a positive or negative effect on activities. A positive risk is that an activity finishes much sooner than planned, making resources available to work on other activities. A negative risk is an activity that is on the critical path that falls so far behind schedule that it causes the entire project to appreciably miss the deadline.

Risks can be categorized as individual project risks and overall project risks. An individual project risk arises from the internal workings of the project, such as with the project team and availability of resources. An overall project risk has a broader impact on the project, project sponsor, and stakeholders, such as delaying other mission critical operations.

The project manager tailors the risk management process based on the size and complexity of the project. Larger, more complex projects that have a critical importance to the organization will have a higher risk than lesser projects.

The outcome of the plan risk management process is the *risk management plan* that identifies risks, the probability of the risk and the impact the risk might have on the project. Probability is categorized by the chance the risk will occur, ranging from very unlikely to almost certain. The impact categorizes the effect the risk has on the project if it occurs as stated, as negligible to severe.

Planning Process Group		Plan Risk Management	
Inputs		**Tools and Techniques**	**Outputs**
– Enterprise environmental factors		– Data analysis	– Risk management plan
– Organizational process assets		– Expert judgment	
– Project charter		– Meetings	
– Project documents		– Stakeholder analysis	
– Project management plan			

Identify Risks Process

The project manager uses the *identify risks process* to recognize events that might place the project in jeopardy. The outcome of this process is the *risk register* that lists all risks and the *risk report* that further defines each risk and summarizes the overall risk to the project.

There are several tools that the project manager uses to identify risks. These are:

– *Assumption and constraint analysis*, which validates assumptions and limitations used when reviewing situations that may occur during the project. The project manager identifies a risk based on what the project manager believes is a risk in the project. The assumption and constraint analysis ensures that those beliefs are well-founded.

– *SWOT analysis* is a technique that examines the project's strengths, weaknesses, opportunities, and threats. Opportunities, such as improving an activity, arise from the project's strengths. Threats arise from the project's weaknesses.

Planning Process Group		Identify Risks	
Inputs		**Tools and Techniques**	**Outputs**
– Agreements		– Data analysis	– Project documents
– Enterprise environmental factors		– Data gathering	updates
– Organizational process assets		– Expert judgment	– Risk register
– Procurement documents		– Interpersonal and team	– Risk Report
– Project documents		skills	
– Risk management plan		– Meeting	
		– Prompt lists	

Plan Risk Responses Process

The project manager uses the *plan risk responses process* to develop strategies to respond to risk during the project. The goal is to have a risk response plan ready should a potential risk be realized, so that the project manager and the project team do not have to spend time reviewing options on how to respond to the risk once it occurs. The outcome of the plan risk responses process is a contingency plan and a fallback plan, each defining events that trigger a response and define response activities. A *contingency plan* contains activities to manage risks when they occur (extinguish the fire). A *fallback plan* contains more drastic responses to severe risks (evacuate the building).

There are three strategies for risks that threaten the project.
– *Avoid the risk* by eliminating the cause of the risk.
– *Mitigate the risk* by reducing the probability that the risk will occur or the impact the risk will have on the project should the risk occur.
– *Transfer the risk* by making another party responsible for the risk, such as outsourcing a risky activity to a vendor or acquiring insurance.

There are also three strategies to address risks that provide opportunity.
– *Exploit the risk* by taking advantage of an opportunity.
– *Enhance the risk* by increasing the probability that the risk will occur or increasing the impact the risk will have on the project.
– *Share the risk* by partnering with other teams to take advantage of the opportunity.

Two other strategies for dealing with risk are to *accept the risk*, realizing that the risk is unlikely to occur or will have minimum impact on the project. This is basically doing nothing. The other strategy is to *escalate the risk* to the project sponsor or appropriate stakeholders when the risk is outside the scope of the project manager to control.

Planning Process Group	Plan Risk Responses Process	
Inputs	**Tools and Techniques**	**Outputs**
– Organizational process assets – Project documents – Project management plan	– Expert judgment – Interpersonal and team skills – Risk strategies – Project management information system	– Contingency plan – Fallback plan – Project document updates

Planning Domain

Plan Procurements Management Process

The *plan procurements management process* identifies activities for acquiring resources and services. The outcome of the process is the *procurement management plan*, *procurement statement of work*, and other documents required to engage vendors to perform work or supply resources to the project. The procurement management plan contains what, when and how elements will be acquired for the project.

The project manager determines the process for qualifying vendors and the method of inviting vendors to be considered for the project. This includes *request for information* (RFI), *request for proposal* (RFP) and other information that the project manager uses to reach the negotiation stage of the contract. Also considered is the type of contract, the change contract process, payment schedule and other activities that occur before the contract is signed.

The *plan procurements management process* specifies the type of contracts that can be used to engage a vendor. These are:

- *Cost plus fixed fee* (CPFF) is where the vendor is reimbursed for cost plus the vendor receives a fee.
- *Cost plus incentive fee* (CPIF) is where the vendor is reimbursed for cost, plus the vendor receives an incentive based on whether or not an objective is reached.
- *Firm fixed price contact* (FFP) is where the vendor receives a fixed price for providing the goods or service.
- *Fixed price contracts lump sums contract* is where the vendor receives a one-time payment for goods and services such as with the purchase of equipment.
- *Fixed price incentive fee contract* (FPIF) is where the vendor receives a fixed price plus a performance incentive such as delivering the goods or service ahead of schedule.
- *Fixed price with economic price adjustment* (FPEPA) is where the vendor receives a fixed price; however, adjustments can be made to the price sometime in the future. This is used for contracts that cover a long time period, during which the vendor's expenses increase. The vendor can then pass along increases.

Planning Process Group	Plan Procurements Management	
Inputs	Tools and Techniques	Outputs
– Project management plan	– Data analysis	– Bid documents
– Project charter	– Data gathering	– Change request
– Project documents	– Expert judgment	– Independent cost estimates
– Milestone list		– Make or buy decisions
– Project team assignments	– Make-or-buy analysis	– Organizational process assets
– Requirements documentation		– Procurement management plan
– Resource requirements	– Market research	– Procurement statement of work
– Risk register		– Procurement strategy
– Stakeholder register	– Meetings	– Project document updates
– Enterprise environmental factors	– Source selection analysis	– Source selection criteria
– Organizational process assets		– Updates

Managing the Project

Direct and Management Project Work Process

The *direct and management project work process* focuses on performing the work that was defined during planning, guided by the charter and other planning documents. The outcome of the direct and manage project +work process is ultimately the project deliverable. However during the course of the project, the project manager will also produce work performance data, record issues in the issue log, and incorporate approved change requests into the project management plan.

Executing Process Group		Direct and Manage Project Work	
Inputs	Tools and Techniques	Outputs	
– Approved change request – Enterprise environmental factors – Organizational process assets – Project documents – Project management plan	– Expert judgment – Meetings – Project management information system	– Change requests – Deliverables – Issue log – Organizational process assets – Project document updates – Project management plan updates – Updates – Work performance data	

Management Project Knowledge Process

Each new project creates a learning experience. The project manager uses knowledge learned from past projects to develop a baseline plan for the current project. New situations occur once the project is underway that cause project managers to take a direction that is different from the baseline plan, sometimes having to find new solutions to new problems. It is important for the project manager and the organization to learn from those experiences and incorporate that knowledge into future projects.

The management project knowledge process formally records knowledge gained throughout the project. This is the process where the project manager and the stakeholder formally record new situations, new issues, and new solutions in the lessons learned register. The lessons learned register is a document that is referenced by all project managers during the planning stages of new projects.

Executing Process Group	Management Project Knowledge	
Inputs	Tools and Techniques	Outputs
− Deliverables − Enterprise environmental factors − Lessons learned registry − Organizational process assets − Project documents − Project management plan − Project team assignments − Resource breakdown structure − Source selection criteria − Stakeholder register	− Expert judgment − Information management − Interpersonal − Knowledge management − Team skills	− Lessons learned register − Project documents updates − Project management plan updates

Project Resource Management Process

The *project resource management process* manages resources once the project gets underway. The project manager uses *resource planning documents* as a guide to acquiring resources in a timely way to ensure resources are available at the time the resource is needed for the work. The project manager assembles the project team based on tailoring considerations for the project and for available staff. Tailoring considers the diversity of the team (background), the location of staff, and industry-specific resources required for the project.

Another key element of the project resource management process is to develop the team. A goal is for the project manager to improve the team's competencies to grow the team and enhance the team's performance for current and future projects. Each project provides the opportunity for the organization to increase each team member's skillset, enabling them to take a greater role in the future.

The project resource management process is also used to manage the project team. The project manager will monitor the performance of each team member and the team as a whole, providing feedback and helping to resolve issues that arise during the project.

Acquire Resources Process

The *acquire resources process* is used to bring onboard resources needed for work on the project. Resources include staff, equipment, materials, supplies, and anything else that is necessary for the project manager to complete the project deliverable. The outcome of the acquire resource process are team assignments, resource calendars and other documents used for resources.

Executing Process Group	Project Resource Management	
Inputs	**Tools and Techniques**	**Outputs**
– Deliverables – Enterprise environmental factors – Organizational process assets – Project documents – Project management plan – Project team assignments – Resource breakdown structure	– Benchmarking – Data analysis – Data gathering – Data representation – Decision making – Expert judgment – Expert judgment – Information management – Interpersonal – Knowledge management – Meetings – Team skills	– Resource schedules – Project documents updates – Project team assignments updates

The project manager typically acquires resources in advance of actual work on the project. This is referred to as a pre-assignment. For example, the project manager acquires a business analyst before the business analysis actually works on a specific activity. The project manager is also likely to create virtual teams from staff throughout the organization. A *virtual team* is a team that comes together to work on a specific activity and then returns to other assignments outside the project once the activity is completed.

Executing Process Group	Acquire Resources	
Inputs	**Tools and Techniques**	**Outputs**
– Enterprise environmental factors – Organizational process assets – Project documents – Project management plan – Project schedule – Resource calendars – Resource requirements – Stakeholder register	– Decision making – Interpersonal and team skills – Pre-assignment – Virtual teams	– Change requests – Organizational process assets – Physical resource assignments – Project documents updates – Project management plan updates – Project team assignments – Resource calendars – Enterprise environmental factors updates – Organizational process assets updates

The Develop Team Process

The purpose of the *develop team process* is to improve the performance of the team while managing the project. In doing so, the project manager must recognize the natural states of team development that occur anytime a new team is assembled. The following are the stages of team development.

- *Forming* occurs when the team gets together for the first time. This is the period when members of the team become acquainted. Members consider each other as strangers. Interactions are relatively formal as members informally establish ground rules for interaction with one another.
- *Storming* then follows as members of the team jockey to define their role on the team. Each is considered an individual, not a team member. During this period there might be hostility as members express their feelings.
- *Norming* is the next stage of team development, in which differences are re-solved, positions on the team are clear, and members know the strengths and weaknesses of each other. They begin to act as a team.
- *Adjourning* is the final stage of team development, in which the project deliverable is completed and the team breaks up. The team embraces success and then moves on individually to another project.

Executing Process Group	Develop Team	
Inputs	Tools and Techniques	Outputs
– Enterprise environmental factors – Organizational process assets – Project documents – Project management plan – Project team assignments – Resource calendars	– Individual and team assessments – Meetings – Recognition and rewards – Training – Virtual teams	– Change requests – Enterprise environmental factors updates – Organizational process assets updates – Project documents updates – Project management plan updates – Team performance assessments

Manage Team Process

The manage team process focuses on motivating the project team to follow the project plan and develop the project deliverables on time and with the expected quality. The project manager monitors performance of each team member and provides feedback to keep the project on track. In addition the manager manages changes in the project to resolve issues and looks for ways to optimize the performance of the project team and the project as a whole.

Executing Process Group		Manage Team	
Inputs	Tools and Techniques	Outputs	
– Enterprise environmental factors – Organizational process assets – Project documents – Project management plan – Team performance assessments – Work performance reports	– Interpersonal and team skills – Project management information system	– Change requests – Enterprise environmental factors updates – Project document updates – Project management plan updates	

Conflict Resolution Process

The project manager uses the *conflict resolution process* to address any conflict that might arise during the project. Conflicts occur naturally during a project caused by misunderstandings, unmanaged expectations, poor communication, and honest disagreement on strategy. The conflict resolution process requires that the project manager be open to resolving conflicts and focus on issues—not personalities—and focus on the current issue, not what led up to the conflict.

The conflict resolution process uses conflict resolution techniques to address issues at the center of the conflict. Conflict resolution techniques are:
- *Confrontation*, which is the preferred method used to address the conflict head-on.
- *Collaboration*, which focuses on incorporating multiple viewpoints into a consensus.
- *Compromising*, which is a blended solution where parties of the conflict give up a position. Neither party gets exactly what they want.
- *Smoothing*, which sets out to minimize the problem, but is usually a temporary solution because the conflict is likely to arise in the future.
- *Withdrawal*, in which one party gives up without resolving the conflict. This is the worst solution.

Control Resources Process

The *control resources process* focuses on monitoring resources, ensuring that the planned physical resources are available according to the *resource plan*. This differs from managing the actual use of resources, which involves actively managing—not monitoring—physical resources. For example, the control resources process moni-tors the availability of the physical resource. Managing the actual resources in-volves addressing issues if the resource is unavailable.

Executing Process Group		Conflict Resolution	
Inputs	**Tools and Techniques**	**Outputs**	
– Enterprise environmental factors – Organizational process assets – Project documents – Project management plan – Resource calendars – Resource requirements – Stakeholder register – Team performance assessments – Work performance reports	– Individual and team assessments – Interpersonal and team skills – Meeting – Recognition and rewards – Training – Virtual teams	– Change requests – Change requests – Enterprise environmental factors updates – Organizational process assets updates – Physical resource assignments – Project document updates – Project documents updates – Project management plan updates – Project management plan updates – Project team assignments – Resource calendars	

Executing Process Group		Control Resources	
Inputs	**Tools and Techniques**	**Outputs**	
– Agreements – Organizational process assets – Project documents – Project management plan – Work performance data	– Data analysis – Interpersonal and team skills – Problem solving – Project management information system	– Change requests – Project documents updates – Project management plan updates – Work performance information	

Project Communication Management Process

The *project communication management process* ensures the project manager meets the information needs of stakeholders by undertaking activities to effectively exchange information. There are two parts to the project communication management process. The first part is to *develop* an effective *communication strategy*. The second part is to *implement the communication strategy* so that all stakeholders receive the correct message in a timely manner.

The communication strategy is based on stakeholder needs. Each stakeholder has specific requirements to exchange information between the project team and the stakeholder throughout project development. Likewise, the project manager has constraints within which to communicate with stakeholders. The project communication management process balances these needs.

The project manager must retrieve stored project data so it can be incorporated into an appropriately formatted message that is distributed to stakeholders. The message can be formal, such as in a formatted document like a project charter; informal, such as email and text messages; or informal conversations. In addition, the project manager must monitor communications and encourage feedback to assure that the message sent was the message received by stakeholders. Any misunderstandings must be clarified immediately.

Executing Process Group	Project Communication Management	
Inputs	**Tools and Techniques**	**Outputs**
– Enterprise environmental factors – Organizational process assets – Project charter – Project documents – Project management plan – Requirements documentation – Stakeholder register	– Communication models – Communication requirement analysis – Communication technology – Data representation – Expert judgment – Interpersonal and team skills – Meetings	– Communication management plan – Project document updates – Project management plan updates

Manage Communications Process

The *manage communication process* enacts the *communication management plan*. This is the process of collecting data, transforming data into information, storing both data and information, and assembling information into a format that is distributed to stakeholders.

Executing Process Group	Manage Communications	
Inputs	**Tools and Techniques**	**Outputs**
– Communication management – Communication plan – Enterprise environmental factors – Organizational process assets – Project documents – Project management plan – Stakeholder engagement plan – Work performance reports	– Communication models – Communication skills – Communication technology – Interpersonal and team skills – Meetings – Project management information system – Project reporting	– Organizational process assets – Project communications – Project document updates – Project management plan updates – updates

Project Stakeholder Management Process

The *project stakeholder management process* is used by the project manager to provide continuous communications with stakeholders based on the project needs, stakeholders' expectations, and the project team's requirements to engage stakeholders in appropriate aspects of the project. A key element of the project stakeholder management process is to monitor and manage stakeholder engagement by maintaining ongoing relationships and then tailoring communication strategies to meet stakeholders' expectations, interests, and the potential impact on the project.

The key to success in managing stakeholders is to engage all stakeholders and not limit ongoing communications to a subset of stakeholders. Furthermore, all team members must be involved in stakeholder engagements. The project manager must also regularly review project risks with stakeholders and encourage close involvement in the project by stakeholders who are most affected by the risk and the project.

Executing Process Group		Project Stakeholder Management	
Inputs		**Tools and Techniques**	**Outputs**
– Enterprise environmental factors		– Communications skills	– Project document
– Issue log		– Expert judgment	updates
– Organizational process assets		– Ground rules	– Project management
– Project documents		– Interpersonal and team	plan
– Project management plan		skills	– Stakeholder
– Stakeholder register		– Meetings	communication

Control Procurements Process

The *control procurements process* is used by the project manager to monitor contract performance and manage relationships with vendors. The project manager ensures that vendors adhere to legal agreements and deliver goods and services according to specifications. Any deviation from the contract may result in a change request by either the vendor or the project manager, resulting in terms of the contract changing to accommodate the deviation in requirements or performance.

Manage Stakeholder Engagement Process

The project manager uses *manage stakeholder engagement* to actively work with stakeholders throughout the project with the goal of having stakeholders feel like a participant in the project within their interests and needs. Stakeholder engagement

Executing Process Group	Control Procurements	
Inputs	**Tools and Techniques**	**Outputs**
− Agreements − Approved change requests − Enterprise environmental factors − Organizational process assets − Procurement documents − Project documentations − Project management plan − Work performance data	− Audits − Claims administration − Data analysis − Earned value analysis − Expert judgment − Inspection − Performance reviews − Trend analysis	− Change request − Closed procurements − Organizational process assets − Procurement documentation updates − Project documents update − Project management plan updates − Updates work performance information

must be a proactive activity for the project manager and the project team in order to foster involvement of the stakeholder in the project.

The outcome of the manage stakeholder engagement process are stakeholder reports and feedback that may result in change requests to the project scope that lead to changes to the baseline project management plan, should change be approved. In addition, there is increased buy-in by stakeholders who actively participate in the project.

Executing Process Group	Manage Stakeholder Engagement	
Inputs	**Tools and Techniques**	**Outputs**
− Enterprise environmental factors − Issue log − Organizational process assets − Project documents − Project management plan − Stakeholder register	− Communications skills − Expert judgment meetings − Ground rules − Interpersonal and team skills	− Change requests − Project document updates − Project management plan − Stakeholder reports

Perform Integrated Change Control Process

The *perform integrated change control process* is a critical element of project management because the process prevents scope creep. *Scope creep* occurs when new requirements are imposed after the project is launched and the new requirements are not considered in the project plan. New requirements often are necessary once the project is underway as new elements become known. The change control process provides structure for considering new requirements and formally incorporating new requirements into a *revised project plan*.

The project sponsor and the project manager form a *change control board* consisting of key stakeholders who weigh the benefits and drawbacks of each proposed new requirement. A case is made before the change control board for expanding the scope of the project. The project manager then presents an impact statement that shows how the new requirement affects the project. Members of the change control board then decide to include or postpone inclusion of the new requirement into the project scope.

Executing Process Group	Perform Integrated Change Control	
Inputs	Tools and Techniques	Outputs
– Change requests – Enterprise environmental factors – Organizational process assets – Project management plan – Work performance reports	– Alternatives analysis – Change control tools – Cost benefit analysis – Data analysis – Decision making – Expert judgment – Meetings	– Approved change request – Project documents updates – Project management plan updates

Project Scope Management Process

The *project scope management process* is used by the project manager to ensure that the project team's work is on elements that are within the project scope. The project scope is determined at the initiation of the project and later through the change control process and becomes the basis for the work breakdown structure and the project plan. It is common that stakeholders have business reasons for expanding the project scope and request changes without fully appreciating the impact the change will have on the project. While the *perform integrated change control process* provides structure to formally evaluate each proposed change, the project scope management process ensures that the project team works on only elements of the project that are within the approved project scope.

The project manager monitors the team's performance by comparing each team member's activity with the assigned activity based on the project plan. Any activity underway that does not adhere to the project plan is questioned and stopped, since the activity is likely outside the project scope.

Executing Process Group	Project Scope Management	
Inputs	**Tools and Techniques**	**Outputs**
– Activity attributes – Activity list – Milestone list – Project charter – Project documents – Project management plan – Project team assignments – Requirements documentation – Scope baseline	– Benchmarking – Brainstorming – Data analysis – Decision making – Expert judgment – Inspection planning – Meetings	– Approved change request – Project documents updates – Project management plan updates – Project schedule network diagrams

Conduct Procurements Process

The *conduct procurement process* is used by the project manager to identify and select vendors to provide goods and services to the project. The project manager uses activities contained in the procurement management plan to request information from vendors, entertain proposals, and enter into appropriate contracts with vendors.

Executing Process Group	Conduct Procurements	
Inputs	**Tools and Techniques**	**Outputs**
– Communications management plan – Cost baseline – Enterprise environmental factors – Organizational process assets – Procurement documentation – Procurement management plan – Project documents – Project management plan – Project schedule – Requirements documentation – Risk management plan – Scope management plan – Seller proposals – Stakeholder register	– Advertising – Bidder conference – Data analysis – Expert judgment – Interpersonal and term skills – Procurement negotiations – Proposal evaluation	– Agreements – Change requests – Organizational process assets updates – Project documents updates – Project management plan updates – Select sellers

Manage Quality Process

The *manage quality process* implements the quality management plan into activities to produce the project deliverable. This is commonly referred to as *quality assurance*. The project manager uses the manage quality process tools to incorporate quality into each project activity. The outputs of the manage quality process are quality reports used by stakeholders to identify issues that jeopardize the quality of the project. Stakeholders then decided how to enhance the quality of the project to ensure the project's success.

These tools are:

– *Alternative analysis,* which identifies approaches to use for an activity to produce quality output.
– *Document analysis* is used to point to activities that may be out of control, placing the project and quality of the project deliverable at risk.
– *Process analysis* examines non-value-added activities that can be removed from the project, decreasing the opportunity for defects and increasing quality.
– *Quality audits* independently examine each activity to identify failures to adhere to quality standards.
– *Root cause analysis* examines the underlying reasons that cause variance in an activity that jeopardize the quality of the project deliverable.

Monitor Process Group	Manage Quality	
Inputs	Tools and Techniques	Outputs
– Lessons learned register	– Checklists	– Change requests
– Organizational process	– Data gathering	– Project documents
assets	– Data analysis	updates
– Project documents	– Data representation	– Project management plan
– Project management plan	– Decision making	updates
– Quality control	– Problem solving	– Quality reports
measurement	– Quality audits	– Test and evaluation
– Quality management plan	– Quality improvement	documents
– Quality metrics	methods	
– Risk report		

Implement Risk Responses Process

The project manager uses the *implement risk response process* to respond to risky events that occur during the project based on pre-determined responses identified in the contingency plan and the fallback plan. Both the contingency plan and the fallback plan list likely and remote risky events that might be experienced; however, there may be times when an unexpected risk event occurs. In these situations, the project manager and the project team must evaluate the event and apply an appropriate strategic response. The outcome of the implement risk response process is an update of project documentation, including the project plan.

Executing Process Group	Implement Risk Responses	
Inputs	Tools and Techniques	Outputs
− Contingency plan − Fallback plan − Organizational process assets − Project documents − Project management plan	− Expert judgment − Interpersonal and team skills influencing − Project management information system − Risk monitoring	− Project document updates

Monitoring the Project

Monitor and Control Project Work

The *monitor and control project work process* is used by the project manager to ensure that the project team produces the *project deliverable*. Once the project plan is completed, the project manager compares the project performance against the project plan to ensure that the project is on course. Any deviation requires the project manager to assess why there is a difference and to implement any corrective or preventive actions to bring the project performance in line with the project plan.

The project manager also continues to monitor the project for risks, thereby becoming proactive by implementing strategies that will respond to each risk appropriately so as to minimize the impact to the project. The project manager also monitors efforts to keep stakeholders informed on the ongoing status of the project as planned.

Monitor Process Group	Monitor and Control Project Work	
Inputs	Tools and Techniques	Outputs
− Agreements − Cost forecasts − Enterprise environmental factors − Milestone list − Organizational process assets − Project documents − Project management plan − Quality reports − Risk register − Risk report − Schedule forecasts − Work performance data − Work performance information	− Alternatives analysis − Cost benefits analysis − Data analysis − Decision making − Earned value analysis − Expert judgment − Meetings − Root cause analysis − Trend analysis − Variance analysis	− Change requests − Project document updates − Project management plan updates − Work performance reports

Monitor Communications Process

The *monitoring communication process* is used by the project manager to ensure that communication between stakeholders and the project team is occurring as planned. The project manager compares actual communication with that which the plan communicates. Any deviations are rectified by the project manager, making sure that stakeholders stay informed about the project and that the project team stays informed about the desires of stakeholders.

Monitor Process Group	Monitor Communications	
Inputs	Tools and Techniques	Outputs
- Enterprise environmental factors - Organizational process assets - Project communications - Project documents - Project management plan - Work performance data	- Data analysis - Expert judgment and meetings - Information management system - Interpersonal and team skills	- Change request - Project document updates - Project management plan updates - Work performance information

Monitor Stakeholder's Engagement Process

The project manager uses the *monitor stakeholder's engagement process* to ensure that stakeholders remain engaged in the project as planned. The engagement plan can be modified by the project manager if there is any deviation between the engagement plan and actual engagement with stakeholders. Modifications are considered, tailoring strategies to keep stakeholders engaged while meeting stakeholder expectations and needs.

Monitor Process Group	Monitor Stakeholder's Engagement	
Inputs	Tools and Techniques	Outputs
- Enterprise environmental factors - Organizational process assets - Project documents - Project management plan - Work performance data	- Communication skills - Data analysis - Data representation - Decision making - Interpersonal and team skills - Meetings	- Change requests - Project documents updates - Project management plan updates - Work performance information

Control Scope Process

The *control scope process* is used to monitor the status of the project, comparing the baseline project scope to the current project scope. The project manager uses the control scope process to ensure that new requirements are requested, properly presented to the control board, and that the control board evaluates each new requirement based on the change control process.

Monitor Process Group		Control Scope	
Inputs	Tools and Techniques	Outputs	
– Organizational process assets	– Data analysis	– Change requests	
– Project documents requirements	– Trend analysis	– Project documents updates	
– Requirement traceability matrix	– Variance analysis	– Project management plan	
– Project management plan		updates	
– Work performance data		– Work performance information	

Control Quality Process

The project manager uses the *control quality process* to monitor whether or not the project team is adhering to the quality management plan. The outcome is to verify that activities are complete and produce elements that meet customer expectations. Any deficiencies are rectified, ensuring that the quality of the project remains at an acceptable level as defined by the quality management plan.

A number of tools are used by the project manager to monitor the quality of activities.

- *Check sheets* are used to gather information about an activity when performing a quality audit. Items on a check sheet typically show expectations and results found during the quality audit.
- *Control charts* are used to plot elements of an activity, illustrating variances from expected results that may indicate failures or defects.
- *Verified deliverables* compare expected deliverables to actual deliverables, using quality control measurements to assure that deliverables meet expectations.
- *Work performance information* consists of data about an activity that includes elements that fulfill the requirements, elements that are rejected and require rework to meet the requirements, and the status of each activity.

Monitor Process Group	Control Quality	
Inputs	**Tools and Techniques**	**Outputs**
– Approved change request	– Check sheets	– Change requests
– Deliverables	– Checklists	– Project documents updates
– Enterprise environmental	– Data analysis	– Project management plan
factors	– Data gathering	updates
– Organizational process	– Data representation	– Quality control measurements
assets	– Inspections	– Verified deliverables
– Project documents	– Meetings	– Work performance information
– Project management plan	– Performance reviews	
– Quality management plan	– Root cause analysis	
– Quality metrics	– Statistical sampling	
– Test and evaluation	– Testing/product	
documents	evaluations	
– Work performance data		

Closing the Project

Close Project or Phase Process

The *close project* or *phase process* is used by the project manager when either a phase of the project is completed or the whole project is completed.

Closing Process Group	Close Project or Phase	
Inputs	**Tools and Techniques**	**Outputs**
– Accepted deliverables	– Data analysis	– Final product, service or result
– Agreements	– Document analysis	transition
– Business documents	– Expert judgment	– Final report
– Procurement documentation	– Meetings	– Project documents updates
– Project charter	– Variance analysis	– Updated organizational process
– Project documents		assets
– Project management plan		

Chapter 10
Project Management Calculations

You never know what you'll be asked during the interview or on a project management test, if you are given one. The previous chapters reviewed the basics that might be asked during a technical interview and more technical PMP exam topics. Think of these as items in your project manager's toolbox—items the interviewer may want you to know how to apply to a project.

Another thing that might come up is calculations. Yes, dreaded by many and embraced by few, there are budget and planning calculations that help to assess a project and make ongoing project management decisions—calculations that the interviewer may question you about. Calculations that are also in the project manager's toolbox.

In this chapter we'll review project management calculations and how and why to use them. Calculations focus on measuring the project—enabling the project manager to determine if the project is moving along as planned or how far ahead or behind the project is compared to the baseline schedule.

Calculations also estimate the future—not using a crystal ball but using statistics to project the project's trajectory. Many calculations focus on money—the budgets, investments, and contracts. Some firms expect the project manager to have a working knowledge of basic finance. Calculations shown in this chapter will give you a leg up on the basics.

You'll notice that calculations used for project management have their own terminology that you need to understand to properly use the calculations. A misunderstanding might lead to plugging in the wrong numbers in the formula resulting in the wrong value—not a good thing during the hiring process. You'll find the explanation of each calculation a great way to help you avoid traps that might trip you during the process.

Calculation names are followed by the abbreviation that is commonly used in formulas. Abbreviations have been excluded from the formulas to avoid confusion. However, you may find that firms will use only abbreviations on tests, if you are administered a pre-employment test. Next, you'll find an explanation of how the calculation is used to assess a project, and the formula. The formula illustrates values and calculations necessary to arrive at the result. Examples below each formula include a word problem and a solution using the calculation.

At the end of the chapter you'll see questions similar to questions found on project management tests, and answers with rationales on why the answer is correct.

https://doi.org/10.1515/9781501506222-011

Planned Value (PV)

Planned Value (PV) is the approved value of the work before actually doing the work. The work might be a work package for a segment of the work pack or the entire project.

The formula is:

$$\text{Planned Value} = \text{Budget for Work Package 1} + \text{Budget for Work Package 2}$$
$$+ \text{Budget for Work Package 3}$$

Example: The budget for designing the order entry system is $5,000 and the budget for building the order entry system is $23,000. The budget for implementing the order entry system is $6,000. The Planned Value (PV) is $34,000.

$$\$34,000 = \$5,000 + \$23,000 + \$6,000$$

Budget at Completion (BAC)

Budget at Completion (BAC) is similar to the Planned Value (PV) in that it is the total budget for the project and is used in other project calculations.

The formula is:

$$\text{Budget at Completion} = \text{Budget for Work Package 1} + \text{Budget for Work Package 1}$$
$$+ \text{Budget for Work Package 1}$$

Example: The budget for designing the order entry system is $5,000 and the budget for building the order entry system is $23,000. The budget for implementing the order entry system is $6,000. The Budget at Completion (BAC) is $34,000.

$$\$34,000 = \$5,000 + \$23,000 + \$6,000$$

Estimate at Completion (EAC)

The Estimate at Completion (EAC) calculation is used to forecast the project performance by projecting the total amount that the project will cost. This is a projection of the total cost of the project when the project is completed and is reported periodically during the project. The following are four formulas used to calculate the Estimate at Completion (EAC).

First formula:
The Budget at Completion (BAC) is divided by the Cost Performance Index (CPI) to arrive at the Estimate at Completion (EAC).

Estimate at Completion = Budget at Completion/Cost Performance Index

---

Example: Let's say that the Budget at Completion is $100,000 and the Cost Performance Index is 0.5, which indicates that the project is over budget. The Estimate at Completion is $200,000.

$$\$200,000 = \$100,000 / 0.5$$

Second formula:
This formula is used when the cost estimate was flawed. A new cost estimate is necessary to project the cost of the remaining project. It adds the Actual Cost so far to the Bottom-up Estimate Total Cost (ETC), which is the result of the new cost estimate.

Estimate at Completion = Actual Cost + Bottom−up Estimate Total Cost

---

Example: Let's say that the estimated total cost of the project was $100,000. However, the actual cost halfway through the project is $125,000. The original cost projection was grossly underestimated. A new cost estimate for the remainder of the project is $150,000 after conducting a bottom-up estimate. The Estimate at Completion is $275,000.

$$\$275,000 = \$125,000 + \$150,000$$

Third formula:
This formula is used when events cause a deviation from the estimated budget but now the project is back on course following the remaining estimated budget.

Estimate at Completion = Actual Cost + (Budget at Completion − Earned Value)

Example: Let's say that the Actual Cost (AC) so far is $50,000. The Budget at Completion (BAC) is $175,000. The Earned Value (EV) is $25,000. The Estimate at Completion (EAC) is:

$$\$200,000 = \$50,000 + (\$175,000 - \$25,000)$$

Fourth formula:
This formula is used when the project is over budget and behind schedule and the project sponsor wants the project completed by a deadline. The formula uses the schedule and cost to project the Estimate at Completion (EAC).

Estimate at Completion = Actual Cost + [(Budget at Completion – Earned Value)/
(Cost Performance Index × Schedule Performance Index)]

Example: Let's say that the Actual Cost (AC) is $50,000. The Budget at Completion (BAC) is $175,000. The Earned Value (EV) is $25,000. The Cost Performance Index (CPI) is 0.5 and the Schedule Performance Index is 0.6. The Estimate at Completion is $100,000.

Estimate at Completion = $50,000 + [($175,000 – $25,000) / (0.5 × 0.6)]

Estimate at Completion = $50,000 + [$150,000 / 0.3]

$100,000 = $50,000 + $50,000

Earned Value (EV)

Earned Value (EV) is used to monitor how well the project is going by using the project plan, actual work, and completed work. The Earned Value formula is the percentage of the completed budget. Here is the Earned Value formula.

Earned Value (EV) = percentage complete × Budget at Completion (BAC)

Here is how to calculate the Earned Value:

1. Determine the percentage of the project that is completed using man-hours as the measurement. Analyzing the project plan will determine the total number of man-hours necessary to complete the project. Summing employee hours for tasks completed determines the number of completed employee hours. Here's how to calculate the percentage of the project that is completed.

Percentage complete = (employee hours completed/total employee hours) × 100

2. Earned Value = percentage complete × Budget at Completion (BAC)

Here's an example:
To calculate percentage, complete

50%, = (350/700) × 100

If Budget at Completion was $50,000, then

$25,000 = 50% × $50,000

Estimate to Complete (ETC)

The Estimate to Complete (ETC) is used to forecast how much more money will be spent to finish the project. The calculation uses the Estimate at Completion (EAC) and the Actual Cost (AC) to arrive at the Estimate to Completion (ETC).
The formula is:

$$\text{Estimate to Complete} = \text{Estimate at Completion} - \text{Actual Cost}$$

Example: Let's say that the Actual Cost (AC) is $50,000 and the Estimate at Completion is $100,000. The Estimate to Complete is $50,000.

$$\$50,000 = \$100,000 - \$50,000$$

Actual Cost (AC)

The Actual Cost (AC) calculation is used to determine the current cost of the project.
The formula is:

$$\text{Actual Cost} = \text{Cost for Work Package 1} + \text{Cost for Work Package 2}$$
$$+ \text{Cost for Work Package 3}$$

Example: Let's say the actual cost for designing the order entry system is $6,500 and the actual cost for building the order entry system is $33,200. The actual cost for implementing the order entry system is $7,100. The Actual Cost (AC) is $46,800.

$$\$46,800 = \$6,500 + \$33,200 + \$7,100$$

Variance at Completion (VAC)

The Variance at Completion (VAC) calculates the difference between the Budget at Completion (BAC) and the Estimate at Completion (EAC). It states how much under or over the project costs at the end of the project.

- Variance at Completion = 0: The project is on budget.
- Variance at Completion < 0: The project is over budget.
- Variance at Completion > 0: The project is under budget.

The formula is:

$$\text{Variance at Completion} = \text{Budget at Completion} - \text{Estimate at Completion}$$

Example: Let's say that the Budget at Completion is $100,000 and the Estimate at Completion is $150,000. Here is the calculation. The Variance at Completion is $50,000, which is greater than 0, meaning the project is under budget.

$$\$50,000 = \$100,000 - \$150,000$$

Cost Variance

Cost Variance (CV) is a calculation that compares the project's budget with funds expended on the project to assess the project's financial performance. This states the amount of the project that is under or over the budget at a reporting period. The project's budget is referred to as Earned Value (EV) and expenditures is referred to as Actual Cost (AC). There are three possible results of the Cost Variance:

- Cost Variance (CV) = 0: Indicates that the project is on target and there is no variance.
- Cost Variance (CV) = negative: Indicates that the project is over budget.
- Cost Variance (CV) = positive: Indicates that the project is under budget.

The formula is:

$$\text{Cost Variance} = \text{Earned Value} - \text{Actual Cost}$$

Example: The Earned Value of the project is determined to be $60,000. The Actual Cost is $70,000. The Cost Variance is –$20,000. The negative value means that the project is over budget.

$$-\$20,000 = \$60,000 - \$80,000$$

Cost Performance Index

An index is a composite statistic that measures change. The Cost Performance Index (PCI) is used to measure the cost efficiency of a project by measuring the composite of project costs. There are two variables in the Cost Performance Index. These are the Earned Value (EV) and the Actual Cost (AC). There are three possible Cost Performance Index values.

- Cost Performance Index = 1: Every dollar spent is returning a dollar of value. Performance is as expected.
- Cost Performance Index > 1: Every dollar spent is returning more than a dollar of value. Performance is better than expected.
- Cost Performance Index < 1: Every dollar spent is returning less than a dollar of value. Performance is worse than expected.

The formula is:

$$\text{Cost Performance Index} = \text{Earned Value} / \text{Actual Cost}$$

Example: Let's say that the Earned Value is $60,000 and the Actual Cost is $100,000. Here is the calculation. The index is 0.6, which is less than 1, meaning the project performance based on cost is worse than expected.

$$0.6 = \$60,000 / \$100,000$$

Schedule Variance

The Scheduled Variance is used to monitor the performance of the project by comparing the Earned Value (the actual value of the project completed) and the Planned Value (the approved value of the work done at this point). This states the amount that the project is ahead or behind the schedule. A positive Schedule Variance indicates that the project is ahead of schedule. A negative Schedule Variance indicates the project is behind schedule.

The formula is:

$$\text{Schedule Variance} = \text{Earned Value} - \text{Planned Value}$$

Example: The Earned Value of the project is determined to be $60,000. The Planned Value was $80,000, which was the estimate value of the project. The Schedule Variance is –$20,000. The negative value means that the project is running behind schedule.

$$-\$20,000 = \$60,000 - \$80,000$$

Schedule Performance Index

The Schedule Performance Index is used to measure whether the project is running on schedule based on the Earned Value (EV) and the Planned Value (PV). There are three possible Schedule Performance Index (SPI) values.

- Schedule Performance Index = 1: The project is on schedule.
- Schedule Performance Index > 1: The project is ahead of schedule.
- Schedule Performance Index < 1: The project is behind schedule.

The formula is:

$$\text{Schedule Performance Index} = \text{Earned Value} / \text{Planned Value}$$

Example: Let's say that the earned value is $60,000 and the Planned Value is $50,000. Here is the calculation. The index is 1.2, which is greater than 1, meaning the project is ahead of schedule.

$$1.2 = \$60,000 / \$50,000$$

To Complete Performance Index

The To Complete Performance Index (TCPI) forecasts the cost performance that can be achieved on the remaining portion of the project. There formula bases the To Complete Performance Index (TCPI) on the Budget at Completion (BAC), Earned Value (EV), Estimate at Completion (EAC), and Actual Cost (AC).

The formula is:

$$\text{To Complete Performance Index} = (\text{Budget at Completion} - \text{Earned Value})/$$
$$(\text{Estimate at Completion} - \text{Actual Cost})$$

Example: Let's say that the Actual Cost (AC) is $50,000. The Budget at Completion (BAC) is $175,000. The Earned Value (EV) is $25,000 and the Estimate at Completion (EAC) is $100,000. The To Complete Performance Index (TCPI) is $100,000.

$$\text{To Complete Performance Index} = (\$175,000 - \$25,000)/(\$100,000 - \$50,000)$$
$$3 = \$150,000 / \$50,000$$

Expected Monetary Value (EMV)

The Expected Monetary Value (EMV) is the amount that should be realized based on the likelihood the event occurs. This is used to help the project manager and project sponsor make decisions that will impact the project. The Expected Monetary Value (EMV) uses the impact of the event and the probability that the impact will occur.

The formula is:

$$Expected\ Monetary\ Value\ =\ Probability\ *\ Impact$$

Example: Let's say that Project A will save the firm $100,000 once the project is implemented. However, the chances of completing the project and realizing the saving is one in four. On the other hand, Project B will save the firm $75,000 and has a three in four chance of being completed and realizing the savings. Project B has a higher Expected Monetary Value.

Expected Monetary Value for Project A

$$\$25,000\ =\ 0.25\ *\ \$100,000$$

Expected Monetary Value for Project B

$$\$56,250\ =\ 0.75\ *\ \$75,000$$

Return on Investment

The Return on Investment (ROI) calculation is used to compute the gain or loss of an investment made in the project or any investment. The result is a percentage of the investment. The higher the Return on Investment (ROI) the more profitable the project is to a firm. However, the firm must consider the risk associated with the project. A project with a high Return on Investment (ROI) might also be a high risk that could lead to project failure, not realizing the expected gain. There are two factors in calculating the Return on Investment (ROI). These are Net Profit, which is the gain beyond expenses, and Cost of Investment, which is the amount invested in the project to achieve the gain.

The formula is:

$$Return\ on\ Investment\ =\ (Net\ Profit\ /\ Cost\ of\ Investment)*100$$

Example: Let's say the firm invests $100,000 to development and implement an order entry system that will increase efficiency. The firm realizes $20,000 in savings in the first year of operations. The return on investment is 20% of the investment.

$$20\%\ =\ (\$20,000\ /\ \$100,000)\ *\ 100$$

Payback Period

The Payback Period calculation determines the amount of time that is necessary for the firm to earn back the investment made in a project, or any investment. Projects with a shorter payback period are better, since the money returned can be reinvested in other projects sooner. Factors in the Payback Period calculation are the Initial Investment and the Periodic Cash Flow, which is the amount of revenue the project generates or saves the firm.

The formula is:

$$\text{Payback Period} = \text{Initial Investment} / \text{Periodic Cash Flow}$$

Example Let's say the firm invests $100,000 to develop and implement an order entry system that will increase efficiency. The firm realizes $20,000 in savings each year of operations. The Payback Period is five years. This means that the firm won't recover its investment until five years after the order entry system is implement.

$$5 \text{years} = \$100,000 / \$20,000$$

Risk Priority Number (RPN)

The Risk Priority Number (RPN) is used to assess risk associated with a project that were identified by the Failure Mode and Effect Analysis (FEMA). There are three factors considered when arriving at the Risk Priority Number (RPN).

- Detection: Detection is the capability of detecting the failure and is assigned a value from 1 to 10 with 1 indicating a high capability of detecting the failure and a 10 a low capability of detecting the failure.
- Occurrence: Occurrence is the likelihood that the failure will occur and is assigned a value from 1 to 10 with 1 indicating a remote likelihood that the failure will occur and 10 indicating a high likelihood that the failure will occur.
- Severity: Severity is the impact that a failure will have on the project if it did occur. Severity is assigned a value from 1 to 10 with 1 indicating a low severity and 10 a high severity.

Risks are identified using the Failure Mode and Effect Analysis (FEMA), then given a Risk Priority Number (RPN).

The formula is:

$$\text{Risk Priority Number} = \text{Detection x Occurrence x Severity}$$

Example: Let's say the Failure Mode and Effect Analysis (FEMA) identified two risks. These are the risks that the loud computing provider will go out of business and the specifications for the order entry system are incomplete, leading to bugs in the system.

Cloud computing provider goes out of business.

$$18 = 1 \times 3 \times 6$$

Specifications for the order entry system are incomplete.

$$360 = 8 \times 5 \times 9$$

The Risk Priority Number (RPN) for the cloud computing provider going out of business is 18 and the Risk Priority Number (RPN) for specifications for the order entry system are incomplete is 360. The risk specifications for the order entry system are incomplete are high (360) compared with the cloud computing provider going out of the business (18). Therefore, the project manager needs to focus on minimizing the risk that specifications will be incomplete.

Cost Plus Percentage of Cost (CPPC)

The Cost Plus Percentage of Cost (CPPC) is used to calculate the cost of a vendor's contract. With this contract, the firm accepts complete risk for the performance of the vendor because the firm pays the vendor's expenses and gives the vendor a fee for work. The fee is a percentage of the total cost. The firm is at risk that the vendor will intentionally increase expenses, since this also increases the vendor's fee.

The formula:

$$\text{Total Contract Cost} = \text{Expenses} \times (1 + \text{percentage fee})$$

Example: Let's say the firm wants to replace all desktop computers with the latest models. A vendor is hired to acquire, configure, and install the computers. The cost to acquire the computers is $100,000 and the cost to configure and install the computers is $15,000. The total cost is $115,000. The vendor will receive a 10% fee, which is $11,500. The Total Contract Cost is $126,500.

$$\text{Total Contract Cost} = \$ 115,000 \times (1 + 0.1)$$

$$\$126,500 = \$115,000 \times 1.1$$

Cost Plus Fixed Fee (CPFF)

The Cost Plus Fixed Fee (CPFF) is used to calculate the cost of a vendor's contract. With this contract, the firm accepts complete risk for the performance of the vendor because the firm pays the vendor's expenses and gives the vendor a fee for work. The fee is fixed unless the scope of the contract changes.

The formula:

$$\text{Total Contract Cost} = \text{Expenses} + \text{Fee}$$

Example: Let's say the firm wants to replace all desktop computers with the latest models. A vendor is hired to acquire, configure, and install the computers. The cost to acquire the computers is $100,000 and the cost to configure and install the computers is $15,000. The total cost is $115,000. The vendor will receive a fixed fee of $10,000. The Total Contract Cost is $125,000.

$$\$125,000 = \$115,000 + \$10,000$$

Cost Plus Award Fee (CPAF)

The Cost Plus Award Fee (CPAF) is used to calculate a vendor's contract. The firm assumes all the risk and reimburses the vendor for all expenses. The contract specifies an amount above expenses that the vendor will receive based on performance standards defined in the contract. The firm has the discretion on how much to award the vendor.

The formula is:

$$\text{Total Contract Cost} = \text{Expenses} + \text{Award Fee}$$

Example: Let's say the firm wants to replace all desktop computers with the latest models. A vendor is hired to acquire, configure, and install the computers. The cost to acquire the computers is $100,000 and the cost to configure and install the computers is $15,000. The total cost is $115,000. The vendor will receive an award fee of $10,000 if performance is satisfactory and possibly receive a $15,000 award fee if the vendor goes above and beyond to satisfy the firm.
Satisfied:

$$\$\,125,000 = \$\,115,000 + \$\,10,000$$

Beyond Satisfied:

$$\$\,130,000 = \$\,115,000 + \$\,15,000$$

Cost Plus Incentive Fee (CPIF)

The Cost Plus Incentive Fee (CPIF) is used to calculate a vendor's contract. The firm assumes all the risk and reimburses the vendor for all expenses. The contract specifies the finance incentive that the vendor will receive based on performance defined in the contract.

The formula is:

$$\text{Total Contract Cost} = \text{Expenses} + \text{Incentive Fee}$$

Example: Let's say the firm wants to replace all desktop computers with the latest models. A vendor is hired to acquire, configure, and install the computers. The cost to acquire the computers is $100,000 and the cost to configure and install the computers is $15,000. The total cost is $115,000. The vendor will receive an incentive fee of $5,000 if the deadline is missed; a $10,000 incentive fee if the deadline is met; and receive a $15,000 incentive fee if the vendor beats the deadline. The Total Contract Cost is $125,000.

Missed deadline:

$$\$120,000 = \$115,000 + \$5,000$$

Met deadline:

$$\$125,000 = \$115,000 + \$10,000$$

Beat deadline:

$$\$130,000 = \$115,000 + \$15,000$$

The Critical Path

The critical path is the sequence of tasks whose duration determines the duration for the project. An increase in duration of a task that is on the critical path increases duration of the project. Tasks may move on and fall off the critical path during the project as the project manager adjusts the duration of tasks necessary to manage the project.

PERT Triangular Distribution

There are several calculations that are used to measure the critical path. The first is the Program Evaluation and Review Technique (PERT) Triangular Distribution formula that is used to calculate duration, cost, and resources estimates. These are referred to as *activities*. The objective is to estimate the duration, referred to as Estimated Activity Duration (EAD). The estimate is the average of the activity optimistic duration (O), activity most likely duration (M) and the activity pessimistic duration (P).

The formula is:

$$\text{Estimated Activity Duration} = (\text{Activity Optimistic} + \text{Activity Most Likely} + \text{Activity Pessimistic})/3$$

Example: The project is to build a new order entry system. Experts were consulted to determine the duration to design screens for the new system. Each was asked to give an optimistic, most likely, and pessimistic estimate. Collectively these are 20 man-days (optimistic), 35 man-days (most likely), and 40 man-days (pessimistic). Applying the formula the Estimate Activity Duration for designing screens is 32 man-days.

$$32 \text{ man} - \text{days} = (20 + 35 + 40) / 3$$

PERT Beta Distribution

The PERT Beta Distribution is a variation of the PERT Triangle Distribution that increases the accuracy of the Estimate Activity Duration by giving more weight to the most likely estimate than to the optimistic and pessimistic estimates and minimizing the impact of each variable by dividing by six rather than three.

The formula is:

$$\text{Estimated Activity Duration} = (\text{Activity Optimistic} + (4 \text{ x Activity Most Likely})$$
$$+ \text{Activity Pessimistic}) / 6$$

Example: Let's return to the project to build a new order entry system and use the same estimates provided by the experts. Collectively, these are 20 man-days (optimistic), 35 man-days (most likely), and 40 man-days (pessimistic). Applying the formula, the Estimate Activity Duration for designing screens is 33 man-days.

$$33 \text{ man} - \text{days} = (20 + [4 \text{ x } 35] + 40) / 6$$

Total Float (Slack)

The Total Float, also known as *slack*, determines how long an activity that is not on the critical path can be delayed without affecting the project deadline. Activities on the critical path have zero float because any delay will delay the project. There are two formulas that can be used to calculate the Total Float of an activity. One focuses on the Last Start (LS) and Early Start (ES) of the activity and the other the Late Finish (LF) and Early Finish (EF) of the activity.

The formula is:

$$\text{Total Float} = \text{Late Start} - \text{Early Start}$$

$$\text{Total Float} = \text{Late} - \text{Early Finish}$$

Example: Let's say you are considering moving a designer from designing screens for an order entry system to another activity. The design process isn't on the critical path, but you want to know how much time you have before the process impacts the project's deadline, or when you need the designer back to design the screens. This is referred as the *float*. You estimate the earliest start time and the latest start time for the designer to return to the project. The earliest is 5 days and the latest is 7 days. The Total Float is 2 days. The alternative formula is used following the same process, except using the early finish and late finish dates.

$$2 \text{ days} = 7 \text{ days} - 5 \text{ days}$$

Number of Communication Channels

Communication with stakeholders is critical to the success of the project. The project manager can measure the complexity of communicating with them by calculating the number of communication channels in the project. A *communications channel* is a line of communication with and among stakeholders (a person or a group). The more communications channels, the more complex communication will be during the project. The number of stakeholders is commonly abbreviated as N in a formula.
    The formula is:

$$\text{Number of Communication Channels} = \text{Number of Stakeholders}$$
$$\text{x (Number of Stakeholders} - 1)/2$$

Example: Let's say you are developing an order entry system. There are 20 stakeholders who have some involvement in the project. Remember that a stakeholder may be a person such as the project sponsor or a working group within the firm, such as the Accounts Receivable department, which is considered one stakeholder. There are 190 possible communication channels in this project, stakeholders communicating with the project manager and among themselves.

$$190 = 20 \text{ x(20} - 1) / 2$$

Take the Challenge

No one knows what will be asked on a pre-employment project management test, except for the folks who create the test. Then again, maybe you'll never be asked to take a test. However, just in case you find yourself in front of a project management test, it might be useful to see what kinds of questions you might be asked. Here are ten questions that follow along the lines of questions asked on project management tests.

Here is the project for the first five questions:

Your project is to develop and implement an order entry system within a year with a budget of $250,000 evenly dispersed throughout the year. Six months have gone by and you spent $166,667 with the project's current value of $125,000.

1. Assuming variance doesn't continue during the remainder of the project, what is the expected Estimate at Completion (EAC)?

    A. $166,667   B. $ 291,667   C. $125,000   D. $250,000

2. What is the schedule variance?

    A. $166,667   B. $1   C. 0   D. $125,000

3. What is the cost performance index?

    A. 0.75   B. 0.25   C. 0.1   D. .020

4. Is the project on schedule?

    A. Yes   B. No

5. Is the project on budget, under budget, or over budget?

    A. On budget   B. Under budget   C. Over budget

6. You consulted experts on how long it will take to define the workflow for the order entry system. The opinions are that 20 days is most likely; 15 days is the best case; and 21 days is the worst case. What duration would you assign to this activity using a Triangular PERT Distribution?

    A. 15 days   B. 56 days   C. 41 days   D. 18 days

7. The order entry system project has 23 stakeholders including the project sponsor all of whom are likely to discuss the project independently of the project manager. What is the number of communication channels for this project?

    A. 484   B. 252   C. 242   D. 506

8. You need to determine if a business analyst can be taken off the activity of analyzing the workflow for new customers in the order entry system to work on another activity. You can't delay this workflow analysis, otherwise the activity will be on the critical path. What is the Total Float if the earliest start is 4 days and the latest start is 10 days?

    A. 14 days   B. 4 days   C. 10 days   D. 6 days

9. You hire a vendor to upgrade the computer network to handle the new order entry system. The activity is to run fiber optic cables throughout the facility and connect computers to the fiber optic cables. The vendor wants a Cost Plus Fixed Fee contract. The vendor estimates that labor and material will be between $50,000 and $75,000 and the fixed fee is $20,000. What would be the maximum expense to the firm for this activity?

    A. $70,000   B. $50,000   C. $95,000   D. $145,000

10. The order entry project has four high level activities. These are to develop spec-
ifications for the order entry system; design the order entry system; develop the
order entry system; and implement the order entry system. Before work begins,
you estimate the cost for each high-level activity as shown here. What is the
Planned Value of the order entry project?
  - Develop specifications for the order entry system = $35,000
  - Design the order entry system = $20,000
  - Develop the order entry system = $45,000
  - Implement the order entry system = $25,000

A.$55,000
B.$125000
C.$70,000
D.$45,000

Answers and Rationales

1. **B. $291,667**
   Estimate at Completion = Actual Cost + Budget at Completion – Earned Value
   $ 291,667 = $166,667 + $250,000 – $125,000

2. **C. $0**
   The formula is:

   Planned Value = Budget at Completion x Current Value
   $125,000 = $250,000x50

   Schedule Variance = Earned Value – Planned Value
   0 = $125,000 – $125,000

3. **A. 0.75**
   Cost Performance Index = Earned Value / Actual Cost
   0.75 = $125,000 / $166,667

4. Yes. The Schedule Variance is zero.
   0 = $125,000 – $125,000

5. Over Budget. The Cost Performance Index is greater than zero.
   0.75 = $125,000 / $166,667

6. **D.18 days**

   The formula is:

   Estimate Duration $= ($Pessimistic $+$ Most Likely $+$ Optimistic$)/3 = (10 + 5 + 3)/3$
   Estimate Duration $= (21 + 20 + 15)/3$
   18 days $= (56)/3$

7. **B.253**

   The formula is:

   Number of Communication Channels $= [$Number of Stakeholders x
   (Number of Stakeholders $- 1)]/2$
   Number of Communication Channels $= [23$ x $(23 - 1)]/2$
   Number of Communication Channels $= [23$ x $22]/2$
   $253 = 506/2$

8. **D.6 days**

   The formula is:

   Total Float $=$ Late Start $-$ Early Start
   6 days $=$ 10days $-$ 4days

9. **C.$95,000**

   The formula is:

   Total Contract Cost $=$ Expenses $+$ Fee
   $\$95,000 = \$75,000 + \$20,000$

10. **B.$125,000**

    The formula is:

    Planned Value $=$ Budget for Work Package 1 $+$ Budget for Work Package 2
    $+$ Budget for Work Package 3 $+$ Budget for Work Package 4
    $\$125,000 = \$35,000 + \$20,000 + \$45,000 + \$25,000$

    The Planned Value of the project is $125,000.

Chapter 11
Enterprise, Extreme, Agile Project Management

If someone tells you she's a physician, after sharing your aches and pains with her, you'll probably ask what her specialty is. There are hundreds of medical specialties and specialties within specialties—probably some you've never heard of and haven't a clue what it is without an explanation.

Project managers are somewhat like physicians—not necessarily in pay and prestige, but in specialties. A specialty might be in an industry, managing projects for a Wall Street firm, or a discipline, managing computer systems projects that cross industries. Another type of specialty is in the project management framework used to manage a project. The most commonly used are the waterfall, enterprise, extreme, and agile project management frameworks. There are others, but these are the likely ones that come up during a project management interview.

The waterfall project management framework was discussed in detail in Chapter 7. enterprise, extreme, and agile project management frameworks were also touched upon in Chapter 7 but you'll probably need more than a touch for the project manager interview. This chapter goes into more details about enterprise, extreme, and agile project management frameworks.

Enterprise Project Management

Projects in organizations may not be seen as an investment. Yet, a large percentage of an organization's budget is allocated to projects. Enterprise project management is a branch of project management that focuses on treating all projects as an investment for the organization and a methodology to centralize some or all of project management.

In the 1990s, the business community realized a lot of time and money was spent on projects; however, those projects were not formally managed. It was during this period when the business community implemented formal project management methodology. Then in 2008, there was another change. The business community realized that much of their budgets were supporting projects. The business community was investing money in projects—money that could otherwise be allocated to bringing in revenue. And so, the birth of *enterprise project management*.

A key element of enterprise project management is to create a portfolio of projects —much like a portfolio of stocks, bonds, and other investments—and manage the project portfolio as an investment portfolio. Project sponsors now had to convince a committee of executives who manage the portfolio that the investment in the project is a better investment than other projects and other investment opportunities. Executives then decide the best investments for the firm.

https://doi.org/10.1515/9781501506222-012

The Project Management Office (PMO)

Enterprise project management is part of corporate governance—high in the organization, directed by executives who define the rules within which managers do business. Think of corporate governance as a state where the board of directors is like the legislators—one is elected by stockholders and the others by registered voters—and the chief executive officer is almost like the governor. "Almost" is the key word, because the chief executive offer is appointed by the board of directors, while the governor is elected by registered voters. The board of directors and the chief executive officers make rules or policies to govern how the organization operates to achieve the goals of the board of directors and make money.

Enterprise project management is housed in a project management office called a project management office (PMO). The PMO oversees all projects in the enterprise—but not necessarily in the way you think. They don't manage projects. Instead, the PMO develops a process for creation and managing a portfolio of projects. Think of the PMO as a facilitator—key executives (not the PMO) decide what projects are included in the project portfolio.

The PMO coordinates periodic reviews of the project portfolio where executives add projects that are good investments and remove projects that are no longer good investments. A project that is on time and on budget may be stopped because it is no longer a good investment.

The PMO also establishes project management standards throughout the organization. For example, they define when to use traditional project management methodology and when to use agile project management methodology. The PMO decides which project management software to use and provides super user support for project managers. The PMO manages shared resources, and some PMOs also manage all project managers. However, PMOs don't generally tell project managers how to manage their project. Many times, project managers report to the project sponsor, not the PMO.

The project portfolio is a group of projects that the executives decide are a valued investment. How they make this determination is up to executives, though the PMO office can provide suggestions about how to do this. The project portfolio is periodically reviewed and pruned to ensure that the project portfolio continues to meet executives' investment expectations.

The PMO reports to top management and is part of the organization's strategic team. The focus of the PMO is to:

- Standardize project management methodologies throughout the organization.
- Find ways to economize on the repetitive nature of projects. For example, Division A may have built a system that can be modified by Division B but Division B is unaware of the system. The PMO is aware of all projects and can share information among project managers.

- Create templates of successful project plans using a project management tool. A template can be used by other project managers to reduce the time spent planning and prevent errors from recurring.
- Advise project managers. The PMO staff develops a body of knowledge that can be used by project managers to manage projects.

Types of Project Management Offices

There are at least three types of project management offices.

- The enterprise project management office oversees projects for the entire organization.
- The organizational project management office oversees projects for a subset of the organization such as a division.
- Special purpose PMO that are set up to address one situation that affects the entire organization, such as consolidating offices into one location or meeting a new regulatory requirement.

Select Projects for the Project Portfolio

The challenge is to determine whether a project is a good investment and remains a good investment. The decision depends on the criteria established by the organization based on expected performance of the project portfolio. The overriding question is: Should the organization commit funds, resources, and personnel to resolve a specific issue? Should the project be financed?

In theory, the decision is based on finances and on profit and loss. How much does the project cost to develop? What is the ongoing cost once the project is implemented? How much will the project eventually save the organization or increase revenue for the organization? Executives use investment analysis calculations to value project proposals.

It is the responsibility of the project sponsor to prove to executives that the proposed project is a good investment for the firm. Part of the proposal is to present alternatives to the project that support the claim that the proposed project is the best alternative.

Let's say the project sponsor proposes to improve an inefficient process by developing an internally built computer application. The project sponsor's proposal should evaluate the following options using cost benefit analysis. Cost benefit analysis considers one-time cost, annual cost, annual revenue, and projected profit for each alternative.

- Do nothing: What is the financial impact of keeping the status quo?
- Hiring more staff to use the current process: What is the short- and long-term cost associated with increasing the number of positions?
- Licensing a solution from a vendor: What are the advantages and disadvantages of using an off-the-shelf product or using APIs from third-party vendors?
- Develop an internal solution: What are the advantages and disadvantages of building it yourself?
- Outsource development: What are the advantages and disadvantages of paying someone else to build it?

Breakeven Analysis

Before making an investment, one factor that executives must know is the breakeven point, which is the point in time when the investment returns the money that was invested. Generally speaking, the shorter the breakeven point, the better the investment, because the firm is exposed to risk associated with the investment for the least amount of time. However, a firm might take a long-sighted approach that lets the market develop gradually, leading to a delayed breakeven point. Conversely, the longer it takes to break even, the worse the investment because during that time period, things can go wrong that jeopardize the firm realizing the benefits of the investment. Furthermore, the sooner the investment breaks even, the more opportunity the firm has to reinvest money that was originally invested.

Let's say a firm invests $1 in a box of Cheerios that it can sell for $5 a box. The investment is $1 and the firm breaks even when the box of Cheerios is sold. The breakeven point is a day if the firm purchases and sells the box of Cheerios in the same day. This means that the firm can reinvest the $1 in another box of Cheerios or in a different investment.

Now, if it takes a week to sell the box of Cheerios, the breakeven point is one week, not a day. The box of Cheerios sits on the shelf for a week, where anything could happen to it and make the box unsaleable, in which case the firm loses the $1 investment. The firm takes the risk that nothing is going to happen in the week to prevent the sale. The firm may also decide to mitigate the risk by hiring a security guard to protect the box of Cheerios. The cost of the security guard increases the investment. Furthermore, the firm loses the opportunity to reinvest the $1 for a week. This is referred to as opportunity cost, which is also a consideration when making an investment decision.

Return on Investment (ROI)

Return on investment is a calculation used to determine the monetary value the firm can expect to receive from an investment. A higher return on investment returns more money than a lower return on investment. Let's go back to the investment in the box of Cheerios to see how this works.

An investment of $1 in a box of Cheerios returns $5 when the box is sold. The return on investment is five times the investment, commonly referred to as a ROI of 500%. An alternative is to invest in a box of corn flakes. A box of corn flakes cost $1 and sells for $1.50. The firm receives $1.50 for every box of corn flakes it sells. The ROI is 150%.

Comparing the return on investment for each investment opportunity helps executives determine which is likely a better investment. However, executives must also consider factors other than the return on investment before making a choice about where to invest.

Time Value of Money

The combination of the breakeven point and return on investment narrows down the true value of an investment. A goal of every firm is to make money from money. The sooner the initial investment is returned to the firm the sooner the firm can reinvest that money in another investment and make more money. This is commonly referred to as the *time value of money*.

Selling the box of Cheerios the same day the firm purchases the box is a much better investment than waiting a week to sell the box. The firm could have reinvested the $1 seven times if the box sold in one day, compared with reinvesting the $1 once if it took a week to sell the box. Furthermore, each day, the firm earned and had an additional $4 to invest the profit from selling the box of Cheerios.

However, the firm must also take into consideration the return on investment. Suppose the firm invested in a box of corn flakes instead of a box of Cheerios. Selling a box of corn flakes in a day also returns the $1 the same day the box is purchased. However, the firm receives only an additional 50 cents, not the additional $4 realized from the sale of a box of Cheerios. The return on the sale of a box of corn flakes enables the firm to reinvest $1.50 compared to reinvesting $5 returned from the sales of a box of Cheerios.

Reality of Selecting Projects

In reality, projects are not judged by their contribution to the bottom line—how much the project saves money or increases revenue. Firms that adopted enterprise project management don't use the investment portfolio model for a number of reasons—primarily because it is difficult to relate projects to the bottom line.

Projects are selected for the project portfolio by using a project prioritization worksheet (Figure 11.1). A project prioritization worksheet is a table that contains factors that executives feel are important to the firm when considering a project for the project portfolio. Factors vary. Commonly used factors are strategic value, ease to accomplish, financial benefit, cost, and impact on resources.

<table>
<tr><td colspan="8" align="center">Sample
Projet Prioritization Worksheet</td></tr>
<tr><td>Project</td><td>Strategic Value</td><td>Ease</td><td>Financial Benefit</td><td>Cost</td><td>Resource Impact</td><td>Overall Priority</td><td>Notes</td></tr>
<tr><td>Project A [name]</td><td>1</td><td>3</td><td>3</td><td>5</td><td>2</td><td>2.8</td><td></td></tr>
<tr><td>Project B [name]</td><td>5</td><td>2</td><td>4</td><td>4</td><td>4</td><td>3.8</td><td></td></tr>
<tr><td>Project C [name]</td><td>3</td><td>5</td><td>3</td><td>3</td><td>5</td><td>3.8</td><td></td></tr>
<tr><td>Project D [name]</td><td>2</td><td>4</td><td>3</td><td>3</td><td>5</td><td>3.4</td><td></td></tr>
<tr><td>Project E [name]</td><td>5</td><td>3</td><td>5</td><td>3</td><td>2</td><td>3.6</td><td></td></tr>
<tr><td>Project F [name]</td><td>1</td><td>2</td><td>2</td><td>5</td><td>4</td><td>2.4</td><td></td></tr>
<tr><td>Project G [name]</td><td>1</td><td>2</td><td>1</td><td>2</td><td>2</td><td>1.6</td><td></td></tr>
</table>

Priority ratings (your best guess or judgments) should be scored as follows:

Strategic Value? Is the project important to our overall strategies? 1 = Highly important 5 = Not important

Ease? Will this project be fairly easy to complete? 1 = Very easy 5 = Very difficult

Financial Benefit? Will this project's deliverables likely yield financial benefit? 1 = Highly likely 5 = Not likely

Cost? Will this project likely cost a lot? 1 = Low cost 5 = High cost

Resource Impact? Will this project have a great impact on our resources (people, equipment, etc.)? 1 = Low impact 5 = High impact

Overall Priority: Average score, all five criteria.
NOTE: The *lower* the score, the *higher* the project's priority.

Figure 11.1: The project prioritization worksheet is used to select projects for the project portfolio.

Factors are listed as column headings and rows are projects that are being considered for the project portfolio. Each executive on the team that manages the project portfolio is given the project prioritization worksheet and asked to rank each project from 1 to 5. The lower the score, the higher the priority.

Each executive decides for themselves on how they arrive at the rank. The executive can make the decision based on information in the proposal; or ask for additional information and assessments—such as analysis by the finance department; or they may use their own judgment. There is no required method to arrive at the ranking. The project prioritization worksheets are collected and consolidated by the PMO then the consolidated project prioritization worksheet is redistributed to the executives who repeat the process. Some modify their ranking based on the consolidated ranking and others don't change their ranking. The

PMO revises the consolidated project prioritization worksheet. At the end, the final project prioritization worksheet is given to executives. Collectively, the team decides how many of the high prioritized projects to include in the project portfolio. The same process is used to review the project portfolio.

Project Portfolio and Project Risks

The project management office must consider risks associated with projects that are in the project portfolio. The success of a project depends on a number of factors. The project management office must encourage executives to consider each factor when deciding if a project remains in the project portfolio.

- Successful development of the project.
- Successful interactions among the project manager, project sponsor, and stakeholder.
- Success in changing the organization's behavior—new projects typically mean introducing something new that might force stakeholders outside their comfort zone.
- Bringing the project in on time and on budget—otherwise, the justification for doing the project might be invalid.
- Objectively measuring the project's progress using statistics.

Risk is the possibility that a desired outcome is not achieved, such as the project not being delivered on time, on budget and being successfully implemented. A key risk factor is that projects are done inconsistently within the organization. This is a sign that a project might fail. Inconsistency leads to missed or misunderstood requirements and requirements that cannot be measured or tested, so no one knows if the requirements were met.

Project managers should spend a lot of time on defining requirements—those that do usually have the highest success rates. Case in point. A project manager for a Wall Street firm spent more than three months developing detail requirements that included explicit workflows. The logic for every decision point was identified and verified by stakeholders. Stakeholders had to sign off on the workflow logic. Work flows and specifications were electronically turned over the programmers who encoded the workflow logic into the application—there were no bugs once when the application was implemented.

The project's progress must be consistently measured to determine if the project is on target, on budget, and on time. Projects that are inconsistently measured become less predictable and are risky to the organization because there is no sure way to measure progress.

Here are red flags for failure.
- Projects are not prioritized—there is no project portfolio, or the project portfolio is not managed.
- The project sponsor and stakeholders don't participate in the program.
- There is too much outside oversight on the management of the project.
- The project sponsor and stakeholders bypass the project manager and go directly to the project team to answer questions and give advice.
- The project manager doesn't manage the project—instead he rolls over and gives into requests from the project sponsor and stakeholder.
- Approvals are made informally.
- The project manager has too many responsibilities without the authority to manage those responsibilities.
- There is no definable deliverable.
- The goal is to implement the project ASAP, even if it is impossible to do so.

Where Enterprise Project Management Fails

Enterprise project management may seem like a way for an organization to wrap its arms around all its projects, but enterprise project management can fail. One of the first failures is project sponsors under estimate work and resources required for the project. The presumption is the project proposal is reasonable, and when it isn't, all of the practices of enterprise project management might fail.

Inaccurate representation of the project is a major fail point in enterprise project management. Whether intentionally or inadvertently, the project sponsor paints a more optimistic picture of the project than reality, and executives are misled. Another fail point is when resources are not available based on the project plan. The problem is that the project manager does not own the resources and managers who own the resources are not involved in project planning. No uniformity in the way projects are proposed and managed is a sure sign of failure. Inconsistency leads to a high failure rate for enterprise project management.

The concept of enterprise project management itself must be sold to executives, project sponsors, and project managers. All must buy-in—otherwise, enterprise project management is jeopardized. Here are a few tips you can use to sell the concept of enterprise project management.

First, test the waters by describing your plans for enterprise project management to executives, project sponsors, and project managers. Hold one-on-one meetings. This is where you'll identify your supporters, detractors, and neutral parties to the idea and why they hold their position.

Be sure to identify the person who has the power to decide if the organization should move ahead with enterprise project management and make sure that person is a supporter. Then help them walk through the stages of adoption.

Stages of Adoption

A common failure is not to give executives, project sponsors, and project managers time to adopt your idea of instituting enterprise project management. Each of us follows the stages of adoption before we adopt a new idea. The PMO's job is to help executives, project sponsors, and project managers walk through each stage of adoption.

First, we must be aware that there is a problem and a solution. Next, we need to explore the solution and take a superficial look to see if there is a possible solution. Then we take a look at the details by examining the solution, trying to uncover reasons that invalidate the solution. And then there is the test—we test the solution under various scenarios. If it passes, then we tend to adopt the solution.

This is similar to buying a car—maybe you became aware of the car on television, then explored the car on the internet before going to the dealership to examine the car and then take the car for a test drive. If all goes well, you might buy the car.

Change the Status Quo

Implementing enterprise project management will change how project sponsors and project managers do their jobs. Change is difficult to accept, especially if they feel that all is going well and there is no need to change. The PMO's job is to clarify the problem and the need to change the status quo. Explain how enterprise project management will change their routine of proposing and managing projects. Most important, anticipate and be prepared to address all concerns.

For example, ask project managers to describe the worst part of their job. They may tell you there is not enough time to plan a project and too much time is spent creating reports for stakeholders. The response: The project management office will create templates of successful project plans for projects that are common throughout the organization. The project manager needs to use the template and tweak the plan to meet their needs. Tasks, duration, resources, and other elements of a project plan are already in place.

The project management office can recommend a project tool that provides dashboard enabling stakeholders to monitor the project without the need of periodic reports from the project manager. A dashboard is similar to the dashboard of a car where key information about projects are displayed automatically updated by a computer.

Minimize Opportunity for Conflict

You can't avoid conflicts when proposing and implementing enterprise project management, but you can minimize opportunity for conflict. Here's how to do it.

- Keep lines of communication open—miscommunication or lack of communication is an underlying cause of conflict.
- Encourage stakeholders to participate in the decision process where possible—this gives them a feeling of ownership in enterprise project management.
- Discuss changes incrementally and well before recommending them—walk everyone through the stages of adoption.
- Be honest—enterprise project management will change the way they work. Sometimes you won't make their job easier. Be upfront and give them time to deal with the change.

How to Run a Project Management Office

Running a project management office requires strategic thinking. The goal is to help the organization reach its strategic goal by investing in projects and helping executives establish criteria to determine which projects are included in the project portfolio. Executives make the decision. The PMO facilitates making the decision. There must be frequent review of the performance of the project portfolio, usually quarterly, to find problems early on. The focus is on business needs, not managing projects.

To implement a project management office as a project, there needs to be a project plan, tasks, dependencies, resources, and costs—everything you expect to find in any project plan. Make sure executives are committed to implementing enterprise project management and a PMO. Don't move forward without a commitment.

Clearly define the role of the PMO. Many PMOs are facilitators and have little direct authority over projects. The PMO facilitates the project portfolio process and standardization. Usually, project managers set standards—the PMO does the legwork identifying best practices in the industry. The PMO is the central scheduling center for shared resources, who keep their reporting line. The PMO coordinates their assignments, but they still report to their boss, not the PMO.

The PMO spearheads the adoption of technology to manage projects in the organization—project managers are the adoption body. That is, the PMO proposes technology and procedures and project managers as a whole decide if the technology should be adopted by the organization.

The PMO focuses on the basics of project management and the project portfolio, facilitating activities with executives, project sponsors, and project managers. Here are the typical activities of a PMO.

- Standardization: The PMO is on the lookout for best practices, standards, and project management tools that help manage projects efficiently.
- Facilitate Key Actions: PMO key actions are to facilitate the project portfolio, scheduling shared resources, and setting project management standards.
- Coaching: The most rewarding aspect of the PMO. Members of the PMO may not be super project managers, but are project managers who have the time to help project managers and project sponsors solve problems.
- A home for all project managers: The PMO manager is the supervisor of all project managers and all projects, and is in the position to assign a project manager and project teams to projects.

Realities of the Project Management Office

In theory, the project management office seems to be the solution to all problems related to project management—it isn't. PMOs are established to improve project success rates and to implement project management standards throughout the organization, not to ensure that projects are a good investment.

There are three measurements used by PMOs to assess projects: cost estimates, schedule estimates, and stakeholder satisfaction. Notice that breakeven point, cash flow, or return on investment were not mentioned. PMOs improve employee productivity by managing resource allocation.

For example, some project management offices implement Microsoft Office Project Portfolio Server, which can be used to create and monitor the project portfolio automatically. Project managers use Microsoft Project and save their project plans to the project portfolio server. Dashboards can be created, showing the project portfolio, all projects, or a group of projects for a project sponsor. The dashboard displays the status of those projects in real time. There are other alternatives to Microsoft Project including Wrike, Clarizen, Zoho, and Smartsheet, but Microsoft Project is the market leader in large part because of its significant advantage in integration with Microsoft Office Project Portfolio Server and Microsoft Office.

Extreme Project Management

In traditional project management, the project manager uses the work breakdown structure to divide the project into work packages and then each work pack into tasks, subtasks, duration, dependencies, resources, budget, deliverables, and milestones. The project manager analyzes the project and creates a detailed plan that tells members of the project team what to do and when to do it.

For relatively smaller routine projects, agile project management is used to manage the project. Agile project is where there is no detailed plan. Instead, the project team works from scenarios or requests, and then fulfills the request.

Think of traditional project management as an orchestra where one person writes the musical parts for all of the instruments. Think of agile project management as a quartet with piano, bass, drums, and guitar. You call out a song and the quartet plays the song perfectly, even without music. Each member has played that song many times and knows their part.

Extreme project management is used to manage complex projects that need to be completed rapidly. Variables in the project are constantly changing. There is high uncertainty and high stress because problems associated with the project may have never been solved before. The project team may find itself doing research to solve the problem. The project is highly visible—and there is no cookie-cutter approach to management of the project.

Extreme project management is focused on reality, not theory.

Usually there is no precedent for an extreme project—there is no map that is going to show the proven path to managing the project. Therefore, the project team must devise new ideas and test them. They must throw those ideas away if they don't work and start over—this is planning, deplanning, and re-planning. These are techniques usually frowned upon in traditional project management. Therefore, the project manager must gain and sustain commitment throughout the project life cycle from the project sponsor, stakeholders, and the project team.

An extreme project is going to the moon. No one knew if it could be achieved. There was no book that told you how to go to the moon. You might say that they were writing the book during the moon project. There are unknowns in an extreme project—such as a part of science that has yet to be explored—but they must be explored as part of the project.

If you've watched the movie *Apollo 13*, you've seen a depiction of an extreme project. Three astronauts are trapped in a spacecraft with days to live unless the project team is able to figure out how to keep them alive and get them back to earth. This was reality.

Options were limited to the capabilities of the spacecraft—the depth of the disaster was unknown. There are many quotes from *Apollo 13* that are true for many extreme projects:

- I don't care about what anything was designed to do. I care about what it can do.
- Stop. Think. Don't do something disastrous—don't make matters worse.
- Failure is not an option.

Tunneling from France to England is an example of an extreme project. At first glance, the tunneling effort seems like any massive tunneling construction project—large and complex. There are plenty of books and courses that show how to manage such a project. The extreme element was the politics surrounding the project. There were two national governments, regional and local governments in both countries that had great influence over the project. Both wanted a say in the design of the tunnel. Imagine managing a project where there were countless influential and powerful stakeholders feeling the need to tell you how to manage the project. This degree of influence is not seen in a typical project.

Managing an Extreme Project

Managing an extreme project requires radical concepts that are not common to managing other types of projects. Decisions are made at lower levels, not by the project manager, because many decisions must be made rapidly—there is no time to consult the project manager on every decision. The project manager is the facilitator and integrator. Team members identify and address problems. The project manager makes sure they have everything needed to do the job.

Planning is done in real-time (called *scenario planning*, rather than centralized planning) before the project begins. The team that is charged with addressing a problem develops its own plan, referred to as *participative rapid planning*. Plans are made quickly, based on the existing circumstance.

Virtual teams come together to address a problem and then move on once the problem is resolved. There may be hundreds of issues that must be addressed by virtual teams. The project manager may empower each virtual team to make decisions without consulting the project manager. This sounds strange because most of us run our recommendations past the project manager and ask for their blessing. You may not have time to do this in an extreme project.

Furthermore, the project manager isn't the expert—the virtual team is the expert and should make the decision. This is like bringing your car to a mechanic. You want the mechanic to decide what to do, not come back and ask you—you're not a mechanic—the mechanic is the expert.

Empowerment to Make Decisions

Empowerment to make decisions is based on trust. The project manager trusts the virtual team—that is, you trust the mechanic—and the virtual team trusts that the project manager will support their decision. The level of trust is important. You may not complain if the mechanic performed a necessary costly repair to your car or fixes something they think needs repairing but you feel works fine. If you have that level of trust, then you will accept the outcome. That level of trust is a necessary ingredient in an extreme project.

Failure is a key to empowerment and trust. No one likes to fail—failure is looked down upon in many organizations. The manager of an extreme project must change this culture.

Failure is good and should be celebrated. Sounds strange, but is it? An extreme project presents new issues, some of which the virtual team doesn't know how to solve—in fact, no one knows how to solve them. So the virtual teams try a logical solution, which fails, and they move on to the next logical solution, and the process continues until a workable solution is found. They learn from failure.

All Information Is Shared

All information about an extreme project is shared with all team members. No one filters information. An extreme project is complex and time sensitive. There is no time to file information. Each team member is expected to assess the value of the information for themselves. A piece of information irrelevant to one team member might be the missing information to solve another team member's problem.

The project manager must ensure that technology is implemented to share information among the project team. The project manager is the facilitator and helps to make things happen but does not make things happen. The virtual team has the job to make things happen by identifying problems and solutions, planning, executing the plan, and assessing results. The project manager makes sure each virtual team has everything necessary to do their job.

Relationship Capital

Relationship capital has everything to do with relationships built between the project manager, virtual teams, and stakeholders. Say that you take over a project. You and stakeholders are relative strangers. There is a get-to-know you period when each of you sizes up the other. It takes time to build trust and respect.

Now suppose you worked for the organization for a while. You worked with stakeholders on other projects, so trust and respect is already built—you have relationship capital with stakeholders. There is no get-to-know-you period.

You may not have time to work through the get-to-know-you period on an extreme project. Therefore, the project manager must include team members who already have relationship capital with stakeholders.

Take the Deepwater Horizon oil spill in the Gulf of Mexico that occurred in 2010 with 11 people killed and 17 people injured. 4.9 million barrels of oil leaked into a 68,000 square mile area. Every night, video of the underwater leak was televised live on the David Letterman Show. The problem was that no one had ever fixed a leaking valve a mile below the surface of the water.

The firm needed relationships with the governors of states affected by the spill. The fastest way to build this relationship is to hire a lobbyist. A lobbyist is a person who has relationship capital with stakeholders, such as a governor. It is not typical that the lobbyist is a former staff member of the governor or former elected official.

The lobbyist might be able to call the governor directly on the governor's personal phone line because they are friends, and then deliver BP's message. The objective is to use the lobbyist's relationship capital with the governor to open a trusting relationship between BP and the governor in the shortest possible time period.

The Project Sponsor

The sponsor of an extreme project is usually a top executive in the organization, such as the CEO or board chairman. The role of the project sponsor is to be Captain Kirk. If you remember *Star Trek*, Captain Kirk was also beamed down to solve a problem when the crew got stumped.

You're looking for the project sponsor to be called in to cut through red tape. You don't want the project sponsor to manage the project—you simply want the project sponsor to remove roadblocks so the virtual teams can do their job.

Real-Time Planning

Real-time planning is critical to the success of an extreme project. Real-time planning is modifying the plan to accommodate changes that occur during the execution of the plan.

Rapid planning is a planning technique that helps make decisions quickly in real time. The virtual team uses rapid planning sessions to develop the plan. Rapid planning sessions are interactive where team members are encouraged to be proactive and participate in planning. All information and ideas are shared, discussed, and evaluated by the virtual team. Meetings are short, about 2 to 4 hours, and have an agenda that can be achieved within that period. A decision is made before the end of the meeting.

A Virtual Team

A virtual team is a team that is formed to address a specific issue. The team disbands once the issue is solved. Virtual teams can consist of employees, outside experts, or anyone who is needed to address the issue. Some team members can join the team for a few minutes via telecommunications to provide advice. Other members remain with the team until the problem is solved.

OODA Loop Decision Model

Decisions are made in an extreme project using the OODA loop decision model because it supports quick, effective, and proactive decision-making. There are four decision points or stages in the OODA loop decision model.

The first stage is to *observe the situation* by collecting information from as many sources as is practically possible—you don't have time to conduct extensive data gathering. The more information you can take in here, the more accurate your perception will be.

Next is the *orient stage*, in which you analyze the data and update your current understanding of reality.

– One of the main problems with decision-making is that we all view events in a way that's filtered through our own experiences and perceptions.
– Be aware of your perceptions. By speeding up your ability to orient to reality, you can then move through the decision loop quickly and effectively.
– You need to process it quickly and revise your orientation.

The *decide stage* is where you determine what to do next based on updated data.

– Decisions are your best guesses, based on the observations and the orientation you're using.
– They should be considered to be fluid works in progress.
– New suggestions keep arriving—these can trigger changes to your decisions and subsequent actions.

Then the virtual team takes action and the cycle begins again.

– Be careful with this emphasis on speed.

  – In some situations, you genuinely need speed.
  – In others, a more cautious, deliberate approach is appropriate.

Let's take a look at an approach to manage an extreme project. You are the chief operating officer and now the project manager for this extreme project. You are notified of the explosion on the oil platform in the Gulf of Mexico. There is oil leaking from a malfunctioning valve three miles below the surface of the water and engineering cannot stop the leak. What do you do first?

Let's assume that you had project management training and you focus on the work breakdown structure. This technique doesn't work because too much is unknown, events are constantly changing, and you don't have time to use the traditional project management approach to manage this extreme project.

You decide to use the OODA loop decision model. It provides a methodology that helps you focus on making sound decisions in a constantly changing situation.

You need to begin to wrap your arms around the problem. Yet the problem is complex, rapidly changing, and you lack the expertise to fully comprehend all the facets of the problem.

Begin by brainstorming with yourself. What areas can be affected by the problem? This is a very high-level assessment. There is a leak so there are engineering issues. Personnel were injured. It is safe to assume there are legal and personnel issues and insurance issues too. There will be costs to address the problem, so finance needs to get involved.

Brainstorming at this level should take minutes and give you a clear direction —you need to gather experts in each area and have them evaluate the impact the problem has on their area. Look carefully—experts are already available in your organization. They are directors of those areas of your business.

Each area that can be affected is complex unto itself. Take a look at government. Your organization has a director of government relations. The presumption is that they are the expert that can address any government issue that arises. That's far from reality.

There are two countries affected: the United States and Mexico. Furthermore, in the U.S. there's the federal government and the governments of Texas, Florida, Alabama, and Mississippi. Each state government is further divided into the governor, legislatures, and state agencies. The federal government is broken into the executive branch and Congress. The executive branch consists of the president and federal agencies, including 15 cabinet secretaries. Congress is simply divided into the Senate and House. We could go on and on, further identifying government officials that may be affected by the oil leak.

And then there are influential people that are sometimes more powerful than government officials who need to contacted. These are political party leaders, political party contributors, former officials, and power brokers. You need to learn if there is an issue with all these stakeholders, also including stockholders, the board of directors, your employees and their families, and of course the press. If so, you need to learn what the issue is and how to address the issue.

Your director of government relations is not the expert in all these areas of government. The director of government relations is the facilitator of those areas and can identify potential or real issues, but virtual teams need to be created to handle each level of government. Virtual team members have relationship capital with governmental stakeholders. Planning and intervention are performed by each virtual team based on their relationship with stakeholders.

After brainstorming, assemble directors of key areas in your organization. Write on a whiteboard what you know of the situation and ask everyone to add to and correct the information on the whiteboard. The goal is to build a sense of urgency and refocus the group on identifying and addressing issues related to the oil leak.

Ask each director:

- What problems are we facing in your area? What governmental problems are we facing?
- What resources do you need to identify these problems?
- When can you present the list of problems?

The whiteboard contains a list of known facts and assumptions. Each director will assess the impact, known facts, and assumptions on their area and identify real and potential problems. The project manager is focused on helping directors create the list.

Directors are required to return within an hour to present their findings. Remember, time is of the essence and the project manager must instill this by setting short deadlines. Directors will confer with their experts during the hour. It isn't realistic to expect all issues to be identified within an hour. The goal is simply to identify the next step in each area affected by the oil leak.

Directors will present a prioritized list of issues in their area and be expected to assemble virtual teams to address those issues using the agile project management techniques to resolve issues each identified. For example, engineering has a prioritized list of technical issues needed to be addressed to curtail the leak. Finance has a prioritized list of financial issues to support engineering and the firm as a whole during this period of unknowns. Legal identifies lists of a wide area of liabilities affecting the firm now, in the short term, and in the long term.

Motivate the Extreme Project Management Team

Accelerators are actions that speed the flow of energy through the project, enabling everyone involved in the project to have a sense of ownership—we call this *skin in the game*. The result is unleashed motivation that spurs the innovation that it takes to solves issues in an extreme project.

The first accelerator is to see change as your friend. Change represents an opportunity to improve the chances of resolving the issues. Everyone involved in the extreme project must have a willingness to start over at any time, junk the plan if it is not working, and devise a new plan. Don't waste time making a poor plan work.

Tap into the fact that people want to make a difference. Make the extreme project a mission, like going to the moon, not a project. The team will see the extreme project as a cause.

You must show each team member how their job contributes to the bigger picture. For example, everyone in the operating room isn't a surgeon, yet they all know how their job will make the surgery a success. People support what they create. Let team members determine how to do their job and influence the outcome of the project.

Keep everything simple. Less process, less project management—few policies, few operating standards. Remember that many extreme projects break new ground where the old rules and methods hinder rather than help.

In addition to accelerators, extreme projects require ten shared values.

1. Trust and confidence. The team, the project manager, and stakeholders must trust each other. This is vital to the success of an extreme project. Henry Ford is quoted as saying, "If you think you can, you can. If you think you can't, you can't. In either case you are right."
2. Confidence. Your job as project manager is to instill the confidence that your team can—then trust that they can make the best possible decisions.
3. Client collaboration. There has to be a constant free-flow of information between stakeholders and the project team.
4. People first. Eliminate barriers so your team can produce quality work. Keep everyone focused on the purpose of the extreme project—use slogans, banners, hats, and other visible means to remind everyone of the goal, such as going to the moon by the end of the century.
5. Be forthright. Everyone involved in the project must be forthright and have honest communication—regardless of the message, there are no reprisals.
6. Result-oriented. Focus on resolving the issue, not justifying time spent on trying to solve the issue.
7. Fast failures. Find out quickly if something doesn't work, so you can try something that might work.
8. Early value. Small successes set the path for success. The project manager must identify issues early in the project that can be easily resolved to set the moment for more challenging issues.
9. Quality of life. Quality of life is a critical value—make sure each team member balances work and personal life. An extreme project is time-sensitive—however, your project team needs time away from the job too.
10. Courage. Everyone involved in the project must face the fear of unknowns in an extreme project and act on what they believe is the right thing to do.

Critical Success Factors

Success of an extreme project also depends on critical success factors being in place. A critical success factor is an element that increases the likelihood of a successful project outcome.

-   Self-mastery. Each team member must learn from experience. The project manager puts in place the skills, tools, and the environment to succeed—the team must resolve the issue.

- Lead by commitment to the team. Create an environment that motivates the team to succeed.
- Keep the structure flexible. Have a light control on the team, allowing the team the freedom to innovate and get the work done. Let team leaders create new structures for their portion of the project without having to get approval.
- Keep communication in real-time. Remove all roadblocks that inhibit the free-flow of information.
- Maintain an agile organization. Develop a friendly culture that embraces change.

Risk Management for an Extreme Project

A project manager of an extreme project deals with unknowns that are assessed once the project is underway. Unknowns present risks and the project manager and project team must manage these risks. The initial step is to assess how much risk the organization can tolerate—is it worth the effort and money to mitigate the risk? Or should the organization simply accept the risk?

Each time you drive, you risk the chance of becoming involved in an accident. Most times you accept that risk and there is no accident. However, at some point you may decide that the risk of an accident is too great.

Categorizing risk is not a clear-cut process. Some situations pose an inconvenience, not a risk. For example, driving in snow flurries is more of an inconvenience than a risk. There are two common ways to categorize risk. First is to ask a subject matter expert to perform the risk analysis. The other is to follow the money.

The goal of an organization is to sustain operations. Operations are sustainable if the organization has money to mitigate risks and recovery from anything that can disrupt operations. Consider this money in the bank. Disruption of the continuous flow of money into and out of the organization is a real risk to the sustainability of the organization. For example, a warehouse fire prevents delivery of product, which in turn means customers will not purchase products that can't be delivered. The organization uses reserved funds (money in the bank) to pay bills and maintain operations until the problem is resolved and the flow of money is restored.

Risk Assessment

Risk assessment is the analysis of factors that can interrupt business operations or interrupt your extreme project. The risk assessment focuses on the basics—breathable air, drinkable water, power, and heat. These are things we take for granted, yet may not be available during an extreme project. You can assemble a virtual team on-site, but you also need to provide resources (food, water, accommodations) for them to survive for the length of stay—without them, the virtual team becomes distracted and focus on their personal needs rather than on the extreme project. For example, there are many teams working on the oil leak. Each team individually has to sleep, eat, shower, and other basic needs that must be addressed, otherwise the team can't work.

The risk assessment process begins with a systematic examination of events that could harm the organization or the extreme project. List the probability of each event. What is the likelihood that the event will occur? Determine if sufficient precautions have been taken to prevent or mitigate these events.

Create a risk assessment matrix that focuses on hazards, the organization's assets, and the impact on the business. List each in the event column, then rank the severity and probability of the event. Severity is the magnitude of the event, such as a storm. Severity is ranked as negligible, marginal, critical, and catastrophic. A hurricane has a catastrophic severity rating on the extreme project. It would greatly hamper the virtual team's ability to manage the project.

Probability is the likelihood the event will occur. Probability is ranked as eliminated, improbable, remote, occasional, probable, and frequent. Eliminated means that steps have been taken to make it improbable that the event will occur, such as the virtual project team relocating to Florida and eliminating the chance that a blizzard will interrupt project planning. There is an extremely low probability that Florida will be hit by a blizzard. However, the event would have an improbable probability rank if the virtual team were already located in Florida.

Each event, including improbable events, must be listed in the risk assessment matrix. Don't assume everything in an extreme project will work fine. Evaluate the risk that things could go wrong, and then develop a contingency plan should they go wrong.

Evaluate the Risk Assessment

Evaluate mission-critical events. These are events that may stop or hamper the organization's operations if they occur. This includes keeping in touch with clients and stakeholders. Set priorities on what to do first based on how long an event might be down and how long it will take to restore it. Determine if there are ways to avoid the potential failure event or at least develop a contingency plan that can be enacted if the event occurs.

Agile Project Management

Agile project management is a methodology used to manager relatively small, routine projects that don't lend themselves to traditional project management methodology. Agile project management is particularly useful for resolving issues in an extreme project by virtual teams and enabling virtual teams to focus on customer value and deliver quality results fast.

The focus is on small batches of work by virtual teams. Virtual teams are self-organizing, self-disciplined, and are well integrated, with discipline needed to address the issue at hand. There is intense collaboration with face-to-face communication. The goal is to achieve small, continuous improvements toward the solution while learning and adapting to change.

Agile practices align perfectly with an extreme project. First is to identify top-priority items and then deliver those items rapidly. There is light-touch leadership because the virtual team is empowered to learn what must be done, plan to do it, then execute the plan.

The Focus Board

The virtual team creates a focus board that contains a list of user stories—these are issues that must be resolved. The focus board is left in a common area so team members can frequently review the status of the project. The virtual team works from the list of user stories resolving one small aspect of the issue at a time and producing a result. The goal is to maintain a sustainable pace.

The makeup of the virtual team changes as new and revised issues are recognized—the virtual team is responsible for resolving the issue—however new team members with expertise missing from the virtual team must join the team to resolve the issue.

Core Roles

There are core roles on an agile project management team. The *product owner* is a member of the team that speaks for stakeholders and writes user stores call *churn*. Think of a churn as a stakeholder requirement. The product owner also manages the order in which user stories are addressed.

The development team addresses each user story and fulfills the stakeholder requirements. For example, the engineering manager needs to fix the leaking valve located three miles below the water surface—this is a user story. The development team must fix the valve and stop the leak.

The *scrum master* facilitates the scrum, the gathering of the team following a period of activity. The scrum master is not the team leader. Instead, the scrum master makes sure the team is focused and has no impediments to working on the issue. The scrum master also makes sure that the team follows the agile project management methodology.

There are ancillary roles in the project. These are stakeholders and managers—anyone who does not have a core role, but can still influence the project. For example, the director of government relations is an ancillary role.

The Daily Scrum

The daily scrum is a daily standup meeting lasting no longer than 15 minutes. Each team member must answer:
- What have you done since yesterday?
- What are you planning to do today?
- Are there any impediments that prevent you from accomplishing what you plan to do today?

Backlog Grooming

Backlog grooming is the hour job of assessing backlog of user stories—large user stories can be broken up into smaller user stories. It is at this point when you can refine the acceptance criteria for user-stories. The goal is to make user stories a viable activity for scrum.

The Sprint

A *sprint*, as discussed briefly in Chapter 7, is a basic unit of development that focuses on an item from the product backlog. The product backlog is lower priority user stories. A sprint is performed within a specific duration. The goal is to keep a sustainable pace. The goal of a sprint is to resolve a portion of the issue. For example, the virtual team has a sprint focused on how to make a valve repair at great depths. The team and other virtual teams working on other aspects of the repair hold a daily scrum to report their status and goals for the next day.

The sprint sequence begins with a sprint planning meeting, during which tasks are identified and commitments are made by the team. Next is the sprint followed by the retrospective, a review identifying lessons learned that can be used for the next sprint.

Sprint Planning Meeting

Before each sprint, there is a sprint planning meeting. This is an eight-hour meeting held at the beginning of a sprint cycle. It is at this meeting where the agile project team decides what work is to be done. After a sprint, there is a four-hour sprint review meeting, where the agile project team determines what work is completed and what still needs to be completed. Completed work is presented to stakeholders.

The agile project team then spends three hours reviewing the past sprint, answering the questions:

- What went well during the sprint?
- What could be improved in the next sprint?

Chapter 12
Staying On Top of Your Game with PMP Changes

The key to successfully landing your next project manager position is to demonstrate that your knowledge and skills have kept pace with changing project management techniques. Yesterday's approaches to project management may not meet today's out-of-the box critical thinking skills needed to deliver complex mission critical projects. You need a diverse approach, as reflected in changes in the PMP exam.

The Project Management Institute recognized that the next stage of the project management evolution is at hand. There is a new value spectrum for project management—predictive project management approaches, along with agile approaches and a blend of predictive and agile approaches called the hybrid approach. Collectively, these approaches align knowledge and skill sets with real-life practices of managing projects.

This chapter helps you sharpen your knowledge to speak intelligently about changes to the project management body of knowledge, giving you an edge over project managers who are behind the times during job interviews.

How Projects Are Really Managed

Theory or reality is a question that professional project managers raise when working their way through the project management body of knowledge, preparing for the PMP exam, and preparing for technical job interviews. Some project managers take the practical approach by studying theory for the PMP exam and applying a hybrid of theory and common sense managing projects in practice.

PMI researched to assess if the theory of project management differs from practice. The conclusion is yes. There is an emerging trend on how projects are managed in the real world and it differs from the predictive style of project management. Today's projects are complicated and require a blend of predictive and agile styles of project management in some instances. As a result of their research, PMI has updated the body of knowledge to reflect how projects are really managed.

PMI research determined there are three areas of project management called *domains* that reflect the next evolution of managing a project. The concept of a domain hasn't changed from the existing book of knowledge. A domain requires a high level of knowledge necessary to effectively manage a project. However, the nature of domains has changed. PMI determined there are three domains in the next evaluation of project management.

https://doi.org/10.1515/9781501506222-013

- People: The people domain focuses on skills and activities that are needed to lead the project team.
- Process: The process domain focuses on technique aspects of managing the project.
- Business Environment: The business environment focuses on connecting the project with the organization's strategy.

Tasks and Enablers

Each domain has a two-level structure. The first level is called Tasks. Tasks are underlying project manager responsibilities related to the domain. Simply, these are activities that the project manager performs when managing the project. For example, in the People domain, the project manager is responsible for managing conflicts. Manage Conflict is the first task of the People domain.

The second level of the domain structure is called Enablers. Enablers are examples of work related to each task. Think of Tasks as responsibilities of the project manager and Enablers as things the project manager can to do to meet those responsibilities.

For example, the project manager is responsible to manage conflicts. In order to meet those responsibilities, the project manager must perform three Enablers. These are: *interpret* the source and stage of the conflict; *analyze* the context for the conflict; and *evaluate*/recommend/reconcile the appropriate conflict resolution solution. PMI lists examples of Enablers—however, that list is not exhaustive. It serves to illustrate the types of actions the project manager can perform. There are other actions not listed that naturally occur during a project that are considered Enablers too.

Need to Know for the Job Interview

What do you need to know to sound on top of your game during a technical interview for a project manager's position? The changes to the book of knowledge as a result of recent PMI research. In some cases, the interviewer is already up to speed on the next evolution of project management techniques and wants to know if you also keep pace with the profession. In other cases, you'll be educating the interviewer on the latest techniques, showing that you are on top of your game.

The following tables contain PMI's enhancements to the book of knowledge for the People Process and Business Environment domains. Consider this as your cheat sheet to the new domains.

People Domain

The People domain focuses on skills and activities that are needed to lead the project team.

Task 1 Manage Conflict	**Enablers** – Interpret the source and stage of conflict – Analyze the context for the conflict – Evaluate/recommend/reconcile the appropriate conflict resolution solution
Task 2 Lead a Team	**Enablers** – Set a clear vision and mission – Support diversity and inclusion (e.g., behavior types, thought process) – Value servant leadership (e.g., relate the tenets of servant leadership to the team) – Determine an appropriate leadership style (e.g., directive, collaborative) – Inspire, motivate, and influence team members/stakeholders (e.g., team contract, social contract, reward system) – Analyze team members and stakeholders' influence – Distinguish various options to lead various team members and stakeholders
Task 3 Support team performance	**Enablers** – Appraise team member performance against key performance indicators – Support and recognize team member growth and development – Determine appropriate feedback approach – Verify performance improvements
Task 4 Empower team members and stakeholders	**Enablers** – Organize around team strengths – Support team task accountability – Evaluate demonstration of task accountability – Determine and bestow level(s) of decision-making authority
Task 5 Ensure team members/stakeholders are adequately trained	**Enablers** – Determine required competencies and elements of training – Determine training options based on training needs – Allocate resources for training – Measure training outcomes

(continued)

People Domain	
The People domain focuses on skills and activities that are needed to lead the project team.	

Task 6	Enablers
Build a team	− Appraise stakeholder skills
	− Deduce project resource requirements
	− Continuously assess and refresh team skills to meet project needs
	− Maintain team and knowledge transfer

Task 7	Enablers
Address and remove impediments, obstacles, and blockers for the team	− Determine critical impediments, obstacles, and blockers for the team
	− Prioritize critical impediments, obstacles, and blockers for the team
	− Use network to implement solutions to remove impediments, obstacles, and blockers for the team
	− Re-assess continually to ensure impediments, obstacles, and blockers for the team are being addressed

Task 8	Enablers
Negotiate project agreements	− Analyze the bounds of the negotiations for agreement
	− Assess priorities and determine ultimate objective(s)
	− Verify objective(s) of the project agreement is met
	− Participate in agreement negotiations
	− Determine a negotiation strategy

Task 9	Enablers
Collaborate with stakeholders	− Evaluate engagement needs for stakeholders
	− Optimize alignment between stakeholder needs, expectations, and project objectives
	− Build trust and influence stakeholders to accomplish project objectives

Task 10	Enablers
Build shared understanding	− Break down situation to identify the root cause of a misunderstanding
	− Survey all necessary parties to reach consensus
	− Support outcome of parties' agreement
	− Investigate potential misunderstandings

(continued)

People Domain

The People domain focuses on skills and activities that are needed to lead the project team.

Task 11 Engage and support virtual teams	**Enablers** – Examine virtual team member needs (e.g., environment, geography, culture, global, etc.) – Investigate alternatives (e.g., communication tools, co-location) for virtual team member engagement – Implement options for virtual team member engagement – Continually evaluate effectiveness of virtual team member engagement
Task 12 Define team ground rules	**Enablers** – Communicate organizational principles with team and external stakeholders – Establish an environment that fosters adherence to the ground rules – Manage and rectify ground rule violations
Task 13 Mentor relevant stakeholders	**Enablers** – Allocate the time to mentoring – Recognize and act on mentoring opportunities
Task 14 Promote team performance through the application of emotional intelligence	**Enablers** – Assess behavior through the use of personality indicators – Analyze personality indicators and adjust to the emotional needs of key project stakeholders

---

Process Domain

The Process domain focuses on technique aspects of managing the project.

Task 1 Execute project with the urgency required to deliver business value	**Enablers** – Assess opportunities to deliver value incrementally – Examine the business value throughout the project – Support the team to subdivide project tasks as necessary to find the minimum viable product

(continued)

Process Domain	
The Process domain focuses on technique aspects of managing the project.	
Task 2 Manage communications	**Enablers** – Analyze communication needs of all stakeholders – Determine communication methods, channels, frequency, and level of detail for all stakeholders – Communicate project information and updates effectively – Confirm communication is understood and feedback is received
Task 3 Assess and manage risks	**Enablers** – Determine risk management options – Iteratively assess and prioritize risks
Task 4 Engage stakeholders	**Enablers** – Analyze stakeholders (e.g., power interest grid, influence, impact) – Categorize stakeholders – Engage stakeholders by category – Develop, execute, and validate a strategy for stakeholder engagement
Task 5 Plan and manage budget and resources	**Enablers** – Estimate budgetary needs based on the scope of the project and lessons learned from past projects – Anticipate future budget challenges – Monitor budget variations and work with governance process to adjust as necessary – Plan and manage resources
Task 6 Plan and manage schedule	**Enablers** – Estimate project tasks (milestones, dependencies, story points) – Utilize benchmarks and historical data – Prepare schedule based on methodology – Measure ongoing progress based on methodology – Modify schedule, as needed, based on methodology – Coordinate with other projects and other operations

(continued)

Process Domain
The Process domain focuses on technique aspects of managing the project.

Task 7 Plan and manage quality of products/ deliverables	**Enablers** – Determine quality standard required for project deliverables – Recommend options for improvement based on quality gaps – Continually survey project deliverable quality
Task 8 Plan and manage scope	**Enablers** – Determine and prioritize requirements – Break down scope (e.g., WBS, backlog) – Monitor and validate scope
Task 9 Integrate project planning activities	**Enablers** – Consolidate the project/phase plans – Assess consolidated project plans for dependencies, gaps, and continued business value – Analyze the data collected – Collect and analyze data to make informed project decisions – Determine critical information requirements
Task 10 Manage project changes	**Enablers** – Anticipate and embrace the need for change (e.g., follow change management practices) – Determine strategy to handle change – Execute change management strategy according to the methodology – Determine a change response to move the project forward
Task 11 Plan and manage procurement	**Enablers** – Define resource requirements and needs – Communicate resource requirements – Manage suppliers/contracts – Plan and manage procurement strategy – Develop a delivery solution

(continued)

Process Domain	
The Process domain focuses on technique aspects of managing the project.	
Task 12 Manage project artifacts	**Enablers** – Determine the requirements (what, when, where, who, etc.) for managing the project artifacts – Validate that the project information is kept up to date (i.e., version control) and accessible to all stakeholders – Continually assess the effectiveness of the management of the project artifacts
Task 13 Determine appropriate project methodology/methods and practices	**Enablers** – Assess project needs, complexity, and magnitude – Recommend project execution strategy (e.g., contracting, finance) – Recommend a project methodology/approach (i.e., predictive, agile, hybrid) – Use iterative, incremental practices throughout the project life cycle (e.g., lessons learned, stakeholder engagement, risk)
Task 14 Establish project governance structure	**Enablers** – Determine appropriate governance for a project (e.g., replicate organizational governance) – Define escalation paths and thresholds
Task 15 Manage project issues	**Enablers** – Recognize when a risk becomes an issue – Attack the issue with the optimal action to achieve project success – Collaborate with relevant stakeholders on the approach to resolve the issues
Task 16 Ensure knowledge transfer for project continuity	**Enablers** – Discuss project responsibilities within team – Outline expectations for working environment – Confirm approach for knowledge transfers
Task 17 Plan and manage project/phase closure or transitions	**Enablers** – Determine criteria to successfully close the project or phase – Validate readiness for transition (e.g., to operations team or next phase) – Conclude activities to close out project or phase (e.g., final lessons learned, retrospective, procurement, financials, resources)

Business Environment Domain

The Business Environment focuses on connecting the project with the organization's strategy.

Task 1	Enablers
Plan and manage project compliance	– Confirm project compliance requirements (e.g., security, health and safety, regulatory compliance) – Classify compliance categories – Determine potential threats to compliance – Use methods to support compliance – Analyze the consequences of noncompliance – Determine necessary approach and action to address compliance needs (e.g., risk, legal) – Measure the extent to which the project is in compliance
Task 2	**Enablers**
Evaluate and deliver project benefits and value	– Investigate that benefits are identified – Document agreement on ownership for ongoing benefit realization – Verify measurement system is in place to track benefits – Evaluate delivery options to demonstrate value – Appraise stakeholders of value gain progress
Task 3	**Enablers**
Evaluate and address external business environment changes for impact on scope	– Survey changes to external business environment (e.g., regulations, technology, geopolitical, market) – Assess and prioritize impact on project scope/backlog based on changes in external business environment – Recommend options for scope/backlog changes (e.g., schedule, cost changes) – Continually review external business environment for impacts on project scope/backlog
Task 4	**Enablers**
Support organizational change	– Assess organizational culture – Evaluate impact of organizational change to project and determine required actions – Evaluate impact of the project to the organization and determine required actions

Index

https://doi.org/10.1515/9781501506222-014